More Advance Praise

"I was so moved by Kevin Sessums's funny, sad evocation of his childhood and teenage years in *Mississippi Sissy*. His youthful instinct for finding the theatrical, musical, and literary locals who opened his eyes to the outside world that he yearned to know about is wonderfully touching."

–Dominick Dunne

"*Mississippi Sissy* is an unforgettable memoir. I think it will strike a strong chord with many, many readers. It's a far different book than *Midnight in the Garden of Good and Evil*, but it cast the same kind of spell over me while I was reading it."

–Mark Childress

"*Mississippi Sissy* manages to be both hilarious and heartbreaking, often in the same moment. It is a poignant story of innocence and sexuality, tragedy and courage. But it is ultimately a tale of perseverance of the human spirit. Kevin Sessums not only has a great story to tell, he is a great storyteller."

–Carole Radziwill

"Wow! What a book! I was both shocked and moved by it. It is said that an unexamined life is not worth living. Kevin Sessums examines his with wisdom and humor and a true writer's sense of grace. This book will create more than the proverbial buzz. It will cause a sensation."

–David Geffen

"I could not put Kevin Sessums's memoir down. A young, white, gay boy, who grew up in a whirl and survived the injustices of class and prejudice, Sessums lyrically narrates his escape from this tyranny of Southern hate. This is the story of an angel with asbestos skin. Were this fiction, it would be on a par with John Kennedy Toole's *A Confederacy of Dunces*."

–André Leon Talley

"A gutsy, moving, richly textured, and immensely funny revelation, and a precisely remembered evocation of the Southern political and cultural landscape in the '60s and '70s."

–Patti Carr Black

Mississippi Sissy

KEVIN SESSUMS

ST. MARTIN'S PRESS ❦ NEW YORK

www.stmartins.com

The "In Memoriam" column by Eudora Welty (pages 304–305) is reprinted by permission of the Eudora Welty Foundation, Inc.

Library of Congress Cataloging-in-Publication Data

Sessums, Kevin.
  Mississippi sissy / Kevin Sessums.—1st ed.
    p. cm.
  ISBN-13: 978-0-312-34101-5
  ISBN-10: 0-312-34101-6
  1. Sessums, Kevin. 2. Journalists—United States—Biography. 3. Gay
  journalists—United States—Biography. I. Title.

  PN4874.S428 A3 2007
  70.92—dc20
  [B]

2006051677

First Edition: March 2007

10 9 8 7 6 5 4 3 2 1

In Memory of
Howard Jean, Nancy Carolyn,
Joycie Otis, and Malcolm Lyle

For Karole, and for Kim,
who trusted me to base two scenes,
for which I was not present,
on his journal entries

Death and life are in the power of the tongue. . . .
—Proverbs 18:21

Contents

Author's Note

This book is a re-creation of my childhood and teenage years. All the people and the names are real. All the events actually occurred. The dialogue—as true to these people and events and what was said around me as my memory can possibly make it—is my own invention. I was not carrying around a recording device when growing up in Mississippi. But what I did have, even then, was my writer's ear. I *listened*. That's what most sissies do when we are children: We sit apart and listen.

My mother once told me that the power of language resides in its sound, even before—especially before—we can comprehend its meaning. The same could be said about memory. When I recall my life in Mississippi, what I hear are the rich sounds of the voices that surrounded me and from those sounds come the words, the movement of conversation. It's the way perhaps a composer hears a symphony before transcribing its notes, making it attainable for others who want to listen just as intently to what he hears. Although there is a kind of alchemy involved, there is an equal measure of faith in one's own voice, the sound into which all others combine.

Acknowledgments

I owe debts of gratitude to the following people.

First and foremost, I'd like to thank my editor, Michael Flamini, and my agent, Nina Collins. For a year and a half they were the only two people I allowed to read the first draft of this book. Their intelligence and innate taste proved invaluable to me. I cherish them professionally. I cherish them as friends.

I would also like to thank all of those who read the subsequent frighteningly thick manuscript and liked it enough not only to finish the thing, but also to furnish me with the quotes about the book that I found so encouraging early on. Their generosity—you can find their names on the book jacket as well as the book's initial page—meant the world to me.

I gave an early version of the book to those people still alive who are a part of my story so they could vet my own memory of our shared past and my accuracy in the telling of it. I am grateful for the trust and scrutiny of each of these people. We all have versions of our own lives, and I was heartened when mine mostly conflated, painfully at times, pleasantly at others, with the respective truths of theirs.

Finally, I have always had a problem remembering names. I panic when I have to make an introduction—even if it's two old friends of mine who've never met before. It is some sort of psychological hiccup, like my recurring stutter when I am nervous still about appearing to be too much of a sissy. But there is a group of names that I can, to this day, reel off without one mistake, one hesitation. They are the Mississippi schoolteachers I had who always encouraged me, whether I was an overly curious child, a confused teenager, or a college kid full of a kind of crippled hope. They are, in order, Miss Bridges, Miss Mills, Mrs. Johnston, Mrs. Hunter, Mrs. Rigby, Mrs. Waggener, Mrs. Thompson, Mrs. Fikes, Mrs. Donaldson, Mrs. Hughes, Mrs. Twiss, Miss Lewis, Mrs. Hays, and Professors Lance Goss and Dan Hise.

Mississippi Sissy

The thing I remember from that night as much as I remember Frank Hains's blood-soaked bed, as much as I remember what was left of his gelatinous head after the crowbar had done its work, as much as I remember how his body had been bound and gagged with his own silk neckties, as much as I remember the instant nausea that those sights can induce in a teenage boy who discovers them, was the way my foot shook on the gas pedal after I cranked up my old Comet and headed straight to Carl's. . . . It was as if the shock and fright of finding Frank had puddled in a frenzy down around my right ankle. And yet the car—red leather interior, no power steering, a radio that longed for FM—did not jerk and sputter as I turned onto the Interstate. It seemed instead to head more smoothly onward with each spastic brush of my scuffed Bass Weejun against the gas pedal. That's the core of the memory that night, of all my memories really: the eerie smoothness of the ride. . . .

Prologue

Ross Barnett, George Hamilton, and Arlene Francis

"When I am asked why Southern writers particularly have a penchant for writing about freaks, I say it's because we are still able to recognize one," said Flannery O'Connor. The first time I read that remark, I laughed at O'Connor's knowing wit and divine slyness. And yet—as in her stories when such wit, such slyness, can curdle together into a kind of wisdom that sits like clabber atop the churned-up innocence of our lives—it also left a sour, long-ago taste in my mouth. It tightened my throat. The first freak I ever recognized down South where I was born half a century ago now was my own reflection in a Mississippi mirror.

I was confronted with a glass of such clabber, served ice-cold with day-old corn bread crumbled into it, on the day of my mother's funeral—November 19, 1964—when my brother and sister and I officially moved in with our maternal grandparents, who lived in the country, a few miles outside a little town called Forest. Our father, a sports celebrity of local renown, had only recently been killed in an automobile accident. His death—he flew from his beloved baby-blue Volkswagen Beetle after running a STOP sign at a country intersection and colliding with a car with Neshoba County plates—made headlines across the state. One year later our mother was now dead of esophageal cancer. Dying so soon after my father, my mother enabled me to utilize what little sorrow I was feeling for him. Her dying deepened it, allowed it to seep forever into my life like the blood that ran from his flat-topped head when it hit that newly paved country road. Red thick yolks of the stuff oozed past his butch-waxed thatch of bristles and blackened even more the fresh asphalt, drawing the flies that buzzed over a neighboring pasture where they swarmed around cattle that looked up, for a second, at the sound of the crash then turned away to focus on their cuds.

Different sorts of headlines followed the death of my mother, my siblings and I being the subject of "human interest" features located next to a bunch of Ladies Club columns in weekly county newspapers, nestled among the stories about high school football, pork futures, and fire-bombed churches. "The Sessums Orphans" became our handle as we were paraded around the state and asked to do some fancy dribbling at the halftime of charity basketball games set up for our college funds in little country gymnasiums. Such places became secular sanctuaries to me. The sweet syncopation of balls bouncing against hardwood during a shoot-around was as competitive, as alluring as that *Rich vs. Roach* record of battling drummers I listened to once I grew up and let my love of Ella Fitzgerald lead me to other LPs. *Gym-na-si-um:* It was the first big word I ever learned. It made masculinity musical to my little ears. I went around saying it softly to myself over and over, proud that I was able to pronounce it, loving how pretty it sounded in my mouth. *Gym-na-si-um:* A man's name was in there, *see* was in there too, the very sound of *mmmmmm*, I knew to say when I really liked something, when it tasted good, when I wanted to taste it again. A gymnasium was also the place where my stern father felt secure enough to show me some tenderness. He had been an All-American basketball player at the state's Southern Baptist institute of higher learning, Mississippi College. Drafted by the New York Knicks in 1956 after my mother had just given birth to me, he had returned home from Manhattan at her behest. A Southern belle through-and-through, she could not see herself managing to survive in the vertical hustle and bustle of a Northern urban high-rise with a squalling new-born to care for. She told my father he had a choice: Either he could play for the Knicks and live alone or come home to her and his child and make a more horizontal life in Mississippi, where there were *lawns*, honey, and languor was an assiduously honed attribute.

At least that is what his older sister, my aunt Gladys—corpulent, overly rouged, incautious of tongue—told me a couple of years after my parents' deaths. I, newly nine, was sitting on the floor next to her chair during a weekend birthday visit at her house in Van Winkle, Mississippi. My brother and sister, rowdy with innocence, were down the street being corrupted by the neighborhood ruffians who ran roughshod through the backyards and alleyways of Van Winkle, equipped with BB guns and Bazooka bubblegum and a few half-smoked Viceroys they had purloined from unknowing, know-nothing parents. But all of that was *out there*. I sat inside and busied myself reading Aunt Gladys's collection of movie magazines, which she kept in a cut-down laundry basket by her Barcalounger. "Such a shame, too, such a shame. Yo' daddy always wanted to play ball against number fourteen, Bob Cousey," she said, mentioning the great Boston Celtic player, as she pushed back in her chair and I perused Dorothy Manners's syndicated column in *Modern Screen* for any mention of George Hamilton or Susan Oliver. I had just seen the two starring in *Your Cheatin' Heart* at a Saturday matinee back at the Town Theater in Forest and fallen madly—confusingly—in love with both of them. "Yo' mama and daddy could fight with the best of 'em. But they were devoted to each other ever since second grade in Harperville, where we all grew up as best we could," Aunt Gladys said, kicking off her waitressing shoes. I stared at her corn pads. I pouted at the very mention of my dead parents and pretended I could not smell her feet. "Never let nobody tell you different. Not even me," she said. "Sometimes I wonder though, what would have become of 'em if they had lived a little longer. Love's a funny thing." She yawned, drifting toward sleep. "So funny I forgot to laugh."

Dorothy Manners mentioned neither George nor Susan. I stood and watched from the window as my little brother and little sister now raced in circles around the magnolia sapling that Aunt Gladys had planted at the front of her house on the very morning of my father's accident, her hands still dirty with the freshly dug-up soil when my grandfather telephoned to let her know the awful news. Kim and Karole competed now with Gladys's gathering snores, lacing the steady stream of her snorts with their bursts of sturdy laughter. Even encumbered with our brief and tragic history, my brother and sister had not forgotten how to summon such a sound. I was jealous of the ease with which the very hum of their happiness always hovered about me. As they hit the ground felled by the hilarity of their nascent dizziness, I too dropped back down on the floor. I opened up a *Photoplay*. I searched again for George Hamilton. Searched for Susan Oliver. Searched for that feeling I had the Saturday before when I slumped in the darkened movie theater and let the tingling I felt for them, a nascent dizziness all my own, alleviate my loneliness.

My father succumbed to my mother's challenge of a more grownup, pussy-yearning kind of loneliness and returned home to Mississippi from New York City. He got a job coaching basketball at a high school in a friendly hick-filled hamlet in the middle of the state called Pelahatchie. Almost immediately—legendarily—he took the eight-member team to the state championship. I've often wondered if the look of sad disdain he always delivered my way was the professional remorse of which my very presence reminded him. I am certain this was his recurring silent plaint: *If only she had not been pregnant with you.* Yet it was more than that. Much more. My father and I were like two magnets with their identical poles pressing against each other. It is my most vivid memory of him: that magnetic force field that brought us always to the brink of closeness. As we got to know each other in the first seven years of my life, the last seven years of his, I came to realize it was less a look of disdain than one of perplexed fear that flitted across his face whenever I came into view. *What kind of creature is this? This is a part of me? Flesh of my flesh? Why don't you want to go out and play with the rest of the boys? Shit—go shoot some hoops, son. Get into some trouble. Why do you want to sit inside laughing with the women all the time? Must you laugh with the women?*

My father was a little over six feet tall. His flattop set off the chiseled features of his face. His eyes were the color of Kentucky bourbon and his ears were a tad too big. Swarthy and smooth-skinned, he appeared to have a bit of Native American heritage hidden away somewhere. Soon after he arrived at the small high school, he decided to change the team's name from the Demons to the Chiefs in accordance with Pelahatchie's own Native American heritage. "You'll be the only little demon left around here," he had told me, shaking his head as he watched me run up and down the old gymnasium (perhaps *prance* is a better word) that summer day, right before school started, when he took his buckets of red, blue, white, and yellow paint in there to get rid of the devil at the center of the court and replace it with his colorful rendering of an Indian chief in a full-feathered headdress. As his work progressed and I tired of my prancing, I curled up next to him and watched his handiwork. He hummed, then sang, some country-and-western tunes sung by vocalists on the albums he loved to listen to: Frankie Laine, Johnny Cash, Ray Charles, Jim

Reeves. He let me, only once, dip the brush into the paint and tip a feather with red atop the chief's dignified head while he sang Reeves's "Scarlet Ribbons," the song he put on the stereo when he wanted to slow-dance with my mother. I fell asleep by his side, my head swimming with his slow-dance voice. The fumes from the paint. The salty, sweaty musk of his bare chest and underarms after he had taken off his shirt and rolled it up for me as a makeshift pillow.

The smell of such gym-housed sweat regularly filled my nostrils. It became an inaugural desire. My father would allow me to come to basketball practice—even let me run down out-of-bound balls—if I kept quiet and out of his way. He would also allow me to sit on the bench with him if the games were not close, in an attempt to keep me from sitting with the cheerleaders and mimicking their routines to the delight of the crowd. But he would never let me into the gym's inner sanctum: the Chiefs' downstairs locker room. No matter how much I begged him, tearfully at times, he would not allow it. The more I was denied, of course, the more I longed to know what was behind that door. Once, while he held me tightly in his arms for some sort of rough comfort—before passing me off to a cute, pudgy little pimply-faced team manager named Jack "Tip" Myers—I saw the locker room door open as my father, furious at his team's loss, strode colossally inside. His entrance halted any thought of horseplay and silenced the room except for the incessant hiss of a row of hot showers. A bit of sweat-infused steam from the heat of those showers—a bare shoulder scurried by—escaped from within and warmed my face before the door was slammed shut by my father's hand. It was the first time I felt my heart break. Four years old, I was inundated with adult emotion. I lunged forward. Pimply-faced Myers pried my fingers from the knob. My father's hidden voice rose. The berating had begun.

The following season, after winning a local tournament, my father surprised me by scooping me up from the cheerleaders. He took me straight into the locker room after the game. The delight I felt was as pure as it was profound. The steam from the hissing showers that had once only teased my curious face was now encompassing me as my father put me down on the concrete floor and the players, stripping off their uniforms—giddy and lithe—were teasing each other with that high school athlete's palaver of "asshole" and "dickhead" and "faggot." Buttocks were bared. Bodies, rank with victory, dodged the repeated snaps of tightly wound terrycloth. A gravelly screech, followed by echoes of shared laughter, bounced about all the concrete when the terry hit its target. My father smiled—a handsome crooked grin of a smile—at all the roughhousing, the random merriment. I tried to smile just like him. I can't remember ever being as happy as I was at that very moment. All attempts at happiness over the years have been failed conjuring acts to replicate those first few moments in that locker room, the one and only time I felt my father truly loved me. "Watch Kevinator for a minute," he told Pimply-faced who was handing out the towels. "I'm thirsty after screaming at those refs all through the overtime. Doncha love overtime games, Kevinator?" he asked, running his hand along the bristles of my flattop, a miniature version of his own. "Gotta get me a RC Cola in the coaches' lounge. I'll be right back."

Left fatherless amid the faint smell of liniment and a landscape of inchoate pubic hair, I felt a pleasing knot inside my stomach. Pimply-faced hit me hard atop my head. "Hey, man!" one of the players shouted and hit Pimply-faced back. "Don't pick on Coach's kid. Just 'cause we pick on you." The player, on his way to the showers, lifted me to his chest, the sweat of his neck slick against my cheek. "You okay, buddy?" he asked me before kissing my scalp and putting me back down on the concrete floor. I scampered over to his vacated locker area. I sat down surrounded by the player's discarded gym clothes. I picked up his jockstrap. Pimply-faced laughed at me.

"What's so funny?" my father asked, coming through the door while chugging his RC. Pimply-faced pointed my way. I hid the jock behind my back. "What you got there, Kevinator?" my father wanted to know. "Want a sip of my RC?" He walked toward me. I looked guiltily up at him. I held the jockstrap out, flourishing it with the pliancy I was developing in my wrist.

A few of the players began to snicker.

"What's going on?" the teammate who had rescued me asked as he headed toward us dripping from his shower. He began to towel off in mid-stride. I would not let his jockstrap go. My father, surprised by my strength, finally pulled it from my grasp. He tossed the strap to the player who now stood naked at my side.

"Here. I think this is yours," my father said. "So . . ." was all he said next. The locker room was quiet. He chugged the rest of his RC. "So . . ." Pimply-faced sneered at me. "Take him to the coaches' lounge while I finish up in here," my father told him.

"Yes, sir," said Pimply-faced, who was glad to grab me a little too roughly. I took one more glance back at the boy who had lifted me to his sweaty chest before I was deposited next door in the lounge. "Coach said he'd be right in for him," Pimply-faced told the three other coaches before he returned to the locker room to collect the latest pile of dirty towels.

My mother had furnished the lounge with fried chicken and macaroni'n'cheese and fatbacked butterbeans, and the coaches had piled their paper plates with the food. The three of them stopped chewing and stared down at me. I put my hands on my hips and stared right back. One of the men, smoking a Winston, resumed shoveling mac'n'cheese inside his mouth next to his dangling cigarette. Hot ashes from the reddening butt flaked away and fell on the floor next to me along with some melted cheddar that did not make it into his mouth. The fear that was now knotting my stomach was not pleasant at all. I folded my arms atop it. The smell of the dying cigarette, the mama-aroma of all that fried chicken, the countenance of a glob of congealing cheese, the slightly whispered snide remark— "Can you believe this sissy is Ses's?"—that sneaked out of the side of the man's mouth along with a serpentine puff of sickening smoke, the longing I had to be back inside that locker room, the *longing*: It all combined in one queasy moment and caused me to vomit right on the man's shoes. "Shit," he said, spitting now some of the macaroni on me. He stubbed out his cigarette and stared down at the mess I had made. The other two coaches began to laugh and choke on their food. "Goddamn it. What's so funny?" the man demanded.

My father entered the lounge with his empty RC. I began to cry. "What's the matter, Kevinator?" he asked, kneeling at my side. I pointed at the vomit. "Sorry," my father said. He grabbed some napkins and, still kneeling, cleaned the man's shoes. "Sorry. He's got a sensitive stomach. He's a sensitive kid. He's sensitive."

The two coaches ceased their laughter. They frowned at my father mopping up the vomit. "That's okay, Ses," said the man, lighting another Winston. "Shit happens."

My father turned to me. That recurring look of sad disdain he could deliver my way stopped my tears. He was even sadder than I was. Then, for the very first time, the sadness morphed into that more perplexed look of fear. I did not take my eyes from his. It comforted me to know that my father, who was afraid of nothing, was afraid of me. I unfolded my arms. I put my hands back on my hips. It was the last time I cried in his presence.

My father was thirty-two when he died. My mother, thirty-three, when cancer claimed her. I was eight. My brother, Kim, was six. Karole, our baby sister, had just turned four. "They called it cancer, but it weren't nothing but a broken heart," was the whisper that wafted with enough velocity above our heads during the aftermath of my mother's burial that it could have lifted my sister's bangs with the draft it left in its wake. We had also to endure a plethora of fat-woman hugs. They enveloped us, one by one, these women, with their sagging folds of soft flesh, and scratched our already ruddy faces with the black woolen dresses they had had in their closets since those days they had patterned their wardrobes after Mamie Eisenhower. They exuded an assortment of fragrances: gardenia, vanilla extract, hairspray, Clorox, coffee, a bit of liquor, Lemon Pledge. The mere presence of Kevin and Kim and Karole in a crowded room back then—"KKK . . . ain't that just precious," was another whisper that always seemed to float about us—could elicit tears from total strangers as well as anything they had at the time in their pockets or snappy patent leather purses: Juicy Fruit gum, a piece of old peppermint, loose change, a handkerchief to wipe our noses. I was given a rabbit's foot at my mother's wake by a very tall man who explained to me that he had played basketball with my daddy. "You need this rabbit's foot more 'n me. Which one are you, Kim or Kevin? God knows you younguns need a string'a good luck. You've had a heap of bad. Too big'a heap. Look at me. Here I go again. *Fuck*." At that, he began to cry. I ignored him and wondered what this new word was he had just uttered because Aunt Vena Mae, my grandmother's older sister, shuddered at the sound of it and abruptly pulled me toward her. She was standing nearby, pouring a bit of Carnation evaporated milk into her coffee straight from its little can. I marveled at the word's power, as Aunt Vena Mae's fingers were actually trembling now with anger as she pressed me protectively against her raw silk dress, its tiny nubs rubbing against my face. Aunt Vena Mae always wore a chunky necklace which would bang against her latest astonishing brooch when she moved about. She pulled me closer to her. I heard the agitated clunk of her jewelry above my head. The silk nubs burrowed into my cheek. Something had just happened. Something other than funerals and tears and the arrival of another plate of food to stick in the refrigerator. *Fuck.* I wanted to know a word like that, a word that could make something happen, one that could push death, if only momentarily, from such a room.

The very tall man, saying, "Sorry, ma'am," unfolded his body from its careful crouch next to me and walked away. I forced myself from Vena Mae's grasp. She sipped her Carnationed coffee and assessed me with her stare, filtering me through all her meanness. Childless, Vena Mae flared whenever children were too long underfoot. "That's just her nervous condition," my grandmother would diligently explain. (Venomous Mae was the name I ended up giving her when I was about eleven—a little fuzz on my upper lip—with a wit that had just as shockingly reached its pubescence.) My grandmother was the youngest of nine children—seven girls and two boys—and Vena Mae was the older sister nearest to her in age. They had grown up in the earliest part of the twentieth century (my grandmother was born in 1904) without indoor plumbing. "When nature called we always had to head to the outhouse in pairs so that one sister could shoo away the chickens and roosters in case a bantam got inside the outhouse and pecked at our boodies or other little private areas," my grandmother had once told me. "Vena Mae and me always made them bathroom runs together. You ain't never seen nobody that could shoo a chicken like Vena Mae. I don't know, there's just a *bond* more'n blood when you grow up with somebody that saves your little private parts from being pecked to death on a December morning."

I sure felt like one of those turn-of-the-century chickens as I stood there waiting for Aunt Vena Mae to shoo me away with one of her meanspirited remarks. I readied myself. My hands flew to my hips. "You would've thought that both Howard Jean and Nancy Carolyn dying would have straightened you out some," she finally said, calling my parents rather creepily by their given names while reaching up with her Carnationed hand to make sure her freshly rinsed, tightly teased curls were staying in place. "You want some of this?" she asked, waving the Carnation evaporated milk at me. "Here you go. Tastes like candy," she said, handing me the little tin container of the syrupy white stuff. She grabbed my face too tightly in her freed grip, bracelets jingling under my chin. She moved in closer. "You're pretty as a girl," she said, taunting me with the compliment, then letting go of my face as quickly as she had grabbed it. "Joycie Otis!" she called to my grandmother, keeping up her litany of given names. "Anything I can do to help? Want me to cut up some more cake? I'd have brought my nigger gal down with me from Neshoba County if I'd have known it was going to be this busy."

I frowned at the latest use of the N-word in front of me, although as far as I could tell it was uttered as often around these parts as the phrases "Jesus is your Lord and Savior" and "Would you please pass that plate of biscuits. They buttered?" But I knew better, knew it ever since I'd used the word in Matty May's presence months earlier on the morning after Sidney Poitier won Best Actor for *Lilies of the Field*. Matty May, our maid, was an old friend of my grandmother's. How I wished my grandmother would have let her help out today like she had asked to do when Matty showed up to hug her neck and weep like a wet baby at the news of my mother's death. "Naw, sugar, we'll just cry too much if you're around," my grandmother told her. "Come on over the next day and help me clean up all the mess. You can take home some leftovers." *But if Matty May were here*, I kept thinking, *I'd have somebody to talk to*. Her name became my mantra—*Matty May Matty May Matty May*—as I tried to remain cool and collected because, truth be told, all I wanted to do was turn over all the tables of food. Pick a fight. Do something more than pout. *Matty May Matty May Matty May*. I gripped the rabbit's foot and felt its yellowed intact claws dig into my palm as I surveyed the clacking throng that had gathered in my grandparents' tan-bricked, flat-roofed, surprisingly modernist house way out here in the piney woods on a Mississippi dirt road. Its bright red front door perfectly matched the red berries that clung to the bushes in the flower beds that surrounded it. I took a swig of Carnation. I looked out the dining room's picture window. Cars were now parked all along the dirt road's sloping shoulder. There was no more room for any in the yard around the countless pine trees that had shed their brown needles into a prickly fawn-colored carpet that completely covered the ground. The needles were great for making walls of forts, and I yearned at that very moment to build one that was impenetrable by all the in-coming pity.

The family's menfolk had gathered out there around the lawned cars, the lacelike autumn shadows softening their faces as the sun filtered down through the bare and long-limbed pines. Two older male cousins tossed a brown pine cone back and forth with Kim who pretended he was Charlie Conerly, an old quarterback for the Ole Miss Rebels. Karole, always at Kim's heels, begged to toss the pine cone, too. A few of the men were in that one-foot-on-a-fender stance that I always saw my uncles take when talking about deer hunting, Goldwater's loss, or "all these outside Commie agitators," who seemed continuously to be invading our state through my childhood, especially during those compressed and awful months that joined 1963 to 1964. Those months when both my parents died. When JFK died. When Medgar Evers died. When those three civil rights kids— Schwerner, Chaney, and Goodman—died up in Venomous Mae's beloved Neshoba County. I watched the breath from the men's mouths fog the chilly air with conversation. A car radio was blaring the news that someone named Horace Barnette had confessed to the FBI about the murders of the three kids and was going to tell them exactly what took place back during the summer.

(That was the summer when my mother was the sickest she had ever been while she lay up in a hospital—Lackey Memorial—which had been built to resemble, rather risibly, an antebellum mansion. As I walked out to the parking lot after visiting my weakened mother one particularly hot, sticky evening, my grandmother tried to explain how life was unfair at times. "We're not gonna tell Kim and Karole nothing. Only you," she said. "We figure you're old enough to take it. You're certainly smart enough to understand the situation. You do understand? God just needs good people with Him up in heaven so He's calling your mama to be with your daddy. She's only got another month or so to live, sugar. God's calling her name. He knows what's best. Listen to me. Listen up. I'm more serious than I've ever been in my whole life: You got to be a man about this. A little man. You can't be no child no more. That'll suit you right fine, won't it? You never seemed to like being one anyway." We reached the car, a black tank-like '57 Buick, all grillwork and hubcaps and headlights the size of Cyclopian twins. "So God did this?" I asked my grandmother. "Yes, sugar. You do understand. I knew you would." She touched the tiny bristles of my flattop. To me God was no better than Horace Barnette. Murderers. Both of them. "Then I hate God," I said. My grandmother gasped and slapped me right across my eight-year-old face. She gasped again. She placed her hands on the hood of the Buick and steadied herself. She began to cry. I comforted her for hitting me. I was—she was right—no longer a child.)

The radio next door in the kitchen's window that November day of the funeral was tuned to the same station as the one out in the parked car. The women surrounding my grandmother in the kitchen stopped their banter. The men in the yard leaned in, listening. "Who's this Barnette fellow?" someone asked. Uncle Benny, the husband of Aunt Lola, my grandfather's no-nonsense hulk of a sister, decided to speak up. A cotton farmer and contractor, Uncle Benny always wore overalls, even when he deigned to wear a tie as he had that day. He also had on that extra hunting jacket he kept clean in his closet for the occasions when he wasn't hunting. Benny usually hung back from conversation, slyly grinning at everyone else's slight buffoonery. When he did finally speak, his voice was a surprisingly soft high-timbred whine.

"I bet that Horace fella is kin to old Ross, sure as tootin'," he told the men. "Bet the Governor—I can't help but call him that, though, God help us, we just got us a new one—bet the Governor told him to add that extra 'e' onto his name so's to piss off that littler Kennedy that can't keep his nose out of our business. If you ask me, they kilt the wrong Kennedy. Shoulda kilt both of 'em while they were at it. We got a deer season and a duck season and a quail season. I say we should have a Kennedy season oncet a year, too." The other men laughed and shook their heads in agreement. A "colonel" in Ross Barnett's gubernatorial campaigns, Uncle Benny was one of Barnett's staunchest supporters. He had given the clownish and diabolical segregationist Mississippi governor enough money every four years to be awarded with the honorific. Old Ross was such a dolt he once began a speech he was giving to the congregation at Beth-Israel Temple in Jackson, Mississippi, with this: "There is nothing finer than a group of people meeting in true Christian fellowship."

"Calm down, Benny," said Erle Johnston, Barnett's ex-press secretary who was the editor and owner of our local newspaper, the *Scott County Times*, in which one of the "human interest" features on the Sessums Orphans had appeared. Under Mr. Erle's own byline, he reported that I was the lone child who had known of his mother's impending death, a bit of personal information I had read over and over wondering why he didn't also report that I had been slapped at the time I was told. Johnston, who, I must confess, always showed my family a generous concern and was the first to encourage my journalistic leanings, was later exposed as the director of a secret agency, the Mississippi Sovereignty Commission—sort of a cracker KGB—set up within the state government to rat-out its citizens and intimidate civil rights workers, sometimes violently, in an attempt to safeguard segregation. "Everything's under control, Benny," Johnston said, getting into his car to back out of the yard, careful not to hit the host of pickups that sat, like a herd, around the driveway next to the gas pump my grandfather had had installed on the property so he wouldn't have to drive his Buick the five miles into town for a few gallons of Shell.

"You heard Erle," one of the menfolk told Benny. "Erle's in the know. Nothing to worry about. But it's a sad state of affairs, ain't it, when you can't scare the coloreds no more and get away with it."

The other men shook their heads grimly. "The mistake they made was killing them two white boys," said Uncle Benny. "That's what made the mess."

I stared out at the muffled discussion and wished I could be as oblivious to such words swirling around me as were my little brother and insistent little sister out there tossing pine cones back and forth, frolicking in the pine straw. How had this happened? How had the three of us been born into such a confusing brew of chicanery, malevolence, and kindheartedness? Standing there at that window, I tried to focus on my reflection and not on all those men who did not know what to make of me anyway. I practiced looking sad. But I could not take my eyes off them: *The men. What kind of creatures are these? They are a part of me? Flesh of my flesh?* I listened to the low rumble of their voices discussing the realities of the day (Martin Luther King's numbered hours, LBJ's treachery), a lilt of hatred that, along with organ dirges and the dutiful mourning of the family's tearful womenfolk, furnished the soundtrack of my childhood. Just as my father's sadness changed to fear inside that coaches' lounge when he looked into my eyes, I looked into them now reflected before me, and watched my own practiced sadness, my own disdain, turn to perplexity, to fear. And then it hit me: *I do not belong here. I will report back one day on all that I have witnessed. I am a spy.*

Yet where exactly should an exotic such as I hang his hat? Where the hell did I belong? The best I could figure was on my favorite television show, *What's My Line?* I breathed on the dining room window and signed in, please, KEVIN SESSUMS, on the misted pane. I closed my eyes and tried with all my shattered heart to hear the cultured clip of the *What's My Line?* host John Daly drown out that low rumble of the men outside and the women in the kitchen, who were carrying on again about Northerners and niggers and how much nutmeg to put in next month's eggnog. I listened as Daly issued his weekly command to enter and sign in, please, on the chalkboard to see if the panel could guess my line of work. I would whisper into his ear, "I am a spy." The panel would be stumped. I would win my fifty dollars. Dorothy Kilgallen would call me "darling," and Daly, hearing her, would ask me to join them as a permanent fourth member of the panel. I would get to wear a tuxedo like Bennett Cerf. Or better yet, an evening gown like Arlene Francis and Miss Kilgallen.

I would sneak into the living room to watch Daly and his elegant panel on Sunday nights at 10:30 when everybody else had gone to bed. The show came on after the CBS Late News. I'd lie on my stomach in the dark and watch the images of the warfare up at Ole Miss the year before, when that preppy Negro James Meredith enrolled and insurgent riots erupted. Federal troops invaded. Deaths ensued. I took it all in as I lay there getting ready to practice elongating my vowels in the manner of Arlene and to shade my laughter with the tone that John Daly employed when displaying his jaded bemusement at one of Bennett Cerf's puns. My favorite segment: when a famous mystery guest was about to walk out and all the panelists put on their blindfolds (or "eye masks," as Miss Francis once called them) in order not to see who was signing in on the chalkboard. I would clasp each little index finger against my thumbs and form an imaginary mask over my own eyes and pretend I could not see. Sometimes, to the consternation of my grandfather who always turned in early, my grandmother would watch the show with me. "Tell you what, sugar. There must have been a run on chins when that Kilgallen gal was born, 'cause the Lord sho'nuff forgot to give her one," she would say, putting a hand to her mouth trying to stifle the sound of her laughter so she wouldn't wake my grandfather. I'd laugh too and describe my imaginary eye mask to her, telling her it was black and velvet and had pearls all around it just like Arlene's did. "Don't you want one like Bennett Cerf's?" she would ask.

"I tell you one thing," I heard her voice now rise above the windowed radio's din and awaken me from my latest daydream of a *What's My Line?* life. "I sure hope there ain't no kitchens in heaven."

"Hush, Joycie Otis. Don't you want to hear who all they caught?" asked Aunt Vena Mae, turning up the radio. "If you ask me—we were discussing this in my women's sixty and over Sunday-school class— those civil rights boys were just looking for trouble coming down here like that where they don't belong. Got what they deserved. This is a sign from God that they should mind their own business. I know Cecil Price. I know Sheriff Rainey," she said, mentioning the two Neshoba County law enforcement officers who everybody was saying either covered up the crime or helped commit it. "They're hicks but they're not murderers. A'course, according to everybody else in this day-and-age no-count country, we're all hicks in Mississippi. Some of us just dress better than others."

"Vena Mae, will you hush up about civil rights! I've had it up to here with civil rights!" said my grandmother, who was starting to cry yet again. She was a small woman, barely five feet tall, but had the lungs of a larger one. I once found hidden in my grandfather's closet an old 1920s photo of Vena Mae and my grandmother in all their bobbed-hair-and-bangs, flapper glory. If Vena Mae—always more voluptuous than her little sister—had a Theda Bara bearing about her as she posed for the camera, my tiny grandmother was more Gloria Swanson: all kohled eyes and boney allure. "I buried Nan today," she said, her voice gurgling for air up through her tears. "I buried my baby."

"I'm sorry, Joycie. I know you did," said Vena Mae. "Where's Lyle?"

she asked, mentioning my grandfather's name. "He should be here tending to you. I'm running out of hankies."

"He got mad at me for getting on him for eating that cold clabber and crumbled-up corn bread he loves so much instead of all this food everybody has brought over. I told him it was rude. He was insulting the women. He just started to cry and headed out back yonder. He's been crying today more than me."

I put down my Carnation milk on the window sill and stuck my new rabbit's foot in my pocket. I pinched each of my index fingers against my thumbs and formed my imaginary *What's My Line?* mask atop my eyes. I pranced through the dining room and into the kitchen.

"Where's that Carnation, Kevin? I just poured myself some more coffee," said Vena Mae. I ignored her and headed for the kitchen door. "Don't you know to speak when spoken to, boy? You and Lyle are going to have some trouble with this one," she told my grandmother, who now was sniffling.

"He don't see you, Vena Mae. He's got his highfalutin mask on," said my grandmother. "Call him Arlene and you might get an answer out of him." Aunt Vena Mae cocked an eyebrow. "He's playin' Arlene," my grandmother explained. "If you want that Carnation, you got to call him Arlene."

"I won't do no such thing," said Vena Mae. "I think I've seen it all now. I swuny. Who the Sam Hill is Arlene?"

"That ugly woman that makes herself pretty on Sunday nights after all them lies on the late CBS news," said my grandmother, wiping her nose.

"Arlene Francis?" asked Vena Mae. She put her hand to her chunky necklace. "She's a Jew! Least, that's what I hear tell."

I slammed the door in Vena Mae's face and went looking for my grandfather. He was in the backyard by himself sitting under a pine tree eating his clabber and crumbled-up corn bread with a soup spoon out of a giant glass goblet. I walked up to him—my imaginary mask still fingered in place—and sat by his side. The needles all around the pine's trunk softened the ground. A few of the tree's huge gnarled roots jutted into view and I snuggled into the crevice created by the two largest ones. My grandfather eyed me with a mouthful of clabber-soaked bread. "What's up, Arlene?" he asked. "You couldn't take it in there anymore, either, hon?" I dropped my hands and dug into my pocket to show him my rabbit's foot. "Who gave you that?" he asked. I shrugged. "That's a fine-lookin' thing," he said as I watched him grapple with some final soggy crumbs of corn bread down at the bottom of the goblet. "Want this last bit?" he asked me. I shook my head. The concoction looked like what I had once vomited on that Winston-smoking coach's shoes. My grandfather started to cry some more but quickly fought back the tears. He surveyed the yard with his brimming eyes. "Look at all this space we got back here," he said, burping up some clabber. "Don't this look like a nice place for a pony?" I shrugged. Somewhere out there in the pastures surrounding us was a flock of throaty birds that must have taken a wrong turn out of Alabama, for they were now sounding as deeply flummoxed as I was feeling. "Listen to them damn crows," said my grandfather. "I hate crows. They remind me of all these civil-righters crawling all over the state—black and complaining and always making the most of a bad situation. But I guess that's what we gotta do, too, hon. Make the best of a bad situation. I know you miss yo' mama and daddy something awful. God knows, I do. I know you probably don't know what to make of your old Pop and Mom," he said, using the names that Kim and Karole and I called him and our grandmother. "But I promise you sitting right here on this day under this tree—I want you to remember this the rest of your life—that nobody will ever love you more than Mom and me. We ain't got much but love to give you. But you can rest assured, hon, that we're gonna give you that." His old eyes filled with tears again, his sorrow magnified behind his thick-lensed glasses. I looked up and saw the long gray hairs in his nostrils clot with snot. He pulled out a handkerchief from his back pocket and haphazardly wiped his big nose. He looked a lot like LBJ. "Oh, Lord," he said and pointed toward the house. I heard the clunk of Vena Mae's jewelry in the distance and turned to see her leading my grandmother toward us. "Better batten down the hatches," my grand-father whispered. "Here comes Veeny. And Jake don't look too happy neither," he said, using the nickname my grandmother was called by those closest to her. I put my rabbit's foot back in my pocket and formed my highfalutin mask with my fingers. "You might have the right idea there, Arlene," my grandfather said, chuckling and making sure that there was nothing left in either the goblet or his nose. He put his handkerchief back in his pocket.

"Lyle, you should be tending to Joycie. I had to find her asthma spray before her grief plumb near smothered her. Here!" Vena Mae said, handing off my grandmother, who sat gingerly on the ground on the other side of me, careful not to snag her funeral dress on any of the tree's exposed roots. My grandfather took off his suit jacket and handed it across my masked face to her so she could wrap it around her thin shoulders in the November chill.

"I better not ruin my dress sitting here like this. It's the first time I've ever worn it. Took me near 'bout one whole hour to find this McCall's pattern up at the Thomas Great M last month," my grand-mother said, referring to the department store on Main Street in Forest. "Nan had taken her final turn toward the worst and I knew I'd be needing a dress like this soon enough. Thought I should be plan-ning ahead for this day. Practical to a fault—that's me. How I kept all my seams straight with me crying at my sewing machine like I done, I'll never know."

Vena Mae stood over the three of us and frowned at the sight. She rearranged her bracelets. "Y'all seen Doots anywhere? It's about time we started driving back. I told him not to sneak off," she complained, mentioning her husband who so seldom spoke after years of marriage to her that one could be forgiven for thinking the woman had purposefully wedded a mute. He owned Moore's Hardware up in Philadelphia and would sit in his proprietor's chair in the front of the store and keep the daily tab inside his silent head. "Our car is blocked in out in the front yard. Who's in charge of moving cars in and out? I heard tell Dickie and Bill was doing that," she said, naming the husbands, respectively, of my mother's two sisters, Jo Ann and Peg. A chorus of laughter erupted inside the house. Confused, we turned toward the sound—all of us as mute as Uncle Doots—and waited for it to subside. "You know, Joycie," Vena Mae said, "if we hadn't had a funeral today, this would have been a *right nice* party. Wouldn't it, Lyle? Wouldn't it . . ." She stopped herself when she saw me staring up at her through my fingered-together mask. "Look at you," she said. "I got news for you, boy. You're more Dorothy Kilgallen than Arlene Francis." She turned on her high heels and headed for the house. "Doots!" she called. "Doots! Where are you? We gotta make Neshoba before nightfall!"

"You got a *right nice* sister," said my grandfather to my grandmother.

My grandmother shook her head as Vena Mae disappeared into the house. "Yep. She's something," she said, taking off her cat-eye–shaped glasses and cleaning the lenses with a dry corner of the handkerchief that Vena Mae had given her. She put the glasses back on. "But I don't know what I would have done without her all these years. Remember when Nan was born? Not an easy birth that one. Vena Mae was there for me for a lot of them down days afterwards. Me having yo' mama, Arlene, was almost as bad as when yo' mama had you. You come out plumb blue. You were a blue baby, sugar.

Weren't breathing a'tall. I had just started working as a nurse's aid back then and come running out of that room just a'cryin'. Thought we'd done had us a stillbirth. I got halfway down the hall before I heard you start t'cryin' yourself. Sweetest sound I ever heard. But why ain't you cried none today, sugar? I was thinking about that while I was cutting up one of Lola's chocolate pies." I tightened my mask. I shrugged. "We were all so relieved when you was no longer blue in the face back then that we pulled a fast one on yo' daddy. You were born around noon and he was over at Lola's having lunch. When yo' daddy got back to the hospital we told him he had twin girls." My grandfather laughed. My grandmother straightened her shoulders beneath his jacket. "Let's see if this really helps," she said. She flicked off her cat-eyes. She placed her index fingers against her thumbs and fashioned her own version of an Arlene Francis eye mask. She positioned it on her face. "Now I understand," she said, winking at me through her fingers. "I always thought you couldn't see nothing when you put this mask on. But I'll be darn, if it ain't just the opposite," she said, now winking at my grandfather over my head. "That's your magic secret, ain't it? I figured you out, Arlene. You can see *everything* when you put this mask on. I can even see them crows yonder."

I dropped my hands. I looked toward the fading horizon. This long, awful, to-be-forever-remembered day was drawing to a close. The crows out there looked like bits of night already arriving. I draped an arm on each of the large roots that surrounded me. I pretended I was on a throne. My grandmother's eyes, still framed by her fingers, filled with her endless tears. My grandfather also began to cry. The crows closed in. "Fuck," I said aloud for the first time.

My grandmother gasped but did not slap me. "What did you just say?" she asked.

"Fuck."

My grandfather went for his handkerchief.

"Sugar, that's not a word Arlene Francis would use," my grandmother said.

I shrugged. "Call me Kevinator," I told her.

1

Skeeter Davis, Noël Coward, and Eudora Welty

"Fuck," said Frank Hains. "I knew I shouldn't have given that last bourbon to Eudora."

It had taken me almost a decade after that day of my mother's funeral, but I had finally found the only equivalent that Mississippi offered to a *What's My Line?* life. Frank—a John Daly–like presence in Jackson—was the arts editor of the state's afternoon newspaper, for which he also wrote a column called "On Stage." Eudora was writer Eudora Welty. We were at a cast party for New Stage Theatre's latest production, *Long Day's Journey into Night*, starring Geraldine Fitzgerald as Mary Tyrone. Frank and Miss Welty were active members of New Stage, and he was playing host that night at Bleak House, the name given facetiously to his antebellum home by the local literati of Jackson. The Dickensian nickname derived from the house's outward appearance of haunted dilapidation where it sat, rather spookily, on a hill opposite Jackson's lone Jewish cemetery. Inside, however, past the vast front porch, Frank—also a gifted set designer—had redone his home with a lovely simplicity. Books abounded. A collection of vintage LPs filled one whole room, alphabetized and all of them encased in brown paper sleeves. Even though he had this wide selection of music, he usually only played Mabel Mercer, his favorite, or Erik Satie or Blossom Dearie. He also liked Fred Astaire—for his voice, not his dancing—which was so like Frank; he was always looking for the different angle, the way to appreciate an artist or a piece of art in his own way so that appreciation itself became a kind of art form. There was even a Leontyne Price album of pop songs arranged by André Previn he loved to listen to for some rueful smiles; especially the Mississippi diva's rendition of "Melancholy Baby" with Previn on the piano and Ray Brown on bass. On the night of that latest cast party he was playing, as a tribute, a lot of Noël Coward, who had died the month before.

Frank Hains went to New York City several times a year to review theater and opera for his newspaper and had begun to allow me to stay at Bleak House in his absence. He also subscribed to *After Dark* magazine, and I would peruse the pages of the slender and sleekly photographed issues when I visited him for their overt appeal to the kind of eroticism I had begun to seek out anyplace I could find it. Frank would stand over my shoulder when a new *After Dark* arrived in the mail and point out his latest favorite photograph by Roy Blakey or Kenn Duncan and regale me with stories about Angela Lansbury, who was often featured in the pages, or Rudolf Nureyev, whom he insisted I resembled in some sort of Slavic/Southern sleight-of-hand. "I should be more supportive of the ballet," he said once, staring at the latest photo of Nureyev that *After Dark* was running. "I'm much more at home in literature and drama and musical comedy and opera. Satie is just about the only thing I can stomach that doesn't have a lyric. That, and Bach, but there's a mathematical genius to old J. B. I find fascinating. I once had a crush on a mathematician when I was, like you, a college sophomore. I know—can you picture me a sophomore? Hmmm . . . why Bach and Satie? *There's a column in there somewhere*," he said, using one of his favorite phrases as he pushed his black-framed reading glasses atop his thin-haired head, a habit of his when a concept for a column occurred to him, as if he were helping his brain to see the idea floating about his skull back there around his bald spot.

Frank's kitchen in Bleak House was as big as most homes. Theatrical posters—along with several of the photographs that Miss Welty had taken of innately elegant dirt-poor Mississippians when she worked as a publicist for the Works Project Administration during the Depression—hung along the walls of the house's "dogtrot," the open hallway that runs through the center of so many Southern homes of the antebellum period. A couple of years earlier, Miss Welty had collected many of the photos of her Depression-era travels in a volume titled *One Time, One Place*. She always preferred to refer to them as "snapshots," however, and recalled fondly the little Rolleiflex camera she toted around with her upon her return from her year in business school up at Columbia University, her eyes readjusting, expertly so, to the reasons that had drawn her back home.

I had first met Frank and Miss Welty when I was still in high school. A mutual friend from Forest had taken me to a book party Frank had thrown for Miss Welty at Bleak House. Although I was only sixteen at the time, I had immediately been accepted into their fold. No eye masks were needed, I discovered, but there were other requirements. A liberal political bent helped. A sense of one's own sensuality. Discernment certainly. And, most important, enough knowledge to know when to join a heady conversation or, better yet, simply to listen while others carried on one around you. I learned more sitting at Frank's big round kitchen table than I ever did in any classroom as he and Miss Welty—who would wander over the few blocks it took to drive her blue Ford Fairlane from Pinehurst Street—went off on Richard Nixon or Vladimir Nabokov, but practically swooned over the poetic justness to be found in Jane Austen and somebody "just about the best" named Henry Green. They liked jazz, too—Miss Welty had done a lot of club-hopping in Harlem—and taught me that bourbon was never to be augmented by anything other than maybe an added ice cube if one *simply must* when yet another Mississippi August demanded such a dilution, and sipping at a slightly watered-down potation was the only reasonable exertion that such heat and humidity humanly allowed. Their refilled glasses—it was my honor to administer the respective cubes—fueled their conversation until they drifted sometimes, not often, from cerebral musings to those of the heart.

They were mostly circumspect when discussing their lost loves. Frank would often allude to his "dusky endeavors," as they had come to refer politely to his interest in young African Americans, some of whom had touched him deeply with their aspirations and narratives of maternal love. Miss Welty welcomed these stories of nuanced carnality, as Frank was careful not to tell her the details. One especially hot night under the glow of the big light that hung over his kitchen table, Miss Welty, her upper lip damp, did hint at the feelings she had for one young man long, long ago. Frank had tears in his eyes as she lyrically, elliptically, without ever admitting the depths of her own emotions but not denying them either, told us of a young poet who could obviously still summon a profound sadness within her all these years after he had moved away from Mississippi, from her, and taken up residence in San Francisco and Italy, places more "welcoming to his kind, to yours," she told us as her voice came to a halt and she perhaps heard only his now lost one in the sudden comfort of her silence. She finished neither the carefully diluted story nor the freshly diluted bourbon in front of her, both making it too dangerous that night, she seemed to reason in her reverie, for her to drive back home to a house forever musty with familial love alone.

———

Years later, my little brother, Kim—a Mississippi obstetrician/gynecologist who has also become a sculptor of some renown—presented to Miss Welty a bronze bust of herself. It was the last year of her life and she had taken up residence in the downstairs parlor of the house on Pinehurst. She was in ill health by then and no longer able to make it upstairs to the bedroom where she had written her short stories and novels, putting their freshly typed pages on her old bed, then cutting them up with a pair of sewing scissors before pinning the paragraphs and sentences back together as if literature of the highest order were indeed the piecework of her life.

Many of her favorite books had been moved downstairs also and were scattered everywhere about her—lined on shelves, stacked on the floor, overflowing a loveseat. An autographed photo of President Bill Clinton sat framed on her mantel. Kim lifted her fragile body from her daybed and gently placed her in her motorized lounger. Her head fell back onto the chair's giant pillow. "How can one accomplish this kind of work and practice the art of medicine at the same time?" she weakly asked him, her teeth slightly bucked as she began to smile in the exact smile-ready expression displayed in bronze before her.

"I kept the bust in my clinic and worked on it between Pap smears," Kim told her.

A twinkle came to Miss Welty's eye. "We should call it *Between Paps* then," she said, always good at titles, even in her weakened state. Kim, relieved by her success at levity, attempted, with the bedside manner he had developed in his medical practice, to engage her in more conversation but words no longer issued from her with the ease they once had. She could remember incidents from years past, according to Kim, but had trouble with the flow of raillery that was a generational marker for a certain sort of gentlewoman of the South, of which she was one of the last and finest exemplars. He finally commented on her collection of short stories, *The Golden Apples*. The mention of that particular title sparked something deep within her. Miss Welty raised her head suddenly from her pillow. Her voice grew strong, assured. "Isn't that lovely?" she asked him. "I stole that from William Butler Yeats," she said and, without hesitation, recited the final stanza of Yeats's "The Song of Wandering Aengus":

"Though I am old with wandering
Through hollow lands and hilly lands,
I will find out where she has gone,
And kiss her lips and take her hands;
And walk among long dappled grass,
And pluck till time and times are done
The silver apples of the moon,
The golden apples of the sun."

She placed her head back on its pillow. She sighed, satisfied with this last rendition of her beloved Yeats she would ever get right. Kim compared his bronzed handiwork to what lay before him: her ancient brow, her white wisps of hair, flesh's feeble decay. Reverie was all that was left her now. Were the words of that other beloved poet in her life haunting her still in the comfort of an even deeper silence? Was it he who had led her to Yeats in the first place? She turned toward the bronze for one last look. She stared into her own eyes.

———

I had been discovered at an earlier party for *A Midsummer Night's Dream* at Bleak House by New Stage's artistic director, Ivan Rider, and cast in a subsequent production at the theater, which enabled me to be even more securely ensconced in the only cosmopolitan bohemia that Jackson, Mississippi, offered. I was at the height of my surly, shaggy-haired teenage beauty back then—more punk than Puck—which was exactly the type that the director was looking for to play the role of the deaf-mute Toby in Gian Carlo Menotti's one-act opera *The Medium*. The production was a local sensation and enabled me to gain a drama scholarship to Millsaps College, the Methodist-supported school right up the hill from Bleak House. Frank not only designed the sets for New Stage, but also taught stage design at Millsaps and oversaw all scenic aspects for the productions of the Millsaps Players. He was even a lighting director, and Bleak House was scrupulously lit so that any guest looked lovelier in its environs. "Well, at least less haggard," he once remarked when I pointed this out to him.

Our friendship—though he was almost thirty years older than I—deepened during the two years we got to know each other. He cast me as the newspaper boy with whom Blanche Dubois desperately flirts in a production of *A Streetcar Named Desire* he directed at the Vicksburg Little Theatre. We would talk and talk in his Pontiac LeMans on those ninety-minute round-trips from Jackson to Vicksburg during the six weeks we rehearsed and performed the play. We became so close, in fact, he sprung an odd request on me while we were listening on the LeMans's radio to a bare-bones country station. At first we had tuned in to the twangy numbers and corny, locally produced commercials as a sophisticated lark, but we discovered the longer we listened to that station, the less frequently our laughter came, and we had actually started to sing along with the weary reverence the now familiar lyrics called for. Frank got his start as a disc jockey over in Vicksburg and had a lifelong respect for the discipline and musical knowledge the job required as well as "the way a d.j. of any stripe must harness the mayhem of station life to soothe the listener into believing the lovely lie that there is order in this world." He sometimes confessed that he was at his happiest spinning records all alone in his little glassed-in cubicle, way back then in 1956, the very year of my birth, as I liked to point out to him.

"I have something I really must ask of you," he had said that night on our drive back to Jackson, already blushing before the request could be made, his voice meekly skimming the surface of Skeeter Davis's toughened alto singing a James Taylor song, which was barely audible now from the radio Frank had turned way down. "I have an old trunk locked up in my closet. It contains . . . well . . . it contains what some might consider . . ." He gripped the wheel tighter. "Itcontainswhatsomemightconsider*pornography*," he said, all the words rushing from him in a jumble and tumbling over that very last one. "There—I said it." I turned my head and smiled out the window at the passing pines, an exit sign or two, some roadkill that looked like another opossum too slow to make it across both lanes of the Interstate. "Promise me, Kevin, that you will dispose of that trunk if anything ever happens to me. Promise me. My West Virginia family cannot find it upon my demise; they simply *cannot*," he said.

"Of course, Frank," I assured him. Though he did not mean for such a request to be regarded as funny by me, it was certainly seeming that way at the moment. I tried not to, but I could not help myself: I started to giggle.

Frank flipped up the volume of the radio just as Skeeter was going after her toughest James Taylor note. "Don't you dare laugh at me," he said. "Don't you dare." It was the only time I can remember his ever being curt as far as I was concerned. "I'm being quite serious. I've never been *more* serious. This is our secret. No, it is more than that. This, dear boy, is a *confidence*," he said, imbuing the word with all the meaning he could muster as he launched into that haughty Mabel Mercer mode that could overtake him from time to time, one that seemed rather out of place in the presence of Skeeter. "I thought about asking Eudora, but there are limits to her empathy. I've watched you closely this past year or so since we've gotten to know each other. Don't ask me why, but I trust you completely. You are remarkably free of judgment and yet you are preternaturally wary. It's a nice combination. You seem to be spying right there out in the open all the time, right there in our midst," he said, nailing me. "It's quite disarming. Eudora even commented on it when she first met you. I asked her what she thought of you—I would not have included you in our sphere without her approval—and she said, 'That child is so ripe with private assessments I'm surprised the skin hasn't begun to bruise. Does he *read?*' "

"Yeah, I read," I said. "I read her fucking short stories. She's no Flannery O'Connor."

"Thank God," said Frank. "There's all that Roman flimflam in Flannery. Eudora is more welcoming. You'll see, dear boy. One reaches a certain age and all one longs for is to feel welcomed." I turned and looked at Frank. Really looked at him. Skeeter was singing the Taylor lyric "All those lonely times when I could not find a friend," and I knew in that moment I had found my first true one. I felt—there is no other word for it—such tenderness toward him as I noticed there were tears beginning to fill his eyes. But he held them back. He did not let them fall. He had too much dignity for that. Too much grace. Those are the two main characteristics that Frank Hains so effortlessly possessed, and to this day, when I am lucky enough to summon one or both of them at the most unexpected of moments, I am certain that it is he—ever ephemeral, ever Frank—who is present and enabling me to conjure such characteristics in my own less dignified, less graceful life. Just as I feel his hand still on my shoulder in those moments, I put my hand on his in that one. "I'll get rid of that trunk if it means that much to you," I told him. "Say no more." And we never did. We never mentioned it again.

———————

By the time of that bourbon-drenched New Stage cast party for *Long Day's Journey into Night*, I had decided to rent Bleak House's front bedroom from Frank for the upcoming summer while I earned some much-needed money working at a Jeans West store in a local mall. I had recently auditioned for the Juilliard School of Drama, at Frank's encouraging insistence, and been accepted for the next term. Manhattan—and an even grander *What's My Line?* life—beckoned. But first I would have to get through the upcoming Mississippi months, which would prove, even with my tragic past, to be among the most difficult days of my life. As I look back on it now, that cast party for *Long Day's Journey* rivaled my first locker room visit with my father for its happy allure. The rooms were echoing with the sound of laughter and music and glasses being constantly filled. I knew Frank was certainly having a ball, for he loved playing host. "I'm the hostess with the most-ess," he would sing under his breath, breezing through the place and making sure everyone was having a good time.

Back in the record library, Geraldine Fitzgerald had just finished singing an Irish ballad, one of the numbers she was preparing for a cabaret show in New York called *Street Songs*. Miss Welty, taking the cue, attempted to perform her own little musical ditty for a few of her friends surrounding her on Frank's low-slung, circa-1969 sofa: Jane Reid Petty, a beautiful petite blonde who was New Stage's resident diva (her performance as Edna Earle in Frank's stage adaptation of Miss Welty's *The Ponder Heart* endeared her to local audiences much less sophisticated than she); Charlotte Capers, Miss Welty's lifelong best friend, who was the head of the Mississippi Department of History and Archives; Miss Capers's protégée at the Archives, a smart-as-a-whip, willowy blonde named Patti Carr Black; and Karen Gilfoy, a mannish Rosalind Russell manqué who decided to be a lawyer while learning most of Cole Porter's catalogue.

"When Eudora gets a little drunk like this, she always likes to show off," Frank whispered to me as we admired Jackson's reigning doyennes assembled before us. "Big Char there can really loosen her up," he said. Miss Capers, in this crowd, was lovingly referred to as "Big Charlotte." She hovered around six feet tall and loved—humorously, intellectually, socially—to throw her weight around. Frank and I were standing sofa-side at the stereo, which gave us a lay-of-the-party view. "Too much bourbon can literally bring out the Bea Lillie in Eudora," he whispered.

"Who's Bea Lillie?" I asked. Frank rolled his eyes at me. Miss Welty's unsteady warble—she was certainly in no Yeats-spouting mood that night—tried secretly to amuse her pals. "Wait a minute," I said, suddenly discomfited, a detail from an awful memory darting to the surface before submerging itself once more. "Is Bea Lillie Mrs. Meers?"

"I have no idea what you're talking about," said Frank. "Mrs. Meers? Bea Lillie—a k a *Lady Peel*, not Mrs. Meers—is a great comic genius. Eudora says her recent autobiography has one of the best titles ever—*Every Other Inch a Lady*. Eudora loved that title so much I didn't have the heart to tell her Lady Peel stole it, paraphrasing a remark Rebecca West once made about some *gentleman* she could not abide. Lillie's voice was once described as that of a bunch of drunken fairies—quite apt for this room tonight—who have been hit over the head with a golden hammer. Shhh . . . listen . . . Eudora does a great Lady Peel."

I looked over and was shocked to see Miss Welty, winking up at us, lower the strap on her dress. Vamping now, she exposed a bit of the flesh on her gibbous shoulder and continued her rhythmic high-pitched patter to her friends' muffled laughter:

Yesterday night—
I went to a MAAAAAHVELOUS party
With Nunu and Nada and Nell . . .

Frank held up the album he had just taken off his turntable. "Noël Coward," he said, pointing to its cover. "Eudora's doing Bea Lillie do-

ing Noël Coward." He put on some Mabel Mercer. "I met him once—
Noël Coward. It was on a New York trip. We were all in the same
room as Cardinal Spellman. Would you mind taking Eudora home tonight, dear boy? She's in no condition to drive herself and I have to
stay around to tend to my guests. This party does not seem to be pe-
tering out. Perhaps I'll get out my *Noël Coward in Las Vegas* record and
play that last cut on it, 'The Party's Over Now,' *very loudly.* Wait here.
I'll convince Eudora it's time to go. Oh, God, she's starting in on 'I'm
a Camp-Fire Girl.' "

"But I want to stay. I'm having fun," I whispered back at Frank
while I kept staring at the dashingly handsome blond-haired thirty-
five-year-old advertising executive, a New Stage stalwart, who was
playing the older son, Jamie, in *Long Day's Journey.* His name was
Carl Davis and he had made it very clear that he had a crush on me.
I was ready to make it very clear that such a crush was a credible emotion. "Can't someone else take Miss Welty home?" I asked. "I think
Carl's ready to make a pass."

Frank placed an avuncular hand on my cheek and softly patted it.
He sweetly, knowingly smiled. "Do as I say," he said. "Take Eudora
home. Trust me—you'll write about it one day."

After Miss Welty wavered a bit on a "Camp-Fire Girl" lyric, Frank
helped me escort her to the front porch. Behind us, the frivolity continued. "Kevin can take it from here, Eudora," he said, kissing her on
both cheeks. "Talk to you tomorrow. Have to get back to my guests."

"You're such a sweet boy to be carting me home," Miss Welty said,
and allowed me to take her arm. My white Mercury Comet was
parked on the little hill that led down to the Jewish cemetery. It had
rained all day and we had to be careful not to slip as we traversed the
treacherously slick blades of grass. I led her to the passenger side of
the front seat and opened the door for her. "I'm fine now," she said. I
let go of her arm and hurried around to the driver's side. When I
opened the door I discovered what Miss Welty just had: I'd forgotten

to clean off my front seat after I worked out that afternoon and my dirty gym clothes were still strewn where I had thrown them on her side of the car. She held my jockstrap pinched between her index finger and her thumb and was carefully placing it on the backseat. Her large rheumy eyes focused on my guilty face as surely as my father's had when it was I who held a jock so long ago in just such a manner.

"Sorry, Miss Welty," I said as she wiped her fingers on her lap, the very same fingers—Fuck, I wanted to say aloud—with which every one of her stories had been typed on her old Underwood, upstairs in her bedroom over on Pinehurst.

She smiled at my embarrassment, then looked out her window at the neighboring grave sites. "Oh, I just thought that thing was a little Jewish ghost," she said, now waving her hand dismissively. "We've all got our ghosts to tend to." She looked back at me. She reached over and tapped my steering wheel with her story-telling fingers. "Now let's get goin'," she said.

2

Stephen Sondheim, Captain Hook, and Dorothy Malone

When I was just getting used to being six years old, in the late spring of 1962, I had a crush on an older woman who lived across the street. She was eight and much more experienced than I. Gangly and snaggle-toothed, she had a dusting of freckles across her tanned nose like a sprinkling of cinnamon. She was, my neighbor, the most breathtaking of tomboys. This was indeed her initial allure for me: that tough coquettishness (fist on a hip, ever-flared nostrils, a sloe-eyed squint that could so easily size up oneself in another's eyes) that I would subsequently encounter during my Greenwich Village years hanging out in the Ninth Circle, a hustler bar on West Tenth Street where Janis Joplin reigned over the jukebox and Andy Warhol, Lou Reed, and Robert Mapplethorpe often browsed the denimed wares. The denim jeans my neighbor wore were handed down from her older brothers and they always drooped enticingly about her waist. Her mother made sure they were also hugely cuffed so that they would not drag the ground around her dusty bare feet. Inside those cuffs she stored her gum, a dead cricket or two, and sometimes the butt of one of her mother's discarded cigarettes, which we would re-light, using the kitchen matches she had stolen, as we took turns precisely wrapping our own lips around the lipsticked stain left on the filter. I never once saw her cough as she downed the cigarette smoke and allowed it to float back up past her freckles. It would be years before she sprouted breasts and sprayed a first spritz of her mother's Avon behind ears that then always protruded from her flopping mop of unbrushed hair. "I don't want them titty things," she would complain. She knew the word "titty" would make me blush and she liked me better when such embarrassment rouged my cheeks. It was this daring daintiness of mine—an unnerving natural grace, often ridiculed as girly—that no doubt attracted her to me. Though we didn't yet know exactly what sex was, we possessed complementary sexualities. It was the basis of our friendship.

"Don't say 'titty,'" I'd tell her.

"Titty titty titty," she'd tease me and defiantly puff out her titless chest as she pushed her hair behind those ears of hers, which she once let me clean with a Q-Tip she pulled from one of her cuffs. We were playing in my bedroom as our mothers sunned themselves in the warm May light out back on a quilt my grandmother had made long ago. We lay on our stomachs atop my bed in the same position our mothers had taken in the yard. We gazed upon them through my bedroom window as they pushed each other's bathing suit down on their shoulders so their tans would look more even when they wore their new strapless sundresses. We silently watched them while they carefully rubbed Coppertone suntan lotion on their smooth and lovely backs, their jutting shoulder blades like the nubs of de-winged angels grubbing around down here on earth. My mother's adored transistor radio, nestled on the quilt next to my father's equally adored little black Chihuahua, Coco, was switched from the country-and-western station my father preferred to one that had been playing the latest hits from the Shirelles and Chubby Checker and Little Eva. Coco seemed to be dancing to the music and this struck my neighbor and me as extremely funny. We stifled our giggles and slid onto the floor. We hid ourselves beneath the window sill.

"Clean my ears for me," she commanded when we had calmed down and she extracted that Q-Tip from her cuff, first wetting the swab with a hacked-up gob of her spit. Wax caked the bit of cotton as I inserted it over and over into her ears, careful not to hurt her. "Now whisper something to me," she said in a voice that hinted there was evil in this world. I froze and watched her masterfully work that snaggle-toothed gap in her grin with her mean little tongue. She cupped a filthy fingernailed hand around an ear still damp inside with her own spittle. "Whisper to me your worstest secret," she said, as if she already knew what my father and I had been up to only a few days before.

I leaned into her. She smelled of Johnson's baby shampoo and the peanut butter sandwiches my mother had made to keep us quiet. Should I tell her what had happened between my father and me even though I had promised him not ever to tell anybody? She was, after all, my best friend. Should I not share with her this first and gravest secret of my life, the one that would be the basis for all the other secrets to follow? I concluded, however, that breaking a promise, especially to my father, was much worse than lying. I decided therefore to do just that: lie through my still intact baby teeth. Don't get me wrong. I had lied many times before. Lies flow as innocently and naturally from a child as flatulence and snot and unchecked laughter. But there comes a time when a child first makes a *decision* to lie and life is forever altered. "I ain't got no secret," I whispered.

She quickly dropped her hand and, snarling with disappointment, pushed at my shoulders the way I had seen my mother dismissively push back her plate of uneaten food when she and my father fought over something at the dinner table. The girl pushed me a second time even harder and I fell on the floor. She then straddled me and held my hands behind my head. "What kind of boy are you? You ain't got no secret? You that much a goodie-goodie?" she asked. A long string of spit—a ritual of ours—oozed past the gap in her teeth but she sucked it up before it could hit me in the face. "We gotta make a real boy outta you," she said. "Come on. I'll give you a secret. I'll give you a good'un," she growled, eyeing me with both contempt and curiosity. She drilled herself into my crotch where she sat on top of me. Another string of spit yo-yoed my way. My own saliva thickened— for the very first time—with something other than thirst.

Releasing me from her grip, she peeked out the window. I peeked next. Our mothers—like my baby brother and sister on the other bed in the room—had, napping now, fallen silent. Even Coco had tired of her little jig and dozed too in the afternoon sun. The transistor radio had seemed to put the whole tired world, except for the two of us, into a perfect trance. "Follow me," the girl said.

"What should I do with this Q-Tip?" I asked, still firmly holding the tiny instrument in my grip.

"Hide it," she instructed.

"Where?" I asked.

"Beds are always the best for hiding stuff," she informed me and, grabbing the Q-Tip from me, hid it beneath my mattress. "Now, come on," she said and led me out the back door toward another neighbor's overgrown hedge.

Behind us, as we sneaked away, the sound of the radio began to fade, the Four Seasons nasally insisting that big girls don't cry. We crawled through the neighboring flower bed that snaked with snapdragons and daffodils and rose bushes along the Simpsons' ersatz log cabin that sat next-door to my little green shingled house. No matter how many times Frankie Valli sang, faintly now, that big girls didn't cry, I sure wanted to, because the sudden stabbing memory of the secret I shared with my father filled my eyes to the brimming. I bit my lip, however, and staunched the flow as I crawled on, following behind my neighbor's butt, which burst forth with one of her patented farts right in my face: a trumpet blast of gaseous bliss. I held my breath—my eyes brimmed even more from the odor—as she almost choked on her own swallowed chortle. "Shhh-shhh," she instructed us both. "The Simpson Lady might be watching *As the World Turns*," she said, using the name we had come up with for Mrs. Simpson, who was so much more dignified than all the other women on our street, her manner more highfalutin, her clothes always just a little too nice. "Don't want to scare her. My mama says the Simpson Lady is more nervouser than usual since all them policemen was here last week." We stood and, bushing ourselves off, scurrried to the hedge where she quickly pushed me face-first into the branches. "Put your hands over your eyes. Don't look," she said, her voice taking on the bossy cadence she used so often when we were alone together. I, as always, obeyed and felt the sudden whoosh of her pulling down my shorts around my ankles. She leaned in and clamped her hands over mine. "Now pull your panties down yourself," she whispered as I slipped my hands from beneath hers and pushed my underwear down to where my shorts waited. "Don't look back," she said as I felt her kneeling now behind me. Her hands, like my mother's on the biscuit dough as I watched her on Sunday mornings, readying it to be rolled out and cut in circles for the baking sheet, kneaded my exposed butt before her fingers separated my cheeks to take a look at where I puckered. "Shoot. It looks just like mine," she said, her voice oddly disappointed. "I seen it, my butt hole, in my mama's hand mirror when I held it down yonder 'tween my legs and peeked at myself." She gave me a sniff. "Hmmm . . ." she said, considering the smell. "Figure that—you don't really stank. You sure you a boy?" she asked, giggling, then pulled me down on my knees and took my face-first place in the hedge. She pushed down the latest pair of jeans grown too small for one of her older brothers. She pushed down her panties. "Your turn," she said. "Go on. Look at my butt hole." I could not move. "Scaredy cat. Here," she said. She spread her cheeks with her own hands and pushed herself toward my face. My nose brushed against her and I got my first whiff of the sickening sweet stench of someone else's ass. "See? I stank worse'n you," she bragged. "I'm more a boy'n you are."

"Who's out there?" came the Simpson Lady's frightened voice from within the house. "Anybody out there? I'll call the police again! I swear to God I will. Who's there?"

The girl and I hurriedly pulled up our pants and rushed across the street before we could be found out. We ran up a hill in the back of her house toward a weedy field where there was an old deserted baseball diamond on which the Baptists had once played softball. I was mortified by our adventure so far, but my friend was holding her sides, she was laughing so hard. She led me into one of the field's creaky old dugouts and collapsed in a convulsive heap on the dirt floor next to a pile of IMPEACH EARL WARREN yard signs. I sat down beside her and silently waited for her laughter to subside.

———

The last time I had been in a baseball dugout was a couple of weeks earlier, at Battlefield Park out toward Jackson between the GE plant and an ice cream parlor where I ordered only vanilla cones no matter how much my father tempted me with other flavors. He was on a summer baseball team (he had played for a short time in a semipro league over in Louisiana when he first returned from New York after his tryout for the Knicks) and enjoyed being once more on the field of play instead of having to sit on the sidelines, where he rather frustratingly now found himself working as a high school coach. He let me sit in the dugout with his team that night. It was from that vantage point I had seen him, showboating as usual, slide head-first into second base and knock himself out—injuring his neck and suffering a concussion—for not only had he collided with the second baseman, but he had also been hit in the head by the ball thrown from behind home plate by the catcher trying to make the inning's final out.

My mother screamed and ran from the stands, pushing past the umpire and the catcher whose face was now showing real concern, exposed as it was by the discarded mask that lay on the red clay dirt at his spiked feet. There was complete silence in the crowd except for my mother's voice. "Howard!" she screamed. "Howard! Is he all right? Howard!"

One of her flip-flops flew from her feet as she ran toward second base. I picked it up as I followed after her. "Daddy!" I too screamed. "Daddy!"

My mother pushed away the second baseman, who was kneeling over my father's body. She turned my father over. "Don't move him," the second baseman told her.

"Is he paralyzed? Is he dead?" she asked. I stood beside her holding her flip-flop and shaded my eyes with it in the glare of the infield lights that ringed the bases atop their creosote poles, gnats and moths and their wattage-hungry brethren throbbing in successive swarms at each globed flood lamp that, if I listened closely enough when I was bored by the game, seemed to buzz right back at them. "Somebody go call an ambulance," my mother said through her tears. "Why won't he move? Why won't he open his eyes?"

The umpire lumbered up and took her back to the dugout so she could calm herself. "Let the boy stay by his daddy till the ambulance comes," he had ruled before grabbing the flip-flop from me so he could kneel before her back at the dugout and slip it on her foot, her red toenails caked even redder with the infield's clay. I sat down at my father's side. I stared at his handsome face and the black streaks of pine tar he had let me finger there for the first game of the double-header, two bold streaks, one beneath each eye, the same war paint major-leaguers used to cut down on the sun's annoyance, he explained to me, so he, like they, could field the ball better.

The second baseman placed his gloved hand on my head and let it linger, the smell of the well-oiled leather enveloping me in the sticky night air, a first hint that another Mississippi summer was not waiting for spring to step aside. "He's gonna be okay, kid," the second baseman kept saying.

"Kevinator?" my father groaned, instantly groggy, when he began to gain consciousness and saw me staring at him. That look of perplexed fear he always had when looking my way was even more pronounced as he tried to decipher what had just happened and how his sissy son had become part of the game he was playing.

"He ain't dead!" I shouted back at my mother in the dugout. "Daddy ain't dead!" I called, my voice sounding as oddly disappointed as my tomboy neighbor's had sounded when she had discovered our butt holes bore such similarities.

————————

"What you thinkin' 'bout?" she asked me now as she sat up, pulled a half-smoked cigarette from her cuff, and fired it up with a purloined kitchen match. Smoke filled the old dugout.

"My daddy," I said.

"He still wearing that neck thing?" she asked, mentioning the thick plastic cumbersome white brace he was having to wear until his neck felt better from the baseball collision.

"Yeah. He don't like it, neither," I told her. "Says he wished he'd a just a'gone ahead and broke his neck if he was gonna have to wear that thing. Makes him mad all the time."

The girl eyed me with a bemusement too advanced for her years. "Take your clothes off," she finally said.

I shook my head no.

"Go on. Do like I say," she said. I continued to hesitate but she moved in closer. "Do it," she demanded. I reluctantly obeyed and lay down naked before her in the coolness of the dugout's dirt floor. Slats of light billowed over me from between the weathered shreds of wood on the walls. She took the cigarette butt from her mouth and flicked it away before reaching down and flicking my penis with the same bit of haughty disdain. "That thing grow any bigger?" she asked, narrowing her already narrow eyes. "Make it grow bigger," she said.

"How?" I asked.

"Think of something you like. That's supposed to work," she suggested.

"Captain Kangaroo?"

"Mr. Greenjeans. Tom Terrific. I don't give a shit," she said, loving to shock me with her easy use of scatology. She continued to flick my penis, each flick taking on the rhythmic jingle of Captain Kangeroo's big set of keys that accompanied his program's theme song, which she was now singing with a one-word gusto: "Jing-jing-jing-jing. Jing-jing-jing-jing. Jinga-jing. Jinga-jing. Jing-jing-jing."

I sat up and crawled over into a corner of the dugout. "Stop it," I told her. "Stop it." I balled my knees up toward my chest and held them there.

"Don't be a baby," she said with the troubling, grown-up flair she could employ when the situation called for it. "You really are a weirdo. Go outside for minute," she told me. "I gotta pee."

"Gimme my clothes back," I whimpered.

"Ain't nobody gonna see you," she said, grabbing my shorts and shirt and sitting on them. "Them Baptists don't never come back here to this old ball field no more. They just use these dugouts to store stuff in like them signs yonder. Softball's a girl's game anyways, my mama says. She says it was too underhanded for a bunch of Baptists. Git it? My mama's always makin' up jokes. She's always sayin' 'Git it?' I gotta pee—*scoot*," she said, charging at me as I headed out into the afternoon sun. I forgot all about my nakedness as I pondered why my one and only friend had to have her privacy to urinate since she had already exposed her butt hole to me. I wondered how high I could get if I started to count. "Okay, you can come back in now," she beckoned me when I got to around twenty-seven. I reentered the dugout. Its dirt floor had darkened and began to take on a noticeable dankness as the afternoon sun shifted and no longer lit the place with its slivers sliding through the slats. I could just make out the outline of my neighbor's eight-year-old body lying back in the shadows. She too was naked now. She lay on her back and had positioned the now upside-down pile of IMPEACH EARL WARREN signs to serve as a pillow, her head centered on the inverted W so that a pair of horns seemed appropriately to be sprouting from her head. Her legs, bent at the knees, dangled in the air, a toe or two teasing the one ray of dying light that dawdled above her and flickered like a tired firefly. "Take a look. You like my crawdad hole?" she asked and fingered herself between her legs.

Together the two of us had often "fished" for crawdads by sticking a needle of pine straw down the moist mound of dirt that was a sign one of the small Southern crustaceans had burrowed itself into the earth. If we were lucky, a crawdad would grab onto the needle when we cleanly jerked it from the hole. I stared at where the girl continued to finger herself and she was right: Her tiny mounds of earth-toned flesh did, in fact, resemble a crawdad's busywork.

"Wanna touch it?" she asked.

I shook my head no.

"Don't be a baby," she said, issuing once more that favorite warning of hers. "If you don't touch it, I'm gonna tell your mama you did. If you do, I won't say nothing," she keenly negotiated. I sat closer to her. She took my hand and guided my fingers to her flesh. She quivered at my touch. She closed her eyes. "Stick one in me," she said. I slowly ran an index finger inside her as deep as it would go. She gasped, but approved. I began to insert the finger over and over until I realized my shirt, wadded up over in the corner, was wetter than it had been before I stepped outside. I pulled my finger free. She opened her eyes. "Don't stop," she said, her demanding tone turning into what sounded remarkably like a plea.

"What happened to my shirt?" I asked.

A devilish grin crossed her face as she put her own finger back inside herself. "I wasn't watching where I squatted when I peed," she told me. "Sorry. It'll dry."

I picked up the shirt and wiped my finger on it. "I'm gonna git in trouble for sure," I said. "My mama's gonna know we been bad."

The girl's grin girded itself for the smirk it always turned into. Sitting up, she pulled on her panties. "We ain't been bad," she said. "It's *tellin'* that makes it bad. As long as mamas and daddies don't know something, then it ain't bad. They the ones that make things bad and good. We just kids. We just do stuff." She next pulled on her jeans. "Fix my cuffs," she told me, back to being the boss. Still naked, I knelt at her feet and, careful not to spill their remaining contents (a few more cigarette butts, a stick of Juicy Fruit gum, two red Lifesavers), creased her cuffs back into place.

We stepped outside after I had pulled on my shorts, she her top. She took my shirt and hung it from the chicken wire that rusted where it had been nailed up along the front of the dugout so a long-ago bunch of visiting bat-happy Baptists could watch the action without worrying about foul balls. "This'll dry in a minute. I promise. You'll see." We climbed up on the bench outside the dugout. She put her arm around me and entwined her right ankle with my left one where our feet dangled and began to swing our legs to and fro. She circled the conversation back to Captain Kangaroo and talked of his comparative coolness to Mr. Greenjeans and Tom Terrific. She calmed my fears about my imminent enrollment in first grade, dispensing advice about eating paste and the vomit-inducing power of the merry-go-round. She told me not to worry, that what had just transpired between us didn't make us man and wife because "you ain't stuck your peter in me yet." She gave me one of her red Lifesavers. She lit another cigarette butt. She belched and made me blush. The air smelled of rain.

"Kevin!" my mother's voice thundered as she, like the approaching wad of clouds the humid spring sky had longed for all day, rolled toward us with the maximum force she too could muster, not tornado-watch–worthy in that summer of tornado watches, but wondrously frightening all the same in her own sudden bluster that could change the day's temperature just as easily, tighten my throat in anticipation of its outcome, make Coco bark. The girl's mother now shouted her name with equal gusto, forming a duet of anger as mine continued to call, "Kevin! Kevin! Kevin!" her worry sung aloud at soprano pitch, my friend's mother's voice lower, an altogether annoyed alto emerging from her throat, ever-phlegmy with the smoke from the cigarette on which she was no doubt puffing.

The girl unwrapped her arm from my shoulder and, burying her own cigarette in the dirt, bolted toward the pitcher's mound. "Come on! Hurry up!" she called, not such a big shot after all. "We're in deep shit," she warned as she ran back and picked up a few sticks that were scattered about the dugout's bench. "Take some of these. Say we were out here looking for stuff." Such a generic cover story seemed dumb, even to dumb little me, but I didn't have anything better to suggest, the truth in the last few days becoming an evermore treacherous option.

Real thunder now sounded in the distance as our mothers appeared, marching toward us over the ridge that led to the ball field. My friend's mother had put on her new sundress but mine still wore her bathing suit and looked madder than any Miss Mississippi who had failed to make it into the Top Ten of the Miss America pageant after winning a couple of preliminaries. Then there it was—not even the continued roll of thunder could compete with it—that aural warning of her displeasure, which, as I look back on it now, was that summer's signal call, a sound that no subsequent one has ever been able to drown out: her well-worn flip-flops flapping against her agitated heels. My baby sister, Karole, was held on her hip and bounced about as my mother's angry stride increased in speed once she spotted me. Coco and my brother, Kim, both came scurrying behind her trying to keep up as they each panted with the toll it was taking on their little legs. Coco—as long as my mother fumed—found the will to bark.

"We're in trouble," I whispered to my friend.

"You sure are," my mother said, somehow having heard me and pulling me toward her out on the third-base line with her Karole-less hand.

"We were just trying to find stuff," my friend said to her own mother, who grabbed one of the sticks from her and began to spank her with it as, sure enough, a cigarette dangled from her fixed and smoky frown. My friend ran in circles around her—her mother kept jerking her about by her wrist—and began tearlessly to yelp each time the stick landed on her thighs. Her mother spit out her cigarette in the infield toward first base and spanked her harder.

I handed my mother a stick so she could start hitting me too but she just threw it on the ground. "Never ever go off without telling us where you are," she insisted and seemed about to cry herself while taking in the scene with a careful sweep of her heightened sensitivities, an ability of hers I was to inherit, like her knack for putting an outfit together or lowering her eyes in my father's presence. Karole began to wail. "You two both know that there's a pervert lurking about," my mother said, mentioning something she called a Peeping Tom that had recently terrorized our neighborhood as she jostled Karole on her hip in an attempt to quiet her.

My friend's mother, tiring of her attempt to elicit tears over on her side of the pitcher's mound, was able to light another cigarette and jerk her little hellion home all at the same time. The price tag was still attached to her sundress and, feeling it scratching at her freshly shaved armpit, she reached up and ripped it off with the yellow-fingered hand that brandished her unfiltered Pall Mall—her newest favorite brand of cigarettes, ever since she had developed a crush on its spokesman, Dale Robertson, that "tall drink of water," as she called him.

Kim picked up the stick my mother had thrown on the ground and tried to get Coco to stop barking and retrieve it. My mother grabbed me by my own wrist now and led her maddening brood back to our little green-shingled house. "Look what you've made me do," she said. "You've made me cross the street in my bathing suit." Tears no longer seemed to be about to surface in her voice. Instead, an unlikely laughter bubbled up beneath it. She shook her head. Her short blond hair fell into place as perfectly as Peter Pan's had back in December when I pointed out the wires that helped Mary Martin fly on television. It was the first time I had ever realized I might be clever enough to debunk any semblance of life's magic. My mother straightened a strap on her bathing suit and regained her composure. "If that Peeping Tom is hiding behind a tree, he's getting a good look!" she said too loudly toward a looming pine, repeating that name she kept using for the pervert, one that sounded to me like he was nothing more than a harmless cousin of Peter Pan's. "Goodness, gracious. Where's your shirt?" she asked, eyeing me with new suspicion, as did an ever-more-curious Kim, who was carrying a now silent Coco and holding on for dear life to one of our mother's bare legs. The smell of her Coppertoned flesh wafted about us. "What have you been up to back there with that girl?" she asked, not wanting an answer. "Go on. Run get your shirt. We'll wait for you."

I retrieved my urine-soaked top from where it hung on the dugout's chicken wire. When my mother got a whiff of it she really was leery of what sort of lasciviousness my friend and I had been up to back in that ball field, but whatever dirty thoughts were going through her mind, she kept them to herself. The rain, right then, violently burst from the clouds that arrived directly overhead and cascaded about us, washing the piss from the shirt I now held above me and scaring Coco so that she shook with the same waves of tiny trembles that seemed to have shot through my mother only moments before when she warded off the kind of laughter that would have been somehow indecent to indulge in within her children's earshot. "You can't play outside the rest of the week," is all that she said as we ran inside the house, the rest of us squealing with delight and dread as we were drenched by the thunderstorm's power. I actually quite enjoyed sitting in my room by myself and was certain she was just being maternally sly, biding her time before my father could get home and mete out a more dire form of punishment, as he was the strict disciplinarian in all our lives. I had yet to be the recipient of one of his spankings from the Big Black Belt when he hauled it out of his closet in order to teach Kim or Karole a lesson.

I climbed into my father's brown leather recliner (an act which, if he were home, would be reason enough to be punished) and contemplated what lay in store for me as I watched my mother dry off Kim and Karole and Coco with the offhanded care of all harried mothers who still wanted to wear their bathing suits on just such days. I refused the offer of the damp towel she then made to me, too busy reasoning in my little head that perhaps I had a bargaining chip with my father since he did not want me to tell anybody the secret we shared, the one I wouldn't even tell my best friend next door. Or would I receive two beatings if I brought that secret up ever again? Were shared secrets something to be wielded at the right moment? Or were they to be woven silently into a closer relationship? Such confusion—my naked afternoon, that out-of-bounds secret I shared with my father, this odd reaction my mother was having to my bad behavior (she seemed rather tickled by it)—caused an hour's worth of tears to surface. I fantasized about how that Big Black Belt would finally feel against my flesh. "Please don't tell Daddy," I pleaded with my mother as I cried and cried. "Please don't tell Daddy. Please. Please. Please. Don't tell him. Please. Please. I'm sorry. Please."

My histrionics, at first so troubling because of their intensity, had begun to bore her by dint of their unrelenting fervor. She obviously had other things on her mind. Kim and Karole needed to be fed. Coco needed to be put back outside in her pen now that the thunderstorm had abated. And she was also expecting the football coach's wife to drop by at any minute. They were planning to perform at a school talent show as a surprise to their husbands, who were the judges, and she had to get ready for her visit. She decided to put her own bargaining chip on the table. "I won't tell Daddy about you if you won't tell him about me and Coach Kirby's wife practicing our song over here this afternoon," she said. "Is that a deal?" I whimpered through the last of my tears and looked at her outstretched hand. I timidly shook it. "That's my boy. We'll just keep everything to ourselves. We're playing on the same team," she said, using the lingua franca of this coach's house so fraught suddenly with secrets. I ceased to cry when it dawned on me that I was the only one there who was privy to all of them. Exhaustion did not dry my eyes that day. My mother's practiced empathy did not. A newfound knowledge did. An inchoate sense of power. "I'm right, aren't I, Kevin? We're on the same team," she said again, needing assurance. I nodded affirmatively. It was her turn to feel better.

But were we on the same team, my mother and I? Or was I on my father's? Those were exactly the words he had used when swearing me to secrecy a few days before. On Sundays we split up into our gender-separated squads, my mother and Karole walking the half block up the hill to the local Methodist church as my father and Kim and I turned right and down another block and settled into a Baptist pew a few minutes later. Sundays were simple to decipher, but there were those six other days of the week. I spent more time with my mother, that was for sure, and knew her moods much better than I knew my father's. He was more mercurial than my mother, who was at least predictable in her own mood swings. When she was alone with her children, listening to that rock-and-roll station on the transistor radio or doing her summer housework in that bathing suit of hers, she was freer, more alive. When she shared cups of coffee and pieces of lemon chess pie with her girlfriends while they laughed at each other's private ribaldry during the boring parts of *Search for Tomorrow*, she seemed even younger than she already was, more girlish. Most of all, when she allowed me to sit with her and her friends and listen in to such girl-talk, thinking I couldn't understand why they all loved endlessly to debate the specific circumcised charms of Eddie Fisher as compared to the speculatively uncut Richard Burton, she was as naughty as my next-door neighbor. I loved her for allowing my ear to be trained in the luridness of private female conversation; it came much more naturally to me than the dogged brusqueness required for the coaching lingo that my father utilized in his job. With him in the house my mother grew more reticent. She lowered her head a bit— like Coco could when she heard his voice as he approached the pen with a handful of dog food that he always insisted was enough for any Chihuahua to eat. My mother kept her wide-set blue eyes cast downward in a mysterious, stoic demureness the very minute my father stepped through the door and demanded our full attention. She was more than careful around him. She seemed to be slightly afraid of him yet comforted simultaneously by the familiarity of such a feeling. A *practiced* fright—she of his powerful allure, he of her separate tastes, each of losing the other—was the basis of their attraction. He had a foul mouth and a devilish sense of humor and—this was key, I think—

kept her laughing as well, the kind of laughter she made sure to save only for him, hence her hesitation earlier in the day at not letting her children know too intimately its timbre. But he never let her forget he was a man with a short fuse. He teased her with its combustive power. She teased him right back, knowing she could ignite him at will. They had been playing this game since their hormones kicked in back in Harperville. I'm certain their sex life was spectacular.

In December 1960 I would often sneak into their bedroom those first few nights after watching *Peter Pan*. I lay in my own bed, freshly tucked in, contemplating why Peter was a blond, forty-seven-year-old woman and wondering whether Captain Hook, with his limp and his lisp, was going to come through my window and take me away to an island of boys who were, like me, lost and stagestruck and a little too lovely. I would wait until all the odd inviting sounds coming from my parents' room—grunted moans, a mew or two of pleasure, my mother's low laughter—had ceased. I would then tiptoe to their door kept slightly ajar in case Karole cried out in the night and sneak over to my father's side of the bed. I would lie on the floor next to him and watch him sleep. For those first few nights, he'd awake and pick me up ever so gently to take me back to my bed, admonishing me for my visits. "You don't belong in there," was his lone groggy refrain. "You don't belong in there. You don't belong . . ." he'd continue, his voice falling back to sleep before the rest of him could, as I watched him shuffle away in his underwear to where my mother slumbered beneath their heavy pile of blankets.

One night as I lay on their bedroom floor staring at his face in repose—bristles of his dark head against the white of the pillow like the penciled forest of wintry pines he had once drawn for me on a blank sheet of paper as we doodled and did not talk—he kicked off that heavy pile of bedcovers during a rambunctious dream and exposed the bulge of his immense erection. My mother's hand—her arm was around his waist where she lay cuddled against him—found its way down inside his underwear and moved the erection about in her grip. More frightened by this sight than anything that could have awaited me if Captain Hook had carried me away, I quickly slid underneath their bed. The mattress creaked above me as they repositioned their bodies.

"Kevin's not down there, is he?" I heard my mother ask.

"Nooooo," came my father's deeply elongated reply, which seemed, as it faded into an "oh" and an "oh" and an "oh," to be nuzzling itself into an area of flesh I would later learn to refer to as another's nape.

"Mmmmmm . . ." my mother moaned. My father moaned back. Their breath kept pace with my racing heart. Trembling from the cold, I waited for the wrestling going on above me to stop. People wrestled when they were mad and hated each other. It was what the boys who made fun of me always wanted to do. Though my mother and father often fought with their voices, I did not want them to fight with their bodies. A foreboding fastened itself to me under their bed that night, as physical a sensation as any that accompanied the thrashing which was occurring overhead, and has never really let me go: *Would I ever be where I belong?* My parents fell silent. I carefully crawled—like Karole—back to my own bed. I waited for Captain Hook.

For weeks afterward, I refused to set foot in my parents' bedroom. Even when my mother would summon me from in there, I would go only as far as the doorway, no farther. My return visit, ironically, involved my father carrying me back in. At breakfast one morning my mother offhandedly accused my aunt Gladys, his cherished big sister, of being a liar. I can't recall the reason for such an accusation, only the epithet itself. My father did not take a moment to contemplate such an assertion on her part. He did not try to argue with her. He in-

stantly, instinctively, reached over the breakfast table past me and violently slapped my mother across her face. She ran crying into their
bedroom. Kim and Karole sat stunned staring at their cereal bowls.
My father scooped me up and carried me into the room with him as
he followed after her. My mother lay on their bed sobbing into her
pillow. He stood me by her and whispered in my ear, "Tell your mama
I'm sorry. Tell her I love her. Tell her. Say it."

"I'm sorry," I said. "I love you, Mommy."

She cried louder.

My father shook me with the full force of those hands of his that
could so effortlessly palm a basketball, scoop up a sissy child, hit the
woman he loved. "No, goddamn it. Say *Daddy*'s sorry. Say *Daddy*
loves you." I stood there on the bed as his grip grew tighter and refused to obey. "*Say it*," he demanded. I remained silent. He knew me
well enough to know that if he became too insistent I, as stubborn as
he, would not budge. He tried another tack. His fingers loosened
their grip on me and he leaned in closer so he could proffer more
softly a futile enticement, his breath redolent of Folger's coffee and
the crispy bacon he had pilfered from my plate. "Tell her I'm sorry
and that I love her and I'll never call you a girl again," he whispered
to me. He had to be joking, I thought. Did he really think this was
going to make me obey him? I *liked* him calling me a girl. It was one
of my favorite things in the world. The way he had settled in to saying it could send welcome shivers down my little spine. His voice no
longer sounded angry and shocked like the first time he said it. Its
tone instead had ripened with his repeated ribbing until it contained
the same sweet sarcasm with which he could tease my mother at
times and take her breath away, a sarcasm outmatched only by the
latest vulgarity-infused persiflage that could so easily fly past his extravagantly pouting lips right before he just as extravagantly pursed
them, knowing she would kiss him just to shut him up. His calling me
a girl and my eye-batting reaction to it—a mirroring of my mother's

only response to such an onslaught of his dirty words—constituted the first stirrings in me of what it meant to flirt. "You girl," I would goad him into saying. "You goddamn girl."

My father had been throwing that word at me ever since I had called forth all my three-and-a-half-year-old charms to persuade my mother to make me a skirt. We had been visiting my grandparents one Saturday in August and I was hanging out with the women in the back bedroom that doubled as my grandmother's sewing studio while they busied themselves with making my mother some new maternity clothes, as she was just beginning to show with Karole. It is the earliest memory of my childhood. They had all been cutting out patterns atop the chenille bedspread on the queen-size four-poster that stood next to the old foot-pedal-powered Singer machine. A small square of material, a remnant from the last carefully rolled out yard, was left over from the final Simplicity pattern they had spread out on the bed and they had wondered what they should do with it, hating to throw anything away if it could be put to use. Aunt Vena Mae was there that day too and she had warned the two other women about the idea I had been brave enough to come up with. "You better not let Howard know about this," she had said, eyeing me with her usual disdain and fanning herself with a copy of *Better Homes and Gardens* magazine. Her golden charm bracelet clanged with the back-and-forth of her wrist, the sound competing with the whir from the oscillating electric fan as it flickered the tissue-thin brown paper of the Simplicity pattern onto which they had let me help them pin the woolen material. "This child is the one that'll get the whupping. Y'all don't want Howard to whup this child," she cautioned, though the way she was looking at me seemed to counter her concern. "I sure hope you're gonna have a real daughter this time, Nancy Carolyn," old Venomous Mae said to my mother as she reached out and touched her teeming stomach. "Maybe it'll help knock some sense into this one," she said, nodding my way. "Convince him he's a boy *by comparison*."

My mother contemplated the concept of a skirt encompassing her son as she circled the extra bit of cloth around my ready body. "Oh, Aunt Veence," she said. "I think he'd look right cute in a little matching outfit."

My grandmother took the remaining pins out of her mouth. "You sure you know what you're doing, Nan?" she asked. "Veeny's right. Howard might not like it. You know what he's like when you get him riled."

My mother and I locked looks. The thought of my father riled up rather riled us too in unexpected ways. "This'll only take a few stitches," she said, and she had the skirt done in no time flat. My grandmother had to agree that I certainly was "right cute" when I modeled it for the women there in the sewing room.

"He's not any such thing," said Vena Mae. "He's not right *nothin'*. And ya'll aren't right in the head for letting him get his way and encouraging him like this. He has to learn to live in this world and this world don't abide boys like that."

My mother grabbed the *Better Homes and Gardens* from her and gently smacked her on her arm. "Hush up, Aunt Veence. I say let him get all this out of his system while he's young. He'll grow out of it," she told the other two women, who exchanged worried looks. "Patsy Kirby told me Dr. Spock says not to be spooked by such shenanigans."

Old Venomous Mae grunted and untangled a few of the charms on her bracelet. "*Shenanigans*—you got that right," she said. My grandmother tried not to laugh. My mother spun me around and made the little skirt blossom in billows about my body. I loved the way it felt as it lifted from the flesh of my legs and fell back into place as soon as I stopped spinning. I ran out to the carport and waited for my father to return from a trip to Harperville, certain that he would love the way I looked as much as I did, no matter what Vena Mae predicted. He drove up as the three women positioned themselves at the kitchen sink looking out the window at the scene about to occur. I sashayed up to my father and begin to spin and spin so he too could marvel at how cute I was. He stopped dead in his tracks and dug his heels into the drive, a gravelly sound that seemed to speak for him since he was struck speechless at the sight. I stopped my spinning and grabbed the skirt in each of my hands and rocked my hips to and fro before him in the way I had seen the petticoated Angela Cartwright do on the TV program, called, appropriately enough, *Make Room for Daddy*. In this way, she teased Danny Thomas when he himself was in the midst of one of his infamous slow burns. My father turned and looked at the three women staring out the window who quickly began to pretend they were washing dishes or cleaning the spotless counter. "Is that a goddamn skirt you've got on?" he asked and lunged at me. I ducked just in time and ran back into the carport. He chased me down and grabbed me by my neck holding me in place. "You think you're a goddamn girl? Is that what you think you are? A girl? A goddamn girl? Nan!" he called. "Get out here this minute! Miz Jake! You, too!" he shouted for my grandmother.

The two of them sheepishly came out the back door into the carport. Aunt Vena Mae stood at the screen door taking in the scene, a look of satisfaction on her Merle Norman-ed face seeping through the wire mesh. "What is this?" my father wanted to know. "Where did a boy of mine get a goddamn skirt to wear?" My mother grabbed me from him and held me to her. My grandmother backed up toward Vena Mae at the screen door. "I made it for him," my mother said, her eyes cast downward toward me where I looked up at her seeking her protection. "He's not hurting anything," she chanced saying.

My father moved toward us both. "The hell he's not!" he screamed. "He's hurting me! He's hurting hisself with such nonsense! He's hurting this family!" He reached down and tore the skirt from my body.

"Howard!" my grandmother shouted.

"I warned you," Aunt Vena Mae said from behind the screen. My mother tried to grab the ripped skirt from my father's grasp and a tug of war ensued above my head. My father won and pushed all the women aside as he strode into the kitchen to get a box of matches. We all followed as he headed straight outside again to the backyard and the big oil drum that served as an incinerator for combustible garbage as well as raked-up leaves and unwanted pine straw. He threw the skirt into the drum and lifted me to his chest. He opened the box and handed me a match. "Light it," he demanded. I looked toward my mother who had always told me not to play with matches. "Light it," he said again. I did not know what to do. He grabbed the match from me and lit it himself and threw it down into the drum where its flame quickly extinguished itself. He tried another match but it too would not stay lit atop the discarded skirt. Marching into the storage room behind the garage with me still in his arms, he found a can of lighter fluid and returned to soak the skirt with squirts from the squeaky can. He plopped me on the ground for a minute and angrily lit one more match. He dropped it into the drum and flames rose suddenly from inside its rusty lip. He lifted me again and made me stare down into the fire. "See that? Take a good look," he told me, shaking me extremely close to the sprouting inferno. "That's what happens when boys try to be girls. That's what happens." My mother attempted to take me from him, but he would not let me go.

"Lyle's late coming home but he'll be back soon from taking inventory up at Dearman's today," my grandmother said, mentioning the hardware store where my grandfather worked, as if his hapless return would somehow calm my father down. Aunt Vena Mae put her braceleted arm around her baby sister and stayed uncharacteristically quiet.

"Howard, stop it," my mother pleaded. "Stop it. Don't blame him. Blame me."

My father turned to her, his face distorted in the red glow from the fire. "I do blame you!" he screamed. "I blame you both. Don't team up on me like this ever again," he said, using that coaching term that would that very day begin to haunt my childhood. "You two are always *teamin' up*." The August afternoon temperature was in the nineties and standing by the fire my father and I both began to sweat with the awful heat he had added to it. My own little three-year-old face was flushed with anger and longing and something as close to hatred as I had ever felt. When I began to cry he handed me off finally to my mother. My grandmother cried also as Vena Mae, knowing her big-sister routine by heart after all these years, calmed her with rote expressions of concern. "Women!" my father said, spitting out the word while looking right at me. "Goddamn women!" He left us there by the dying fire. We heard him once more crank the car and spin out of the gravel drive.

"We've still got a maternity dress to finish," said Vena Mae, patting my grandmother's shoulder. "Let's get back to the sewing machine," she said, taking charge of the situation. "I'll make us all some ice tea. I hear Kim in there crying now. All this commotion must have woke him up from his nap."

My grandmother dried her tears with the lone strip of fabric my mother had not used for the burned-up skirt. "We'll just keep all this from Lyle," she said, dabbing at her eyes.

I climbed beneath the sewing machine when we got back in the room with the half-made maternity clothes. I pouted and watched my grandmother's old bare foot work the pedal, blue veins branching out toward her toes like an inky rendering of a gnarled oak tree ruined not by root rot but a palsied landscape artist's choosing to go out sketching once his brushes began to scare him. "Here," said Aunt Vena Mae, "you want to play with this? Will this cheer you up?" she asked and bent down to pass her unclasped gold charm bracelet to me. She jingled it in front of my frowning face until I took it.

The women remained silent and drank their tea. "Kevin, come out from under there," my mother finally said. I stayed put.

"He's fine," said my grandmother, and let me push the pedal for her with my hand when her foot tired and she gave me the go-ahead. I tried on the bracelet but, slipping from my tiny wrist, it fell into my lap. I plopped it instead on my head like the crown that Mary Ann Mobley wore in all the local newspapers my grandmother kept in her clippings box when Mobley made it to the big time up in Atlantic City the year before. The gravel drive came to life again when my father pulled his speeding car to screeching halt out front. My grandmother sewed faster, pushing my hand away with her veiny foot and going to town on some final seams. "You better give me back that bracelet," Vena Mae said, and reached down to snatch it from my head.

My father slammed the back door. His footsteps headed our way. He stopped at the door of the bedroom and took in the scene. No one spoke. He reached for the *Better Homes and Gardens* that was now sitting on the white chest of drawers. He rolled up the magazine in his fist then told me to follow him into the living room. "Haven't you done enough, Howard?" my mother asked him, but pushed me toward him nonetheless. "Must you spank him?"

My father said nothing. He picked me up and took me to the living room's sofa and sat down next to me. He put his arm around me and unrolled the magazine. We sat looking at the pictures of the beautiful homes and lovely yards and he asked me which ones I liked best, which colors I preferred, which pieces of furniture looked the most comfortable. "Someday we're going to live in a house like one of these," he said and held me tightly to him. "I promise you that, Kevinator," he said. He kissed me on top of my head. "Your mama deserves a house like these. You deserve it." We flipped the pages and pointed to something when it pleased us. He quietly sang a verse of

Johnny Horton's "Battle of New Orleans," his favorite song that summer. He let me hum along. I've never felt as safe.

———————

"Go on. Tell her I love her. Tell her I'm sorry," my father kept up his commands while I stood my ground on the bed that morning as our own battle was joined. "Do it and I promise-cross-my-heart-and-hope-to-die I'll never call you a girl again," he said, sounding not like a father at all with that cross-my-heart silliness.

I remained completely still, completely silent until he began to shake me again, this time much more violently. "No! Stop!" I shouted. "You're hurting me!"

My mother flipped over at the sound of my distress. "Are you proud of yourself now?" she asked with an exaggerated sob. "You've hurt us both."

My father let me go and fell to his knees. "Please, Nan. Please. I'm sorry. I love you," he said, his voice cracking. He reached for her but she jumped at his touch, scurrying to the other side of the as yet unmade bed.

"Don't hurt her!" I yelled, and tried to slap him across his face like he had slapped her earlier. He swung his arm up in self-defense but I dived for the floor before he could land a blow.

"Howard! Stop it! Howard!" my mother screamed.

My father rose and grabbed the Big Black Belt from his closet. "That's it," he said, raising it toward me. "I've had enough of this." I ran from the room as my mother reached across and slammed the door shut behind me. The bottom half of the leather strap, which he had swung for the first time my way, caught in the slammed door and lay in the hallway at my feet. The door then cracked open for a second and the Big Black Belt was slurped back inside like the tongue of a panting chow. I put my little ear up to the suddenly locked door and heard my own parents' own panting now behind it, the sound of the belt's buckle falling to the floor, my father's muffled voice softening from "sorry" to "shh-shh-shh" to "shit, Nan, oh, shit . . . Nan . . . Nan . . . shit . . . oh, shit . . ."

I watched Nan—as I often referred to my mother in my thoughts when my father wasn't around—return from that bedroom of theirs after my urine-soaked adventure in the deserted dugout. She had taken off her bathing suit and was parading around the house now in her bra and panties as she, humming to herself, straightened pillows and dusted surfaces and ran water over an ice tray and poured three glasses of her overly sweetened tea—one for her, one for the football coach's wife who was about to arrive any minute, and one for me. Kim and Karole insisted on cherry Kool-Aid. She asked me to stand up on the couch and help her fashion about her whippet-thin body the toga she had made from an old bedsheet as she prepared herself for the final rehearsal she and Coach Kirby's wife were going to have before the big talent show. "Remember now. This is our little secret," she said when the doorbell rang and Miz Kirby—a Donna Reed look-alike—came giggling inside, the two women giddy with their plans, pleased with themselves for having found this diversion from the boredom that dulled so many of their days. They weren't much more than girls, barely past thirty and stuck in a small Mississippi town with husbands that hadn't taken them out to eat on a Friday night since the men had put the word Coach in front of their names and the two women had to live their lives feigning interest while seated on the backless bleachers of muddy ball fields and half-filled gymnasiums. Like my mother, Miz Kirby quickly stripped down to her bra and panties. She pulled her own toga out of a Jitney Jungle grocery sack.

"These don't look right for ancient Rome," said my mother between sips of tea and snapping her brassiere straps with her fingers, then snapping Miz Kirby's. "Tell you what, I'm not going to wear a bra," she claimed, her eyes widening at what she heard herself saying. She began to lower her straps. "Dare I?" she asked, issuing that low inquisitive whisper I often heard her use when she was in one of her excitable moods. "Dare I?" I sat down on the sofa and petted Coco, trying to calm her trembling. My mother still had not put her out in her pen, which was dangerous in and of itself, as my father forebade the dog in the house. Coco and I watched as my mother and Miz Kirby unsnapped each other's bras. They positioned their breasts inside their makeshift togas while my mother explained how I had mysteriously disappeared earlier in the day with "that little eight-year-old Huck Finn hussy who lives across the street. Came back smelling like a toilet." She tried not to, but couldn't help it: that for-my-father-alone laughter burst forth from her. Coco's ears pricked up and trembled right along with the rest of her short-haired, stubby four-legged torso.

"Maybe he's not such a sissy after all," Miz Kirby managed to say between her own hoots of derision, a sound not Donna Reed–like at all.

"Now, honey, don't talk like that," my mother said, but could not stop laughing. She laid a hand on her short blond hair and smoothed it to her scalp in an attempt to calm herself. "Look how sweet he is pettin' on that Chihuahua. He might be a sissy but he's my sissy," she cooed right at me as she bent down, giving Coco and me a good look at her breasts, small nests of flesh, which almost spilled right in our faces from where she had tucked the tiny things in her strangely wrapped sheet. She kissed me on the cheek and tickled our family's Chihuahua under its proffered chin. I took a gulp of tea, then offered some to Coco, who lapped it right up. "No, honey, don't do that. That's nasty. I've got to get that dog back outside in a minute," she reminded herself. "Really, now, Kevin, don't do that," she continued, pushing Coco's face away from the iced tea and taking the glass from me. "I swear to you, don't you tell your daddy anything about all this." She put my tea back in the kitchen and returned to the living room chewing the ice from my glass. "We're going to surprise your daddy and Coach Kirby when we open up the March of Dimes charity talent show this weekend up at the gym. They're the judges and this'll give 'em a shock. They'll get a kick out of it. At least we hope so. The cheerleaders have convinced us they will. It's already printed in the program that the cheerleaders are supposed to open the show singing 'Sad Movies (Make Me Cry)' by the Lennon Sisters. But we're gonna come out instead. Your daddy's going to get a surprise going-away party at the end of the night, too," she said, happy to confirm yet again for me that our days in this hick burg were numbered since my father had accepted a new job at a junior college in another county where the bleachers were at least nicer and her Friday nights would be free of high school sports.

"Any news about that Peeping Tom business over at the Simpsons?" asked Miz Kirby. "That's plumb creepy. You'd think in a place like this, stuff like that wouldn't happen."

"Nothing yet," my mother said. "But that policeman they sent out to question everybody up and down the street could make Barney Fife look like Tab Hunter. Poor boy. They'll never catch that Peeping Tom if that little skinny thing is all they've got out looking for him."

I watched the Kool-Aid–lipped Kim and Karole, herded together over in the corner, playing in their private world of tiny toys. My mother and her friend ignored the three of us as they put on silly frizzy wigs, painted freckles on their faces, and blacked out a couple of teeth in each of their mouths. They looked like Lucy and Ethel about to get into another fix, a game of dress-up that my mother and I often played when we were bored, my role, even for my taste way back then, too often that of Ethel. I tried to quiet Coco who was yapping now at their costumes as they kept talking about the Peeping

Tom and trying to guess who it possibly could be. I stared, happily shocked, at my mother's antics as she and Miz Kirby began their awkward dance routine, verbally stumbling through the lyrics of "Comedy Tonight" from *A Funny Thing Happened on the Way to the Forum*, which had opened on Broadway that month according to Ed Sullivan when he had introduced the number on his show. There was no cast album yet so they had made up some of the words from memory and kept laughing at their rudimentary rhymes that would have made Stephen Sondheim's own hair frizz. I applauded wildly when she and her friend finished their routine. Coco yapped louder. "Oh, God. Kevin, honey, do your mama a favor and take that dog back out yonder to her pen," my mother told me. "We'll wait to do our encore until you get back. Skedaddle," she said as she brushed some of Coco's short black hair from the couch with her hand. I looked over my shoulder as I headed outside and saw her trying to help Miz Kirby coordinate her dance steps to the song's jaunty rhythm.

I placed Coco in her penned-up spot in the yard and started to run back inside so I wouldn't miss any of my mother's performance. "What are you running for, little man?" asked the Simpson Lady where she knelt at her prized flower beds and planted even more bulbs in there between the rose bushes. Her voice stunned me and I stopped dead in my tracks. A sun bonnet framed her beautiful face. My father once said she reminded him of a classier version of Jane Russell, but he told my mother "you're my tiny-assed Marilyn," when she got upset at the compliment he had paid their raven-haired neighbor. "Cat got your tongue?" the Simpson Lady asked. "Or has that nasty little Chihuahua got it instead? That thing never shuts up, does it? Did I just hear your mother in there singing with somebody? Whose car is that parked there in your driveway? Couldn't make out what they were singing exactly, though their voices sounded pretty. Of course, anything would sound pretty compared to the yapping back in that pen. My husband is going to have to speak to your daddy about that dog again real soon." She fashioned the brim of her bonnet in a more pleasing angle. "So what's going on inside your house this afternoon? It sounds like such *frivolity*," she said, that last word spoken with so much longing in her voice I thought it must be something nice she wanted for herself even though I had no idea what it meant. She turned her attention back to her flower bed and rearranged the plastic cushion she used beneath her pink pedal-pushers so she wouldn't get her knees dirty when she knelt and did her digging as she scooted along. "I think there must have been some sort of animal crawling around in here. Some of these plants have been flattened," she said. "You haven't let Coco play over here have you?" she asked. I shrugged and stared at her. I thought of my friend's crawdad hole and, more troublingly, of the Simpson Lady's. She had just started emerging from inside her family's log-cabin cottage after the trauma of the Peeping Tom incident a few days earlier. I stood for a moment watching her weed the flower bed then ran up the back steps and opened the door to my kitchen. Ethel Merman's voice blared a few notes from *Gypsy* as I entered the house. When I turned to shut the door I saw the Simpson Lady look up from beneath her bonnet, her eyes bearing down on me as the *frivolity* she said was hidden in my house seemed to sadden her by its proximity instead of its presence.

"And now for our encore," my mother announced after taking a big bow in front of me when I settled in on the couch again. She and Miz Kirby broke out singing "Together, Wherever We Go" right along with the cast album from *Gypsy* that Miz Kirby had brought along with her toga in that Jitney Jungle sack. When they finished the number, I applauded wildly once more. My mother took off her frizzy wig. She plopped it on my head. The telephone rang. When she answered it, a worried look came over her flushed face. "Could you go by the Jitney and pick up some milk first? And some Sunbeam bread. And some . . . ah . . . cherry Kool-Aid. Kim and Karole drank the last of it this afternoon," she lied, as I had seen her make a fresh pitcher, dumping all those cups of sugar into it, making it even sweeter than her tea. "Thanks, honey. See you soon."

"Howard?" Miz Kirby asked.

"Yes. He says his neck is killing him so he's skipping his last P.E. class and coming straight home. Your husband's covering for him. Hurry. We've got to get this stuff off our faces. I've got to hide my costume. Here," she said, picking up Miz Kirby's bra from the floor and throwing it to her. She pulled the frizzy red wig off my head. "Oh, God! I just know we're going to get caught!" she said, and the women started to giggle in their panic. They helped each other snap their brassieres back in place—first giving me a noticeable flash of nipples—and reassured themselves that their performance wasn't just foolishness on their part. Miz Kirby slipped back on her shorts and shirt. My mother pulled on some plaid shorts herself and a white blouse. She made sure its collar was turned up against her neck just-so, in a kind of trademark style statement she always made à la Dorothy Malone, one of her favorite stars. She once told me that in the months after my birth she went on a mad moviegoing spree with me swaddled in her arms. "It was the only place you'd stop crying from your colic. Maybe it was the smell of the popcorn or the movie music or the air conditioning or whatever was going on on-screen, but you quieted right down and seemed kinda hypnotized by it all," she told me. I'd ask her again and again to recite the names of all the movies she'd seen when I was a baby and it was "just-the-two-of-us," as she always put it, when she was trying to get me to take a nap when I was almost past my toddler years, the litany like our own private lullaby: *The Searchers*, *The Man Who Knew Too Much*, *Around the World in Eighty Days*, *The Ten Commandments*, *The Bad Seed*, *Baby Doll*, *Bus Stop*, *Giant*, *High Society*, *The King and I*, *Anastasia*, *Lust for Life*, *Friendly Persuasion*, and her all-time favorite, *Written on the Wind*, in which a shameless Malone "finally ended up wearing her hair in a chignon. Do you know what a chignon is, sugar? Let me tell you," she'd whisper as I drifted off to sleep.

My mother didn't break stride that afternoon as she tidied up the house after my father's surprise phone call and slipped on the scuffed-up pair of moccasins Aunt Vena Mae had bought her for her birthday at the Choctaw Indian Fair up in Neshoba County. Miz Kirby helped her make some more ice tea and vacuum the couch of Coco's little black hairs before we accompanied her outside to wave good-bye as she backed out of the drive. I looked over and saw that the only sign left of the Simpson Lady's presence was the plastic cushion she had left next to the flower bed. My mother and I hurried back inside the house. I watched as she hid her toga and wig under the skirt of her bed where she had been keeping them. She then put Kim and Karole down for their nap and ran to the kitchen to pour the fresh pitcher of cherry Kool-Aid down the drain. When she came back into the living room it dawned on her that Miz Kirby had left the *Gypsy* cast album behind. "Shoot. It's too late for me to call her once she gets home so she can come back and get this. Here, Kevin," she said, handing me the album. "Take this thing outside and hide it. Can't chance your daddy finding it in here. Hide it good. I'll call Patsy later and let her know she left it." I looked up and saw that my mother, in her frenzy about my father's imminent arrival, had forgotten about her blacked-out front teeth and looked as lovely as the naughty little snaggle-toothed tomboy who lived across the street. Should I point this out to her? Or should I wait and let my father wonder what was going on inside her mouth? The latter struck me as the more interesting idea, but before I could make a final decision she hurried me along. "Go on, Kevin," she said. "Do like I say. Your daddy will be here any minute."

I took the *Gypsy* album and headed out the door toward our backyard. At first I thought I might put it in Coco's doghouse but decided that she would chew it up. I next spotted the Simpson Lady's knee cushion over in her yard and considered hiding the album underneath it, as they looked to be about the same size, but thought better of that idea after I tried it out and realized you could see the album beneath it if you looked really closely. Should I throw it behind one of her rose bushes or use the gardening trowel she had left behind with her other tools and just dig a hole and bury it in her flower bed? That's when it occurred to me: The best hiding place would be to stick it deep into the Simpson Lady's overgrown hedge where the tomboy had earlier made me push down my pants and sniffed at my butt hole. I scurried on tiptoe to the hedge and wedged the album deep inside the branches. "Who's out there?" the Simpson Lady called, her voice like a sentinel's bugled warning ever since she had been spied on through her bathroom window the week before as she soaped herself up in her tub while her twelve-year-old son—who had inherited his beauty from her—sat on the pot and worried about his homework and wondered if he should try out for the church choir. "Really! Who's out there?" came her querulous voice. "I can hear you! Who's out there?" I kept right on scurrying until I made it back to my house and heard the Simpson Lady's backdoor open just as I shut ours.

My heart was jumping inside my chest when my mother made her way into the kitchen and we heard my father pull up in the driveway. We stood at the backdoor's window, orange and turquoise toreadors darting about the curtain's pattern, a bull or two staring back at us from the untied sash that dangled toward the doorknob when the curtain was drawn against the afternoon sun that added too much heat to the already overheated kitchen. We listened as my father got out of the car and exchanged pleasantries with the Simpson Lady who had walked over to her flower bed to retrieve her knee cushion and gardening tools. My mother fidgeted with her white collar. She turned it up even higher on her neck as she strained to hear exactly what they were saying outside. The Simpson Lady laughed. "Howard can make anybody laugh," she said, more to herself than to me as she ran her finger along the dangling sash, her fingernail, resting now on the knob, the same color and size as the dash of red held by one of the toreadors in front of a charging bull. "All right. Let's Loretta Young it," she said and winked my way, the inculcation of her love of show business and the names of stars she always dropped into our conversation a continual aspect of our closeness. She swung open the door. She moccasinned it down the back steps. I followed after her as my father stiffly turned toward us, his neck still encased in the huge white plastic brace the doctor had made him wear after his baseball collision. (It looked as if he, always the kidder, were mimicking my mother's love of white turned-up collars.) The Simpson Lady had taken off her sun bonnet and her hair was brushed into a perfect brunette pageboy about her beautiful face, her green eyes the same color as that overgrown hedge in back of her. She was, as my mother often had to admit, "quite lovely." My father put one of his large hands on my shoulder and made sure I felt the full pressure of it as I looked away from her loveliness and over toward that hedge. His palm purposefully worked itself up against my own stiffening neck, rubbing it with a combination of affection and warning, each carefully disguised as the other. I could see the pink lettering of the *Gypsy* album peeking through the hedge like buds about to blossom deep within the thicket. "Coco!" my father called out to the dog who always went a little crazy at his presence. "Coco! No! Stop it! No! Stop!"

"Howard, I don't mean to be a nag," said the Simpson Lady in her nicest voice, "but that Chihuahua really must find a companion or something to quiet its barking. My nerves are bad enough these last few days."

"I know. I'm sorry," said my father. "She'll calm down soon. She's in heat. I finally found a mate for her over just this side of Jackson. Met a breeder between innings at Battlefield Park," he said. "She'll quiet down once she has a litter. It quieted Nan down once she had one," he joked. My mother rolled her eyes, but laughed along with the lighthearted ripple that surfaced from within our neighbor's long white throat, which was all the amusement the Simpson Lady could manage to muster in her wary state. "Good Lord, Nan. What's wrong with your mouth?" my father asked, having caught his first glimpse of my mother's blacked-out teeth.

"You look as if you've been eating too much licorice, dear," said the Simpson Lady and pushed some of her stray licorice-colored hair behind a pierced ear. A lone pearl sat burrowed into her lobe as if an albino ladybug, shunned by its red sisters swarming in her flower bed below, had gratefully alighted there. "You're not pregnant again, are you?" she asked.

"When I'd eat too much chocolate as a boy, my daddy'd always say I looked like I'd been sucking on a sow," said my father. The Simpson Lady allowed a less amused sound to ripple her body. She twisted the pearl in her ear.

My mother quite visibly blanched and stared down at me. "No, I'm not pregnant. Kevin and I were just fooling around today," she said, thinking as quickly as she could for an excuse for her snaggle-toothed look. "We were playing Lucy-and-Ethel. It's one of our favorite games when we're feeling silly," she continued and reached up to remove the black duct tape she had used on her two front teeth. She mussed my hair and moved her hand down along my father's, which still rested against the back of my neck.

"I've told you to stop letting him play that," my father scolded her as I felt their fingers entwine. "You're not dressing him up, too, are you? I've warned you—no pretending he's a woman. Not even Ethel goddamn Mertz." The Simpson Lady ignored this bit of family business and bent down to pick up her gardening tools. "You ought to buy a Chihuahua pup from us when Coco has her that litter," my father propositioned, turning his attention back her way. "They make good watchdogs. Their barks are bigger than their bites—but that's true for most of us."

"Howard and his schemes," said my mother. She lifted her hand and put her arm around my father's waist. On tiptoe in her moccasins, she kissed him on his cheek above the plastic brace. "He's always got a scheme going," she said, alluding to his selling of World Book encyclopedias, breeding that little Mexican bitch out back, and planning on starting a Black Angus cattle farm with a buddy from here in Pelahatchie. "I'm glad to see you're out gardening again," she told the Simpson Lady. "We all certainly hope they catch the pervert that scared you so."

"Yes . . . well . . . ," the Simpson Lady said. "My own family will be getting home soon. I'm going back to work at the phone company tomorrow. It is nice to see you all. Things are getting back to normal. My first petunias bloomed today. Life goes on."

We parted and my father opened the car door to retrieve the small sack of groceries he had been asked to bring home. My mother put them away in the kitchen once we were inside. She looked in on Kim and Karole as I watched my father carefully remove his white plastic neck brace and put it on the kitchen table. It was much hotter inside the house than in the breeze that was beginning to ease the late-afternoon humidity out back and I longed to feel the cool firm mold of that neck brace against my bare sticky legs again where my father had days earlier let me secretly straddle him. He reached into a box of Frosted Flakes. He pulled out a fistful and crunched them in his mouth, the muscles of his temples flexing as he chewed. No mention was made of our clandestine life. He stood at the backdoor and parted the curtain on the window and watched the Simpson Lady still standing there admiring her gardening skills. He waved her way when she saw him staring at her. "What are you doing?" asked my mother when she came back into the kitchen.

"Just checking to see if she's all right," said my father, dropping the curtain and rubbing his neck. "She can't seem to get enough of that flower bed. It's like she's afraid to go inside her own house anymore after all that's happened. That flower bed does seem to make her feel better."

"You can't seem to get enough of her, as if she's *your* flower bed," said my mother. "You're always stealing a look at her. Don't think I don't notice. *I see you.*"

"'Thou shalt not steal,'" I said, a little something I had picked up sitting on that Baptist pew each Sunday down the hill.

"What's that supposed to mean?" my father brusquely asked my mother, ignoring my comment and keeping up the conversation they each considered a private one because I was still too young in their eyes to understand the implications of such language. Dumb adults. Sissies always understand. "Sounds like you're trying to accuse me of something," he said, keeping at her and, out of the corner of his eye, watching me start to push his brace about the table, careful not to let it touch the two pieces of black duct tape that my mother had used on her teeth and stuck there on the tabletop on her way to Kim and Karole. "Come right out and say it if you're going to accuse me of something. Don't get all Fancy Nancy with me," he said, using the nickname he employed for her when a fight could easily ensue.

"No accusations. Only, appropriately enough, *observations*," said my mother, always glad to show off her smarts in these moments. She was, as she too often reminded him, the salutatorian of their senior class back in Harperville. She waited for his next remark, prodding, she hoped, some vulgarities to fly about the room and thrill her in ways she could never really understand, only feel. Fancy Nancy was readying herself for a long night. Maybe even a lurid one. Risky? Not exactly. "Heightened" is the word she preferred. "Patsy, sometimes everything feels so *heightened*," she confided to Miz Kirby when they were taking off their bras and prattling on about things they thought were just as private.

"Honey, you know you're the only one for me," my father said and turned down her white collar to kiss her on her neck.

"Why did you take that brace off?" she asked, pushing him away and turning her collar back up. "You know the doctor said you had to keep the brace on until you went to bed."

"Why don't we go to bed right now, then?" he asked and went for her again.

"Howard! Not in front of Kevin!" she said.

"Maybe he can learn something," he said, leering at her and making her stifle her illicit laugh. "My neck's not the only thing that's stiff."

"Howard!" She shoved him away once more, then—she couldn't help herself—she pulled him toward her again. They kissed passionately, forgetting I was sitting right there. I kept pushing the neck brace about the table, concentrating on trying to make myself cry by using the tears I had kept in reserve from earlier in the day. That would make them pay attention to me. It wasn't working, though. Ever since I had thrown up in the coaches' lounge and watched my father clean it up, I had been unable to cry in his presence. How could I ever again cry in front of him after seeing how perplexed he was by me, how my presence actually kind of frightened him. I bet I frightened him even more now, I was able to figure out, because we shared a secret he did not want me to tell. No matter how hard I tried, the tears would not come. So I decided this was my chance to shuck my Ethel Mertz role and play Lucy for once. I *pretended* to cry in that loud wailing way Lucy could when Ricky got mad at her. That did the trick. It shocked my parents into noticing me. Their lips parted. They pushed away from one another. "Honey, what's wrong?" my mother asked, startled by my outburst.

I cried louder in my Lucy-mode.

"Answer your mama, boy," said my father.

My mother came and knelt by my side. "Tell us what's wrong, sugar," she said and stopped me from pushing the brace around the table.

I whimpered. Had I really fooled her? This was a better crying job than Lucille Ball could ever muster. It was in that moment I first thought I might want to be an actor when I grew up. I whimpered a little more. I made sure I looked right at both of my parents before I spoke. "Whose team am I on?" I pointedly asked.

They took their eyes off me and stared at each other. No response from either was forthcoming.

I repeated the question: *"Whose team am I on?"*

"We're all on the same team," said my mother, contradicting her earlier warning to me when she swore me to her side. "Aren't we, Howard?" My father looked like he wasn't so sure about that. He studied me. His face filled up with that perplexed fear he had of me. What answer did I want him to give? he seemed silently to be asking. Was I about to divulge what I promised him I would not? He reached for his neck brace and put it back on. The front doorbell sounded. "Who could that be?" my mother, moaning, wondered aloud. Staring back at us, she went to answer the door, first making sure her collar was pushed up in the exact Malone manner that pleased her so.

"What are you up to?" my father angrily whispered at me. "I could tell you weren't really crying. That's the one tough thing about you. You don't never cry—at least not in front of me no more. You better watch your step, boy."

"You better watch yours," I said, surprising us both. Had I just threatened him? I was feeling rather *heightened* myself. My buddy, that Huck Finn hussy across the street, would be proud of me for so effortlessly appropriating her tough-girl attitude. All I needed was one of her mother's old lipstick-stained cigarette butts dangling from my mouth. My father really did not know what to make of me. He grabbed another fistful of Frosted Flakes and stuffed them in his mouth. I watched his temples move.

My mother, right on cue, entered the kitchen with whorey little Huck and her Dale Robertson–besotted mama, who was still pissed off, still wearing her new sundress. The Coppertone my mother had earlier slathered on her hadn't worked. The woman's shoulders were severely sunburned, which probably made her even more cranky. "Okay. Tell Kevin and Mrs. Sessums what I brought you over to tell them," Huck's mama sternly told her.

My friend looked down at the linoleum floor and stuck her hands into the pockets of her oversized jeans. "I'm sorry I got you in trouble, Kevin," she said. "It was all my fault. I'm sorry, Miz Sessums. I promise not to make Kevin do dirty thangs ever agin."

"Good girl," said her mama, who explained that her daughter had confessed to our "escapades in the dugout," as she had described our little adventure, and told my mother she would fill her in on the disquieting details later. "How's your neck, Howard?" she asked.

"Fine," he said. "Coming along."

"Glad to hear it," said the woman. "Now, *you* come along," she said to her daughter, and grabbed her by her shoulder as they headed back home. My bad-ass buddy began to whistle—quite deliberately—the theme to *Captain Kangaroo* as she looked back over her shoulder at me. My father puckered up himself and joined in the tune.

My mother came back into the kitchen after seeing the two of them out. "What's going on?" my father wanted to know, halting his whistle when he lost track of how the theme ended. "What was that all about?"

I stared up at my mother, my eyes pleading with her not to tell on me, my plans suddenly going awry with the arrival of our neighbors. "Oh, Kevin. Your daddy's not going to spank you," my mother said. "Forget about that Big Black Belt." She wrapped an arm around my father. "Everything considered, he'll probably be proud of you. Let me tell him. You'll see." She turned to help my father fasten his neck brace. "Kevin and that girl were caught playing doctor or whatever back in one of those old Baptist softball dugouts behind her house," she said. "They were very naughty as far as we can tell. But *boys will be boys*, right, Howard?"

My father scowled at me before breaking out in exaggerated laughter. "Way to go, Kevinator! Maybe there's hope for you yet!" My mother joined in his laughter, which led them to kiss again for a very long time, careful not to muss the stiff white collars around each other's necks. Punishment I could have dealt with, but I wasn't expecting to get laughed at and then completely ignored. I realized in that moment I was on neither of their teams. They would always be on one and I would be on another.

Someone knocked at the backdoor. We all jumped at the sound. Had Huck and her mama forgotten something? My mother gathered herself, her head spinning in the way only my father could make it spin. He reached over and wiped a bit of his spittle from her lip. My mother opened the backdoor and there stood the Simpson Lady holding Miz Kirby's *Gypsy* cast album.

"I'm sorry to bother y'all," she said, "but I found this. Think it belongs to you," she said as she bent down to hand the album to me. "I thought I saw you playing around my hedge earlier and was curious when I saw something stuck into it. Does this belong to you, little man?" she asked. My mother, blushing, took the album from her and thanked her for returning it. That did it. I had had enough. Things were spinning out of control. "Dare I?" I kept hearing my mother's voice echo inside my head. "Dare I?" "Dare I?" I ran to my parents' bedroom. I grabbed the frizzy wig from under their bed and plopped it on my head. I dragged the toga behind me and headed for the kitchen. When I got back, I grabbed the duct tape from the table and stuck it on my own two front teeth and began to sing—in my sissiest mode—all the words I could remember from "Together, Wherever

We Go." Out back, Coco barked. Karole, waking up from her nap, began to cry. Kim came toddling in. The three adults didn't know what to make of me. Perplexed fear resurfaced on my father's face. The Simpson Lady looked embarrassed for us all. Defeat darkened my mother's blue eyes. Kim picked his nose.

What transpired the rest of that night is rather a blur. As clear as the day leading up to it has always been in my memory, the night it-self sort of floats in front of my face, just out of reach. I feel like the Simpson Lady, who knew someone was at her window but could not see them, who remained scared to know too much. This I do know: I know that a battle erupted as soon as the Simpson Lady bid us farewell and my father demanded to know where I had gotten that costume and why I was singing that song and what "goddamn non-sense" was going on. My mother confessed about her plans to perform at the charity event and he forebade her to do it. Forebade her. Frosted Flakes were all we had for dinner that night. I was told to take Kim and Karole outside to play with Coco by the light of the back porch. Whatever frivolity was, the opposite of it was taking place now inside my house. "Coaches' wives are like preachers' wives. They have a *place* in the goddamn community and it's not for goddamn sure showin' off all snaggle-toothed and parading their snatches around on stage!" My father shouted loud enough for Coco to bark in the way she did only at the sound of his voice, the excited, incessant percussive yaps of her lower register set off by quick little growls. The Simpson Lady's son came over, ostensibly to play with us, but obvi-ously trying to ferret out some information for his mother. I didn't mind. He was especially beautiful by the light of that lone bare bulb by the backdoor that barely illuminated our yard. "You gonna sing in the choir?" I asked him. He seemed shocked by the question. My fa-ther, controlling himself, called us back inside. Kim and Karole were grateful to fall asleep but gratefulness was the last thing on my busy mind. I had long ago given up on Captain Hook offering me safe harbor with a bunch of like-minded boys. I knew I had to lie there on my bed biding my time before I could someday escape. And what about that other secret? It was still intact. I had missed my chance to tell it. Would I tell it yet? "It's *tellin'* that makes it bad," the Huck Finn hussy had theorized about our own now detonated secret. Had she been right? Deep in the night I heard my mother crying behind a closed bedroom door because something had been forbidden. The sound of her utter sadness was seeping too deeply into me. My father's stubborn, angry voice did nothing to block it out. I searched under my mattress for the Huck Finn hussy's dirty Q-Tip and stuck it into my ears, pretending to clean the sound away. It did not work. I stood at the window. My face found the moon's light. I mimed taking off a brassiere. I stripped my bed of its sheet and fashioned a toga about my own body. A kind of collar resulted and I turned it up like Dorothy Malone. My mother continued to cry, but I forced myself to listen for the memory of her soprano instead perfectly hitting its earlier happy notes. I lip-synched to that remembered sound, not to the one flooding the house at that moment, and tried to come up with the words from the first song she had rehearsed that day with Miz Kirby, "Comedy Tonight." The only lyric that came to mind was, "Something *familiar*. Something *familiar*. Something *familiar*." It was a refrain that no doubt haunted the Simpson Lady who seemed to sense she might know who the Peeping Tom was, just like it was haunting me. It haunts me still. "Something *familiar*. Something *familiar*." I lip-synched those words over and over. I paraded my snatch around. I waited until my mother's tears had finally ceased, until even the furtive whispers that followed had faded, until the house around me was as quiet as my ever-moving mouth.

3

Johnny Weissmuller, Margaret Hamilton, and Katherine Anne Porter

Early on, I coped with having the distinction of being the sissiest boy in Mississippi by befriending an imaginary black girl who had appeared at my side one Saturday afternoon in my grandparents' house, where Kim and Karole and I had recently taken refuge after our father had been killed in his car accident and my mother had begun to succumb to cancer. My mother had attempted, after my father's sudden death, to go back to school to get her teaching degree in English. She had only a diploma from a local business college and the thought of spending the rest of her days as a secretary who, as a beautiful widow, would be fair game for the wanton advances of a seersucker-wearing cracker boss in some Mississippi backwater, made her eyes brim with even more tears. "Just between us, Kevin, 'shorthand' sounds to me more like a deformity from which some poor soul might suffer, a physical affliction rather than a secretarial skill," she said. I had asked her late one night why she was going back to college and she explained to me in her own way—amusing herself before she felt the need to amuse others—how much she loved language and how certain she was that the secretarial pool was not a place where her talents should be moored. "I always wanted to teach English but I had you children to raise and your daddy . . . well . . . he wouldn't . . . let's just say I had to raise him, too. Let's leave it at that."

She was allowing me to stay up late with her that night while she wrote thank-you notes to all the people who had sent her sympathy cards and brought over casseroles after my father's funeral, her careful, inky cursive script filling her creamy stationery in an attempt, line by line, letter by letter, to shape her deepening sense of loss into something as indelible as that very ink, a legibility somehow lessening such loss, grief becoming but another of her duties to perform with a presumptive Southern grace. All that clandestine joy she once shared with me when my father wasn't around had vanished now that my father Was Not Around. All she was capable of sharing from then on was the grown-up sorrow she could not share with Kim and Karole. No show tunes had been sung since my father's car accident. None of her naughty laughter had made itself known in my vicinity. "Words should not be turned into squiggly little things like bugs to be squashed upon a page," she continued, elaborating on her hatred of her secretarial skills when we stayed up whispering to each other that night as my brother and sister so easily slept. She stroked my face, my cheek an excuse for her to take a break from addressing the stack of envelopes she had to send to all her friends who still had husbands who were alive.

Her sadness, so sudden, so ferocious, was turning the welcome frivolity of her love of moviegoing, show biz gossip and rock-and-roll on the radio into something darker, richer, deepening it into the literary bent she'd always kept to herself but now hoped to render into something that would help her pay the rent. It was a sadness that seemed to surpass even the loss she felt for my father and encompass what she was just beginning to sense: the loss of herself from encroaching disease. That night, even before the initial duties of her widowhood were completed, she was already letting go of being my mother and, while still in my presence, becoming my memory, a memory she sensed I would keep alive for my sleeping siblings, for my ever watchful self, for the curious strangers who would someday read the inky words that I too would carefully line up along a page, this very one, line by line, letter by letter, to tame my own loss into something indelible, legible, my own sense of duty finally fulfilled. "I've always lived my life as if I were taking down shorthand dictated by someone else," she said. "Don't you dare do that. You be your own special word, Kevin. I know people call you a sissy. I know Daddy did a lot of the time, God rest his soul. Even I've called you that in my own way when I'm beside myself, and teasing the nearest person to me seems the only solution to the severity of one of my dark moods." She stopped and almost cried again in my presence, but decided she had better not for I had witnessed too many of her tears in the preceding days. She stared instead right at me with her blue eyes. She handed me her pen and a piece of her stationery. "Write it down. Write down that word. S-I-S-S-Y." I obeyed and wrote the letters as large as I could across the paper. "Now, whenever anybody calls you that again you remember how pretty that looks on there. Look at the muscles those S's have. Look at the arms on that Y. Look at the backbone that lone I has. What posture. What presence. See how proud that I is to stand there in front of you." She paused, seeming no longer to ponder the letters on the page, but instead what her future might be. Would she really live long enough to become an English professor at some two-bit junior college, or would she die never knowing what would become of her children? Would we someday, like her, stay up late at night with our own sissy sons and try to explain away the cruelty in the world to them? Her blue eyes fluttered as if a swoon were coming on, a look she got when her dark moods passed and she was about to be fun to be around once more. "The souls of words reside inside their sounds, Kevin. Always remember that. That's where the music is in language," she said, sounding like her beloved Miranda in Katherine Anne Porter's *Pale Horse, Pale Rider*, her very favorite book. When Miranda encounters her old Cousin Eva on a train home to the South, she remarks that Eva, a Latin teacher, had told her not to bother about the sense of a Latin sentence when she was a girl, but to get the sound in her mind, trusting the music inherent in any language to lead her onward. "Even a word we think of as a mean one can be pretty if you listen to it in the right way," my mother insisted. "Meaning has no meaning if you train your ear to listen to how lovely language is. It has its own scale. But don't ever scrutinize it," she warned. "Feel it. Form it in your mouth." She took a deep breath as if she were about to hit one of her high soprano notes in a secret lyric. "Sissysissysissysissysissysissy," she instead incessantly whispered in my ear and began to tickle me. "Say it with Mommy. Sissysissysissysissy." I did as I was told, gladdened to hear the hint of happiness hidden somewhere still inside her. "Sissysissysissysissy," I called myself, our voices melding into a sibilant giggle we shared inside that strange and ugly little house into which we had just moved, without my father to threaten to hit us with his Big Black Belt or to hold us in his arms and say he was sorry or to fill the rooms with his butch-waxed smell, his fragmentary whistle, his loving, wary looks aimed our way.

My mother abruptly stopped her part of our giggle. I quieted mine in turn. We sat in silence as she stared down at her unfinished thank-you notes. She handed me a new roll of stamps to start licking for her, trusting me to put them on the envelopes just like she had instructed me. "And, God knows, Kevin," she said, turning again to the matter-of-factness of our task, of all the tasks that now faced her. "If I'm ever going to put more than another opened can of Chef Boy-ar-dee spaghetti and meatballs on the table for you children, I'm going to need a better diploma than the one I've got. That is, if I make it that far. Let's pray what I'm feeling inside is just the final throes of heartbreak and not something more horrible." She stopped, touching her throat with a different kind of tenderness than that with which she had just touched my cheek, her fingers more tentative, less certain of their mission as they sought not to soothe but to search out something they could not yet quite decipher. Turning her gaze from mine, she then looked out the window across the moonlit field where the Hinds Junior College Hi-Steppers, a precision dance team of preening freshman and sophomore coeds, practiced their halftime routines in the afternoon sunshine five days a week next to our dank little house on that shaded and spooky cul-de-sac. My umbrageous memory of the place—furnished not only by the gigantic oak that hovered over us for the few months we lived there, but also by the unremitting mourning that spread out from my mother and covered us all—was relieved from time to time by sitting at that same window and watching those Hi-Steppers practice in their sequined outfits glistening in the afternoon sun. The oak rustled against the roof that night as I sat watching her contemplate the moonlight where it fell on the now empty field she had forbidden us to play on when those sequined coeds were out there kicking and carrying on. I waited for her to speak. It was the first time she put a word—one I could not understand except to know that it must be as horrifying as it sounded—to the fear that was forming along with the tumor inside her, a fear that was more threatening to me at that point than any tumor, for it was obviously, unlike the tumor, contagious. I had caught it. "I wonder, Kevin. Mommy really does wonder: Can heartbreak *metastasize?*" she asked, then returned to writing her thank-you notes.

———

Hinds Junior College in Raymond, Mississippi, where my father had been a track coach and Physical Education teacher for only a couple of semesters at the time of his death, not only had given my mother a full scholarship, but also that old run-down, badly shingled, abandoned faculty house for us to live in. This was after the school had forced us to move out of one of the newer brick versions where my parents, in the last happy months of their lives, had spent so many of their nights playing Scrabble with other faculty couples. Scrabble was my father's favorite board game because of the glee he felt when forcing the other players to accept the dirty words he liked to come up with when he'd link his letters to the ones already on the board, the merriment he caused now only a memory for us in the ugly house's eerie silence, the only sound in that moment the scratchy resumption of my mother's cursive writing against the blank pieces of stationery, a tiny echo of the oak scratching at the roof overhead. I watched her write until her hand began to cramp and she led me to her bedroom where she had me pull shut for her once more the forest green and azure drapery my grandmother had made as a housewarming present, the deeply hued fabric lending the room an algae-filled, undersea quality, especially when the only light allowed in it was the oft switched-on reading lamp by her bed. Understandably, my mother was having trouble sleeping after the suddenness of my father's death and found that if she held me to her, spooning with me atop her blue bedspread, she could drift off for a while, giving me the option of staying there with her through the night or making my way back to my own room like the little man she was insisting I become. "You're the *man* of the house, now, Kevin, being the oldest and all," she would reiterate for me when I insisted on being only seven, not sure that I wanted to be what was being demanded of me within the family structure left us. When holding me too tightly to her did not induce the sleep she so needed, she found that if she read aloud to us her own form of bedtime stories both our eyes would maybe tire. She much preferred adult fare to fairy tales and began to pass on to me during those "bedtime story" nights her love of literature, even of the lighter variety. She kept a copy of Helen Gurley Brown's *Sex and the Single Girl* under her Bible, now greatly ignored because of her anger at God. She would dip into Brown's how-to manual from time to time during those lamp-lit nights when she found that current bestseller the pick-me-up (a few recipes, some racy advice, a randy comment here and there, which she'd try to explain to me) that she needed in her new single state, before her moroseness would settle in once more and she turned for comfort to her most cherished of writers, Katherine Anne Porter. *Ship of Fools* was the author's first big hit. It had just come out that year, around the time of my father's death, and the thought of Porter having her own bestseller on her hands seemed the one thing other than Helen Gurley Brown's sexual bromides that cheered my mother up a bit. She loved reading aloud to me from *Ship of Fools*, her favorite scene concerning how one of the characters had died trying to save a drowning bulldog.

She also kept her dog-eared copy of *Pale Horse, Pale Rider* at the ready and pointed out that Miranda, the main character of the book, was eight years old, just like I was about to be, when she introduced me to her in the first section of the initial novella in the collection, *Old Mortality*. I can still hear my mother reading to me over and over those very last words in the story in her soft Southern accent during the hours when sleep was refusing all entreaty. It is a passage in which Porter lets us know the very essence of Miranda's developing character, the passage that has always served as a kind of outline for me to follow when looking back over the years and attempting to crack my mother's own complicated personality. "What is the truth, she asked herself as intently as if the question had never been asked, the truth, even about the smallest, the least important of all things I must find out? and where shall I begin to look for it?" Miranda finally muses in *Old Mortality* as she looks around at her life in Louisiana, just as I look now at mine in Mississippi. "Her mind closed stubbornly against re-membering," Porter writes of Miranda, "not the past but the legend of the past, other people's memory of the past, at which she had spent her life peering in wonder like a child at a magic-lantern show. Ah, but there is my own life to come yet, she thought, my own life now and beyond. I don't want any promises. I won't have false hopes, I won't be romantic about myself. I can't live in this world any longer, she told herself, listening to the voices back of her. Let them tell their stories to each other. Let them go on explaining how things happened. I don't care. At least I can know the truth about what hap-pens to me, she assured herself silently, making a promise to herself, in her hopefulness, her ignorance."

Those nights lingering over Porter's prose with my mother led me to other writers who gave me just as much solace in my own weary solitude when my teenage years commenced, a solitude that in and of itself was a way to connect with the very memory of my mother dur-ing those first few months in that green and azure bedroom without her husband, when she taught me that a companionless soul could comfort itself with the beauty of a well-chosen word, a well-written sentence, a well-parsed phrase. Salvation, she imparted, was offered in a paragraph's perfect form when one was capable of reading it with understanding, with empathy, with purpose. All such contrivances—words, sentences, phrases, paragraphs—could be combined into a lifeline one could throw to oneself. So it was that, as a teenager, I turned, always with her hushed voice in my head, from Katherine Anne Porter to the poets Muriel Rukeyser and Anne Sexton and W. H. Auden and David St. John, as well as the mighty Iris Murdoch, E. M. Forster's *Maurice*, and, of course, Flannery O'Connor, a little Faulkner, and Miss Welty. But it all started back in my mother's empty bed, that little reading lamp of hers illuminating not only her favorite pages of Porter's prose, but also, in some greater sense, her need to pass on to me a love of language that would linger with me, she seemed to intuit, long after any memory of her visage had become blurred and distant, a diaphanous face that, yes, only words would be able to sketch someday, once I tried visually to conjure her and found I could not.

On other nights I'd discover her alone with our stereo, its mahogany cabinet my father's favorite piece of furniture, listening to his cherished country-and-western singers or playing over and over his favorite album, Brother Dave Gardner's *Ain't That Weird?* Gardner was an ex-preacher who had become a stand-up comic, a man my father insisted was "one of them reformed Bible-thumpers, a gol'durn atheist when you get right down to it, who believes that a good belly laugh can save a bad man's soul better than any goddamn Son a'-God." Preaching such a sacrilegious belief to his friends and in-laws, he made them all sit and listen to Brother Dave, daring them to laugh at the jokes and the rambling redneck-loving stories on the album, which, of course, they did, finding my father's delight at his own bad-boyness as amusingly seductive as any of Brother Dave's punch lines. My mother, after my father's death, would sit and listen to Brother Dave go through his slightly subversive cornball repertoire and no longer crack a smile.

Other nights, when I longed for her to read another of her selections from Katherine Anne Porter, she would lock herself up in her bedroom and cry herself to sleep without the benefit of my company. I once knocked on her door when I couldn't sleep myself because of the sound of her tears so close by in the next room. She finally let me in and I found her on her bed with the Scrabble board opened up before her as she arranged the letters to form all the dirty words my father liked to spell. She reached down to scramble the letters so I could not make out what she was doing, although I already knew enough of the words. My father had tried to toughen me up with early knowledge of such language as I sat listening to him argue with his buddies about the merits of the Mickey Mantle versus Roger

Maris debate that seemed to consume him during the last full summer of his life. He was one hundred percent a Maris man and made sure I understood every word he used to make his case before the manly conversations turned to pussies and cunts and the careful consideration of Hollywood's big-titted women—Mansfield, Monroe, et al.—compared to the smaller-titted variety. "Women almost as pretty as my own little-titted Nancy Carolyn," he'd continue his commentary, always loving the way my mother's two names fit in his mouth, their having comfortably settled into his cheek after all my parents' years together like a juiced-up chaw of tobacco, its sluice, like the lovely flow of her name, a form of relaxation for him, a resultant moment of sweet release when either expulsion occurred. "Janet Leigh, let's say—she's got little'uns like Nancy Carolyn," he'd keep on regaling them, as sure of his delivery as Brother Dave was. "Or—who else? Oh, yeah—a looker like that skinny bitch Audrey Whatshername. I reckon that little Audrey gal ain't got nothing bigger than a couple of mosquito bites, but, boy oh boy, I'd like to scratch them mamas for her," he'd say, grinning that lopsided grin of his, all of his laughing buddies, Mantle men and Maris men alike, finally agreeing that it was indeed that latter kind of little-titted women, especially their favorite, someone named Juliet Prowse, who, in an attempt to compensate for their bra size, could probably suck the best cock in show business. "How big you think Frank Sinatra's dick is?" I remember him once asking. "He acts like it's big as mine, but I bet it's no bigger'n Kevinator's here," he said, rubbing my head and making everybody laugh even more.

My mother and I sat studying the scrambled Scrabble letters in our silence until, brightening, she asked me to help her pick up the huge tan *World Book* unabridged dictionary embossed in red and gold lettering, which was kept under her bed along with the Scrabble set. "Let's learn some new words," she said, deciding to practice her teaching skills on me. It was the first of many nights when I'd sit with her on the bed and we'd get out the Scrabble tiles and go through the gargantuan dictionary picking out words in order to spell them correctly, then focusing on their numbered meanings. She also taught me about subjects and predicates and adjectives and adverbs while sitting in the middle of that bed with all those Scrabble tiles between us. "We'll take a week for each letter of the alphabet and see how many words we can spell and learn," she said that night, opening the dictionary up to the A's. It was during the fifth week, when we'd made it to the E's, that her health began to decline to such an EXTENT (one of the words she taught me) that it could no longer be ignored. Her tears that night surfaced not from sadness, but from the physical pain she was suffering. It was after studying the words EXOTIC and ELITE and ELIXIR that she made me make the call to my grandparents as she lay on the bed barely able to whisper the instructions to me, telling me each word to tell them as if such an S.O.S. were part of the teaching duties she was trying out on me. It was one of our last nights in that ugly little shingled house, a frightening hubbub of activity ensuing inside her dimly lit bedroom (never again an enclave of the intimacy I alone shared with her) as we were rescued by doctors and preachers and grandparents and aunts and uncles who that night descended upon us once that first call went out. A decision was subsequently made, after my mother's diagnosis of cancer a few days later, that she and Kim and Karole and I would move in with my grandparents. Goodbye to the Hinds Hi-Steppers and her private readings of Katherine Anne Porter—although I made sure to hide her copies of *Ship of Fools* and *Pale Horse, Pale Rider* among my own belongings at her suggestion before anybody could arrive that night. They were secret treasures I would dip into after she was dead, in order to summon her voice, a voice that was attached to the very rhythms of Porter's prose, until the copies, threadbare from perusal, were lost by a shipping company during my transatlantic move to Paris. They were in a small box of other books the shippers misplaced. I'm still not over the loss. I wanted them around me for sentimental reasons once I attempted to make a home for myself in a land where the comfort I found in the English language would prove to be not a refuge but a hindrance, deepening a loneliness that continued more forcefully to creep into my being while I sat, day in and day out, and stared at the empty chairs across from me at Café Flore or choked down Nutella-slathered street-vendor crepes and questioned whether I ever again would have a conversation with anyone other than my silent self. During my year in Paris I missed my mother more than any other time in my life. I knew, as my silent conversations swooped from my past to that Parisian present and back again, how cute Nancy Carolyn would think all the little African girls were that I encountered on my long and winding walks through the city. I'd conjure Nancy Carolyn to accompany me and pretend that she was commenting on their tiny faces, lovely and alien and proud, some so black they looked oddly blue in the Parisian sun that stubbornly lingered on those late-summer evenings, when my imaginary mother and I would meander until nine o'clock rolled around, sometimes till ten, and I made my way back to the Pont Neuf where I'd watch the sun finally set. The little African girls, not quite old enough to be safely ensconced in their first year at some Muslim preparatory school out in the northeastern edges of the nineteenth arrondissment, held their harried immigrant mothers' hands and hid their sweetly embarrassed faces from me when I made a point of acknowledging their presence, their smiles too quickly buried in the flowing, colorfully printed skirts of their mothers, the richly dyed fabrics that formed so many of the bubas and wrappers and head ties as deeply blue and briny green as the heavily woven drapery back in that bedroom in Raymond, Mississippi, which I pulled shut for the last time for my own mother that awful night full of hastily culled family members who lurked helplessly in the blue-green shadows of the room, drapery I can to this day feel beneath my fingers as I stood in the corner and rubbed the nub of its wide, burlap-like weave over and over, waiting for my mother's pain to subside as she was carefully lifted from the bed and put into the ambulance, my hands fumbling for the cords as she cried out my name, unable to move toward her, unable to open the drapery back up, unable still.

———

That Parisian summer was not my first experience with imaginary female companionship. Perhaps the reason I was so taken with the faces of all the little African girls is that they reminded me of the imaginary girl who "befriended" me after I moved in with my grandparents. Back then, I just thought she looked like a miniature version of Matty May, my grandparents' maid. It never dawned on me that I would be able one day to compare my friend to African immigrants with whom I shared Parisian sidewalks as a grownup who had become brave enough to move worlds away from a Mississippi country road where he, a child, was not brave at all, but cowered grief-stricken in the culvert under his grandparents' gravel drive. I'd crawl as far inside the culvert as I could and lie down and listen to Kim and Karole and the fat little Derrick boys from down the road, whose parents owned the ramshackle chicken farm one pasture over, play cowboys and Indians until all their little necks would go grimy in the heat, the crevices turning black with dirt, "nigger beads," my grandmother would call the summer filth that gathered there. She'd try quickly to swab their necks with a damp dish towel as they raced inside the kitchen for the red Kool-Aid they still drank by the gallon before they galloped off for more of their Kevin-less fun. As soon as they were safely playing all those freshly Bush Hogged acres away from me, I'd crawl back outside the culvert and carry on inside with my secret trove of Katherine Anne Porter. I'd pretend I could make out all her words as I hid inside my grandmother's sewing closet with a flashlight I had stolen from one of my grandfather's drawers. My new stuffed animal, the green curving phallic form of Cecil the Seasick Sea Serpent, listened intently as I whispered in his earless presence all of the story I could remember about that German ship, those fools, the drowning bulldog.

My imaginary friend, a replacement for Cecil once she had arrived on the scene, was a tiny thing just like Matty May, who was but a bent slip of a woman, a comma typed onto the white world around her. My friend's eyes were as sly and mischievous as Matty's and she had the same oddly smoky smell. Her hair was also worn like Matty had worn hers all her life, plaited in flat precise rows to her head and culminating in a few tiny pigtails down around the top of her neck, a few around her ears. Matty was always running her tongue around in her mouth as if she had just eaten something delicious or was about to say something equally so. Epiphany had a tongue just like her.

She first appeared to me—my Epiphany—when Matty May and I had finished watching our umpteenth rerun of Johnny Weissmuller, still the love of my life, in one of his Tarzan movies that Jackson's Channel 12 would air as a Saturday afternoon double-feature with episodes of *Jungle Jim*, his 1950s television series. Those were touch-and-go days back then, when my brother and sister were out in the yard playing their own make-believe games with those fat dumb-ass Derrick boys while I shut myself off indoors to ruminate on the death of my father and how my mother was insisting on following in his footsteps. Her love of him, I was just figuring out, was proving to be greater than her love of us. "Naw, now," Matty May assured me when I first ran this theory past her during a commercial for Cowboy Maloney's appliance store during one of the Tarzan movies. "Naw, now, child. Naw, now. Don't you think no such thing." This is when my imaginary friend, waiting silently till Matty had excused herself to take down the load of laundry she had drying on the clothesline, told me that an African witch doctor had conjured her for my benefit and that her name was Epiphany. She also got tough with me right off the bat. "That old darkie was wrong," she said. "But you was, too. Yo' mama loves yo' dead daddy different'n you. She don't love him no more'n you. That's the firstest thing Epiphany's here to tell you. But you just keep a'listenin'. I got—Lawd be—a lot more to say."

I had asked my grandmother only the Sunday before in church what the word EPIPHANY meant, wondering if I would have learned it myself a few months earlier if my mother had not gotten sick that night in her bedroom and we had kept up our study habits. The preacher that Sunday, after mentioning my mother by name in his prayer, had, during his sermon, pursed his lips powerfully around those four perfect syllables, e-pi-pha-ny, in order to pronounce them (he was rather prissy himself, now that I think of it) with an urgency, a fervor, and my grandmother had whispered down at me, my head in her lap, "Oh, honey, that's just a pretty name for a little nigger girl," showing no compunction at all for using the N-word in a house of worship since the preacher himself often used the word from the pulpit when railing against the civil rights movement by citing chapter and verse from the Bible as evidence that separation of the races was the righteous stance to take in such times.

I, on the other hand, no longer used the N-word myself after Matty May had set me straight on the morning after the Academy Awards show in which Sidney Poitier won Best Actor for *Lilies of the Field*. I had walked into my new bedroom at my grandparents' house that Tuesday morning where she was making my bed before I caught the bus for school. "How you doin'?" she asked, the greeting she always started the day with when she'd first see me, the salutation sounding more like "How y'dwine'?", that "dwine" the most welcome of endearments to my young ears. I initially found the sound of it peculiar, privately laughable, but quickly grew to rely on its regularity, knowing that as long as Matty made a point of asking after my well-being then I would be "dwine" okay.

"Did you watch the Oscars last night, Matty?" I had asked her that morning. "Can you believe a *nigger* won Best Actor?"

Matty May sat down on the bed. A long slow sigh slid from her. She reached over and took a sip of the Tang she liked to drink instead of a morning cup of coffee. "Oh, baby . . . ," she kept saying over and over and running her palm along the chenille spread. "Oh, baby. . . ." The look of sad resignation in her eyes—all slyness had disappeared from them—was the same I had seen in my mother's only the day before in her hospital room, a look of utter fatigue, defeat. "I thought you was different, child. Lawd be, if they can get you t'sayin' such things, there ain't no hope. No hope." She started to cry. I sat down next to her and reached out and held her hand. I turned her palm over and, as I loved to do when taking a nap with her sitting at my side, I gently rubbed her calluses with my fingers, amazed by their toughness and how very tender they made me feel. "No hope. No hope," she kept repeating.

"Nigger's a ugly word?" I quietly asked her, trying to understand this newest storm of tears in my presence.

"Child, it's d'ugliest. Jesus never say nigger in d'Bible. God made us colored folk in His own image too, you know. So if we a nigger, God a nigger, too. You think about that. And you think about old Matty cryin' here like this, if you ever think about sayin' that agin." I looked up at her and asked her what I should call her then, since my grandparents, careful never to curse around me, used the word several times a day within my earshot. She straightened her bent shoulders and roughly pulled me up by the collar on the shirt she had just ironed for me to wear to school. She stood me up right in front of her. She always made sure to use a sweet tone when addressing me, but not in that moment. Her voice took on a hard edge, not lashing out at me exactly, but making me notice the angry dignity with which it was suddenly imbued. "Ah-woe!" she said, that special exclamation she always used for emphasis when she wanted your attention and was sure to get it. "I got a name, child. Call me by my right name—Matty May. That's got a pretty sound to it. You don't need to use some ugly name when my mama give me two pretty ones. Sometimes when I'm shopping at Paul Chambers," she said, referring to the owner of the general store where many of the country folk in the area shopped for groceries, work clothes, and gasoline, "and I hear some white fool use that word around me I just say my name over and over in my head to drownt it out, Matty May Matty May Matty May. Now I got a new one I can use—Poitier Poitier Poitier," she said, practically singing the name, her face aglow with pride. "Sounds almost as pretty as my own."

I helped her make up the rest of my bed that morning. "Matty May," I asked, "when somebody calls me a sissy at school, can I say your name over and over in my head to make it go away?"

She teared up again. She offered me the last sip of her Tang. I took it, defying my grandparents' admonition never to get a colored person's germs. "Child, you can use old Matty's name all you want," she said, kissing me on top of my head. "Plenty of me to go around now that I got something as pretty as Sidney Poitier to pronounce inside myself."

I was anxious to tell Matty about my new friend when she appeared, but Epiphany said she would keep me company only if I, in turn, kept her a secret. I agreed, quite comfortable with such a request, for secrecy was becoming, along with death, the twin motifs in my life. Though she was no older than I—I was now eight—Epiphany's imagined voice had a knowing tone to it as she would drawl her favorite appellation for me, "Chiiiild," in her rather drawn-out and stilted Swahili-tinged lilt, using Matty May's own favorite name for me but stretching that vowel even further than Matty May could until it sounded like I did when Matty made me open wide so she could see how sore my throat really was, and if "you sho'nuff just mightn't better stay in this here bed and let ol' Matty make you—ah-woe!—a hot totty out'a Tang and a tea-spoon of that Old Kentucky 'cause Miz Jake and me done fount where Mr. Lyle hides it up yonder on that top shelf in the kitchen behind them extra sacks of Martha White Self-Rising Flour."

Matty May was always the voice of reason in my young life. And Epiphany? Perhaps she was only my own adult voice arriving too soon inside my head because of the tragically grown-up circumstances that crowded my thoughts in those days. I do know that for the few months I made pains to mimic Epiphany during my most private moments—her akimbo stance, her head tilted just so in contempla-tion of how we had both arrived in such a place—she was as real as my lingering sorrow. Indeed, she was the very cure my sorrow de-manded. Her presence was a dare to it.

From the moment she alighted, fully formed, out of the very light of the television screen, Epiphany was constantly by my side. I can't say I was shocked by her presence, or even spooked by it, for I knew that I had created her. She was not real. I was bereft, as close to crazy as a kid can be when his parents' lives are kicked out from under him, but I was not crazy enough to believe Epiphany was a flesh-and-blood little girl. I see now she was a way to witness the narrative of my life, which by the age of eight had become too difficult for me to compre-hend any longer as a participant. Epiphany was the first character I would make up before I ever tried my hand at writing fiction or mag-azine profiles or fashioning a memoir into fable. I almost always re-mained indoors amongst the grownups—a welcome relief from the constant play of six-year-old Kim and four-year-old Karole as I sat perfectly still, saying nothing, hearing everything—and Epiphany, unseen to them, sat by my side and held my hand. She was a way to keep myself calm, to keep myself company there in the middle of them all, a confidant with whom later I could share my increasingly well-formed opinions about all the conversations we'd sat through regarding a rash of subjects, including the future of Kim and Karole and me ("Should we divide 'em up or keep 'em together?"); all the unkind names they could come up with to call a Kennedy; the continuing debate concerning who was prettier, Linda Lee Mead or Mary Ann Mobley, Mississippi's back-to-back Miss Americas from a couple of years earlier; whether watermelon was better with or without salt and whether watermelon-rind pickles, one of Aunt Lola's specialties, were worth the effort of working in a hot kitchen to put them up in such unrelenting heat; the hordes of hateful Ivy Leaguers descending on us all that summer and "looking down their noses at good God-fearing folks like us"; how Fannie Lou Hammer had "showed off her fat self up in Atlantic City at the Democrat convention," according to my grandmother when she felt like complaining about everything in life, not just the Ivy Leaguers, "making the whole country think we can't handle our niggers down here—why can't they all be as sweet as Matty there, huh, Matty—but old Fannie Lou got one thing right when she said she was sick and tired of being sick and tired, I feel like that myself almost every day I breathe"; how Elvis, a good Southern boy, must hate "them sorry Beatles"; how the Communists were winning; how funny Red Skelton was; and how many BTUs were needed in the Fedder's they were planning to buy at cost from Mr. Dearman up at the hardware store where my grandfather worked so they could air-condition the sewing room once my mother moved home from Lackey Memorial now that they were able to get a hospital bed in there for her. A friendless boy's invention, Epiphany was a much-needed ally in a place where allies were nonexistent. Epiphany understood, in her obvious otherness, how I felt in such a world. She even mothered me from time to time, after she took it upon herself to point out that my sick mother, as much as she loved me, never really mothered me, treating me more like a sibling.

"Chiiiild, y'all act like y'all sisters," she said, sitting up under the sewing machine with me after school one of those days my mother was recuperating at home in her new hospital bed. Proud of my reading talents for which she rightly credited herself, my mother listened as I read to Epiphany from a page or two of *Pale Horse, Pale Rider* before something called a morphine drip, the newest device wheeled into the room the day before, began to do its work and she drifted off to what had been promised us all, a painless sleep. Epiphany and I sat there and watched her as she reflexively moaned at whatever nascent dreams were beginning to sweep through her unconscious. Since the new Fedder's air conditioner had been put in the sewing room's window, the two of us had staked out that spot underneath the old Singer as our favorite meeting place. Epiphany loved it when I'd let her push my grandmother's foot on the sewing machine pedal while my grandmother was whipping up some new dotted Swiss shirts for Kim and me to wear to school and talking to my mother about whether "Lady Bird's a nigger-lover like the rest of that bunch," or what new mischief Coco had gotten into that afternoon, or what had happened on one of her soap operas that day when Matty had ceased being the maid at one o'clock and reverted to being her old friend as they had their coffee and pieces of coconut cake and watched *Another World* and, appropriately enough, *The Doctors*. Epiphany hated all that Katherine Anne Porter I kept making her listen to when I was practicing my reading skills on her. "Chiiiild, I'm a child. You a child. Why you keep reading all this grown-up bullshit to me?" she finally asked me one day, her mouth as salty as my father's. "Ain't you got no chirren shit you can read? How about that story about that other girl with the pigtails from where I come from?"

"What other girl from Africa?" I asked.

"No, chiiiild. I come from out'a the TV. I didn't come from out'a no

Africa. You always getting that mixed up. I keep telling you, Tarzan wasn't no ape man. He wore more makeup than Jane. Almost as much as Cheetah," she'd say and slap my own knee when laughter overtook her. "Comin' out the television is a shitload more EXOTIC than coming out'a Africa, stupid head. I'm talkin' 'bout that girl that sings about them rainbows and's got that dog I'd like to give a poison bone to." Epiphany had a phobia about canines. Coco made her crazy. She insisted I keep them apart. "Didn't I see a copy of *The Wonderfulest Wizard of Oz* around here somewhere? Or what about all that Dr. Seuss nonsense your mama's real two sisters keep giving you? Read that shit to me."

I pouted and went to the bookshelves next to the dining room and brought back the copy of the abridged illustrated version of *The Wonderful Wizard of Oz* that Aunt Pat had bought me. She was another of my grandmother's older sisters. She lived down in Woodville and was a few years past Venomous Mae in age. Aunt Pat, a retired elementary school teacher, was the spitting befuddled image of Aunt Clara on *Bewitched* and loved to present us with the badly painted, slightly cracked ceramics she proudly brought forth from the kiln she kept in an attic apartment in the rambling family homestead down in Woodville. "Let's buy you a book. You love books. Not many boys love books, but you're one of them. I see that. I certainly do," she said to me one afternoon in that voice of hers that waddled in the air just like her round hips did when she dawdled about doing whatever struck her fancy. She took me to the Ben Franklin Five-and-Dime on Main Street in Forest after a particularly upsetting visit with my mother before the doctors decided that morphine was the only option left them. "Looks like all they've got is some Zane Grey paperbacks and a bunch of comics. Who's this Lulu?" she said, perusing some brightly colored pictures. "This won't do. Not right for you. Oh, here. Look at this," she'd said, and handed me the book with L. FRANK BAUM in big colorful letters printed across the bottom in a palette even brighter than Lulu's. I agreed to the purchase and when we got home I put it on the shelf next to the gigantic World Book dictionary and never thought of it again.

Aunt Pat, bless her easily harried heart, had volunteered to look after us while my grandmother tended to my mother at the hospital during a few of the most difficult weeks of her illness. Though she was an astute babysitter when it came to keeping us amused with games, helping Kim and me with our homework, and telling us all bedtime stories—her favorite, and ours, was one about an elfin creature called Hop On My Thumb—she became flustered when household duties were to be performed. She more than once burned our morning toast, which Kim and Karole and I insisted be sprinkled with cinnamon sugar and buttered just so, with four pats, one in each corner, then baked in the oven until golden, not simply browned in the toaster and spread cinnamonlessly with homemade muscadine jelly. Her scrambled eggs were never soft enough. She ignored the bacon in the refrigerator. Tang confounded her. There was a discussion one night about her fraying nerves and she departed before she was supposed to, heading back to her kiln, glad to tuck her tail, much like Coco was doing more and more as so much distress and confusion in the house likewise confounded her in Tang-like proportions.

I plopped back down on the floor beneath the sewing machine with *The Wonderful Wizard of Oz* and began to read to the satisfied, though oddly saddened, Epiphany. Chapter One concerned the cyclone, which I informed Epiphany we called a tornado in those parts. She smirked at me like she always did when I told her something she already knew. By the time we got to the munchkins in Chapter Two, my mother was stirring from her morphine dream and Epiphany motioned for me to go over to her and step up on the kitchen stool placed next to the tall hospital bed so I could be closer to her and feed her some of the crushed ice my grandmother kept in a thermos there on the table next to the bed, a job that made me feel I was being helpful when helplessness was all that I remember from those days. The crushed ice would keep my mother's mouth moist and make it feel more comfortable, and maybe even allow her eat a popsicle, the only bit of sustenance she seemed able to keep down. I stared at her mouth and longed for it to be able to sing once more for me. I even longed for the hymns that took the place of the show tunes during the few weeks of remission she enjoyed after we had moved in with my grandparents following her diagnosis. A solemnity had understandably overtaken her during those days, which lent itself to lyrics about Jesus and the cross and what awaited her in heaven, a boilerplate of platitudes set out beneath the notes of the treble clef inside the thin, scruffy, old brown Cokesbury hymnals used by my grandparents' Trinity Methodist Church. Instead of Sondheim and Jule Styne, she had turned to John Wesley tunes, and on many Sundays inside Trinity's new A-framed sanctuary, one that acoustically seemed able to summon the Holy Ghost, she sang solos in her still clear soprano or, from time to time, duets with an alto-voiced flame-haired beautician named Ozella Weems, two of their stand-out numbers being "Whispering Hope" and "Sunrise Tomorrow," which were suggested by the church's organist, Grace Speed, a white-haired, old-maid, first-grade teacher whose name made me realize how economical beauty could be, how unexpected in its origin. When Miss Speed discovered I had inherited my mother's perfect soprano in a little-boy version, she had me later singing the same solos my mother had sung in church when she was alive. I'd pretend I was lip-synching to my mother's voice—as I had that night of secrets back in Pelahatchie when I stood in the moonlight at my bedroom window—but her high notes really would, there in the church, miraculously sound from my throat. My own soprano was the lone physical approximation I had left of her. I hated singing those church solos, but I did it anyway so I could feel my mother's presence inside me. It was how she reached out to me from wherever death had taken her. It was the closest thing that remained of her touch.

"Did I hear you reading again out loud?" she asked me now, as I stood on that stool next to her bed. Allowing the piece of crushed ice to melt in her mouth, she stared at my face as if I were her own imaginary friend that no one else could see. "Mommy is so proud of you when you read. Always read. Never stop reading. You still have Miranda hidden away?" she asked. "You're my own little Miranda. Put us together, in fact, and we equal one whole Miranda by now. Though I don't know if I'm going to come through all this with the same flying colors that she did . . . if this were only influenza . . . I'm afraid I'm going to meet Adam's fate," she said, sounding downright biblical as she evoked Miranda's boyfriend's name, a piece of crushed ice slipping from her mouth. Although her breath was putrid with morphine, I had come to love the stink of it, equating it with the limited time we had left together. I placed the bit of ice back on her tongue. "I'm so sorry you have to see me like this, Kevin. Mommy is so sorry," she said and turned her face away from me toward the wall.

Something strange was happening to Epiphany's face when I started reading to her from *The Wonderful Wizard of Oz*. It was, no doubt about it, slowly disappearing, turning away from me in her own way. She became more faint with each chapter I read to her. When I commented on this after Coco's funeral—she had been hit by one of the many cars she had begun to chase on the road in front of my grandparents' house, almost as if she had worked up the courage to throw herself in front of the wheel that killed her in a suicidal attempt to escape us all—Epiphany just frowned, her mouth hazy in the twilight as we sat by Coco's grave, which my grandfather had dug in the corner of the backyard out toward the pond. He had also made a wooden cross to mark the grave and my grandmother had printed COCO on it with a Magic Marker, her tears overwhelming her when she began to say a prayer as we lowered Coco, her little Chihuahua body wrapped in plastic, down into the hole. Suddenly, from behind us in the house, came the faint sound, growing more intense, of my mother palming over and over the little hotel desk bell kept by her bed, the repeated ping-ping-ping of it—the signal that she needed to go to the bathroom—competing with the crickets that always came to sudden life at the end of each Mississippi summer day. "Oh, God. I got to go see about Nan," my grandmother interrupted her own prayer. "Nothing seems to stay in her stomach. I thought morphine was supposed to make you constipated. That's what Rogers told me," she said, citing, as was her wont, Lackey Memorial's head nurse, for whom she had unbounded respect. "Amen," she remembered to say, then headed into the house. Karole and Kim, forlorn, their eyes as usual fixed on each other, followed her inside. My grandfather excused himself and went for a walk around the pond. He stared down at himself in the water.

I stayed where I was. I whispered to Epiphany, "I guess you're glad Coco's dead."

Epiphany's eyes hardened. I loved the fact that she never cried, never once, but looked at me more fiercely when something upset her. Hers was the one tearless presence in my life; for that alone she will always have my gratitude. "Just 'cause I don't like dogs don't give you no right to say such a awful thing," she said, lighting into me. "I'm sad the damn thing's gone. I'm sad for all y'all. I'm sad so much sadness is all around this place. Sad sad sad sad sad," she said, spitting out the word like it was that awful little piece of licorice she had tricked me into trying the week before that I had spit right at her. "It's all too sad out here," she said. "When you're sad back home inside the TV you can just go on down the street and watch Mr. Ed's mouth move or play Barbie with the Beaver or hang out with Alice Kramden and Trixie Norton and try not to pee in your pants when they start telling each other dirty jokes. Alice'll even give you a puff off her cigarette. Where I come from, sad don't mean what it means out here. It ain't real. I was warned, though. Especially by Topo Gigio and Hoss Cartwright. They was right. They said I wouldn't like it. All this shit out here is too damn real."

"I saw President Kennedy get kilt on the TV," I told her, staring down at the fresh mound of dirt now covering Coco. "I saw his funeral. That was sad. That was real."

Epiphany sat thinking about what I had just said. One of the Derricks' skinny cows from their small herd came up close to us from their neighboring pasture and stared at us across the barbed-wire fence. You could smell the Derricks' chicken houses in the distance, the warm breeze blowing from that direction musky with feed and the feathery dust that the swarms of baby chicks could muster when I would sneak off to their farm by myself a few years later and hide away in one of those long unventilated structures, my movement setting the chicks off as I waded through them, their soft down brushing against my ankles in their dumb excitement, an ebbing and flowing of deafening chirps as they stirred up the wood chips scattered on the dirt floor, the choking odor of their slimy, greenish bits of chicken waste clotting in the chips sending me back into the sunlight as soon as I had quickly masturbated.

"The world's gone crazy, ain't it," Epiphany finally said as she fixated on that chicken house smell. "Real folks done started dying where I come from. And here I am a fake person dying out here," she lamented. "That's what Topo and Hoss told me would happen. I should'a listened to that little'un and that big'un. But, chiiild, I wanted to come help you so bad I told them it didn't matter. You ever watch Miss Whatshername on *Romper Room* when she says that romper-bomper-stomper-do shit and asks if all her friends had fun at play and says she can see you through her magic mirror? That mirror really works. I borrowed it from her one time when she was sleeping off that Schlitz she stole from a commercial and saw you watching us

all on TV. You near 'bout broke my heart with all your hankering not
to be no chiiiild no more. That's when I knew I had to come visit you.
Even Alice and Trixie warned me about all this when they were lettin' me smoke one of them cigarettes and teachin' me them dirty
jokes they tell behind their dumb husbands' backs. Them husbands
smell bad. You don't want to stand downwind of them two. Alice and
Trixie told me that once I rounded up some laughter for you that I'd
start to fadin' on you. You'd lose my signal. I was just so sick of
bein' . . . what's that word that your mama's Katherine Anne and her
Miranda are so nuts about?—*immured?*—yeah, that's it . . . I was so
sick of bein' immured in that make-believe bullshit, I traded livin'
forever for livin'. Some of us do. Not many of us, but some. Mostly
the ones like me who are in the background and bored and so full of
hankerin' for stuff ourselves. You keep thinkin', chiiiild, that I was
your wish come true when I come out of that TV and sat down beside
you. But didn't you ever stop to think that you was *my* wish come
true, too?"

"Don't fade away, Epiphany," I said. "Please. I won't have a friend
in this world if you fade away. Please don't."

"Don't worry. You ain't gonna have to bury me. Nosiree. I'll spare
you that one. Epiphany ain't gonna have no funeral. Won't burden
you with another one of them things. Before too long I just won't be
here no more. I'll just be part of the air that you breathe. Part of your
brain that remembers stuff. Chiiiild, ain't you figured that out yet?
That's what I am—I'm you."

She reached out and held my hand.

"You think Coco's in heaven?" I asked her. She shrugged. Out by
the pond, my grandfather's sudden sobs surged forth from him, the
sound, like the pond's surface reacting to the rock he had just skipped
fiercely across it, rippling that chickenhouse breeze and banking up
against my mother's ever continuing moans of pain back up there in
the house. The cow next to us mooed at all the ugly human noise it

was having to deal with as it walked away toward its herd, its hooves squishing the fresh patty it had just left behind. Epiphany and I unlocked our fingers and put our hands to our noses to staunch the patty's aroma, as rank as any of my mother's morphine-laced droppings which I had gotten a whiff of the day before when I happened by the opened bathroom door and saw my grandmother wiping her sore raw bottom with a warm bath cloth before she ordered me to close the door after saying, "Don't you dare look at this, don't you dare." But I did.

"Dogs don't go to heaven, chiiiild," said Epiphany, answering my Coco question, her voice muffled behind her fingers. "They all go to that mean bitch Lassie's show," she said. "I've seen it with my own two eyes. They all line up and that bitch lets 'em sniff at her. That's—Lawd be—dog heaven for you: sniffin' Lassie's hole for all eternity." We softly laughed at this latest bit of celebrity gossip enabling us to get through another nightfall of a grandfather unable to fight back his tears, a grandmother who grimly coped with her renewed maternal shit-cleaning duties by attempting to coax my mother back to health with misplaced baby talk, and a mother, uncoaxed, whose hair was cleansed when sprinkled with a sickeningly sweet-smelling powder-like concoction called "dry shampoo." Weeks earlier, I had volunteered for "hair duty." When my grandmother was finished with tending to my mother in the bathroom, I went inside and carefully pulled the tiny plastic teeth in the concoction's accompanying comb against her tender scalp to loosen the powder into my palm. "Honey, stop, now, stop . . . it stings . . . stop . . . feels like a falcon's claws," she said to me as I attempted to spruce her up a bit and tuck her in before I tried to fall asleep myself. I held my eyes shut and waited for another round of her cries to subside and delirium to set in, her moans becoming the lowing that would fill the house once the neighboring cows fell silent.

By the second week of October 1964 I had made it up to the twelfth chapter of *The Wonderful Wizard of Oz* and my mother, perhaps bored out of her morphined mind by my choice of childish reading material, had moved back to Lackey Memorial for her final hospital stay. She'd be dead in a month. Epiphany, by that point, had weakened almost as much as my mother had but insisted I continue with our reading every day after I got home from school. We'd meet beneath the Singer sewing machine and, ignoring the empty hospital bed stripped bare of its sheets, we tried to get to the end of the book before Epiphany faded away completely. I wondered at that point who would disappear from my life first, my mother or my imaginary friend. "It ain't like I don't already know how this story turns out," Epiphany said, consoling me when I mentioned this to her. "Oz ain't that far a'- piece from Africa where Dorothy and me come from. Ifen I climb up in one of them TV trees enough I can see its emerald ass. Munchkins everywhere. But let's you and me stop for a minute, chiiiild. Let's talk for a spell. What you got planned for Halloween?"

I shrugged. "I don't know," I said. "Maybe I won't go as nothing. Everybody's too busy with my mama dying for me to bother them with stuff like that."

"What do I keep tellin' you?" she asked, her continuing exasperation at me the one thing that would not fade.

"I'm a chiiiild," I said, rolling my eyes and mimicking her accent.

"And what do chirren do?" she asked.

"They dress up for Halloween," I told her.

Epiphany looked at me with her hollowed-out eyes. I could see right through them. I'd win first prize in the costume contest at the school carnival for sure if I could go as Epiphany for she was looking for all the world like a real ghost. Or maybe I could go looking like my mother, all pallid skin and puny bones and blond powdery hair flat against her flaking scalp. "What are you supposed to be?" Bobby Thompson would ask me. He was the prettiest boy in my class. "I'm a' about-dead mama," I'd say, fluttering my eyelashes at him. Maybe he'd feel sorry for me. Maybe he'd like me more.

"Sooooo . . . ," Epiphany said, eyeing me as best she could. "Tell me. You have to have some secret idea as to what you'd really like to go as on Halloween. Go on. Tell me. We'll start plannin' it. It'll be the last favor I'll do you."

"Arlene Francis," I said.

"No way! One of them carpetbaggers on *What's My Line?*" Epiphany asked, appalled by the suggestion.

"She's not a carpetbagger," I said. "I know what a carpetbagger is. It's a book my mama said was trash when she tried to read it. Arlene Francis ain't trash." I pouted and I put the book down. "I want to be Arlene Francis."

"Chiiiild, let me let you in on something. *Arlene Francis* wants to be Arlene Francis. I didn't come out of the TV to turn you into no hoity-toity. Us sho'nuff residents of TV can't stand folks like her and that piece of work Bennett Cerf and Betsy Palmer and Peggy Cass and Kitty Carlisle. Don't even get me started on Henry Morgan and that Bess Myerson bitch. Art Linkletter? I don't like the way he uses us chirren for laughs. Chirren ain't punch lines. We got feelin's same as growd-ups. Oh, I could go on and on. They all trash. They all carpetbaggers. Real folks shouldn't put down stakes in the land of TV. It's hard enough for the likes of me there without them crowdin' in. All your kin is right. I don't believe in integration neither. Real folks should stay put out here outside the TV where they belong."

"You didn't stay put. You come out here," I told her. "What's the difference? You're integrating us."

Epiphany stared at me with a combination of regret and contempt. "I'm integratin' *you*, chiiiild. Nobody else can see me, fool. Arlene Francis? I swuny." We sat in silence contemplating my Halloween idea. "Ain't nobody at that carnival gonna know who the hell you are if you go lookin' like a middle-age woman who lives in New York City and puts on airs," she finally said. "Plus, pearls don't work on a person your size."

"Arlene don't wear pearls," I told Epiphany. "She always wears a heart'a diamonds."

"Pearls. Diamonds. What's the difference. Your grandmama near 'bout fainted that time she walked in on us when we was in her jewelry drawer a'tryin' on her clip-ons. What you think she's gonna do if you dress up like Arlene Francis?"

"She knows I like her. Sometimes I pretend I'm her already. I don't answer to nobody unlessen they call me that. My grandmama says she'd rather die of the grippe than do such a thing."

"You ain't gonna catch me callin' you no Arlene Francis neither," said Epiphany. "Don't worry. We'll come up with something else for you to go disguised as for Halloween. But we gotta come up with it soon. Chiiiild, listen to me. Look over thisaway. Can you even still see me?"

I turned to scold her for asking such an awful question. But she was right to ask it. I could barely make out her face in the air beside me. All thoughts of fighting with Epiphany about Arlene Francis flew out of my head at that moment. I could not bear the thought that she would no longer be a part of my world. And I most assuredly did not want to end her time here with me with a disagreement. "All right. You win. We'll think of some sort another Halloween costume, you and me," I told her and tried to find her hand to hold, but it had already completely disappeared. Her face was all that hovered next to me now.

"Read on," she said, her voice softer than it had ever been and, if possible, more insistent. "Do like I say, chiiiild. Read on. *Read.*"

I obeyed and turned my attention back to *The Wonderful Wizard of Oz.* I continued the chapter regarding the one-eyed Wicked Witch of the West and how she she sent the crows and the bees and the wolves in her thrall out to kill Dorothy and her friends but they were violently thwarted each time by the Tin Man and the Scarecrow. It was when I read the incantation that the witch came up with to summon her flying monkeys, "Ep-pe pe-pe kak-ke ziz-zy zuz-zy zik!" that it dawned on me who I could go costumed as to the Halloween carnival in a couple of weeks. "The Wicked Witch!" I squealed with delight. "Epiphany! I can be the Wicked Witch for Halloween!"

I turned to see what her reaction would be to this brainstorm but Epiphany was no longer by my side. Instead, sitting right where she had sat, as if the incantation had conjured her, was dear old Matty May. "How y'dwine?" she asked, Epiphany having transmogrified in that instant into my grandmother's maid. Or had my grandmother's maid months earlier transmogrified into Epiphany? Back then, in the days to come, I reasoned as best I could, when I tried to figure it all out with my eight-year-old brain, that each had literally blended into the other, that they had been in CAHOOTS, a word I had learned with my mother during our C-word week. As I try to figure it out today, it's as good an explanation as any I can come up with, other than the fact that I might really have been crazy with too much grief as my mother's death approached. CAHOOTS is the kind of word that suits them both. CAHOOTS it will have to be. Although Epiphany was certainly not real, the vivid memory of her anchors my sense of reality during those dark days between the deaths of my parents. In many ways, she is more vital in my thoughts today than my parents, whose flesh deceived me, defeated them. I do remember Matty once overhearing me carry on a conversation with Epiphany and warning me at the time, "Child, don't you start talking to yourself on top of all the other troubles that's going on in this here house. Matty don't know much," she said. "But Matty knows this—when a soul be talkin' to itself it be talkin' to the devil. You hush up now. You got something to say, you say it to old Matty. You know I don't never have a never-mind for you."

Matty May's face registered a deep concern when I turned to her with the Wicked Witch idea. My own expression, an amalgam of emotions, must have been one of astonishment and confusion and anger at Epiphany's exit from my life. She had not even said good-bye. "What's wrong, child?" asked Matty. "Do like I tell you. Read on. *Read*. This here book is just gettin' good. I liked that part when the Scarecrow wrung all them birds' necks. As good as in that *Noon Wine* stemwinder that that Porter woman come up with about when Mr. Thompson, think that was his name, kilt that carpetbagger with his ax when he come to get that nice crazy man who played the harmonica. That *Noon Wine* is Matty's kind of story. You read it 'bout as good as you read this'un here about Miss Dorothy and her dog. Makes me think of Coco, though. Po' thang."

"Where's Epiphany?" I asked, tears beginning to sting my face. I tried to climb from under the Singer and hit my head. "Where is Epiphany? Where is she?" I asked louder.

"Calm down, child," said Matty, pulling me back to the floor. She checked my scalp for blood. "You want me to go get you some Tang? That always calms you down. Let me see that head. Let me see that bump. Naw, now, Matty don't think you gonna need no Merthiolate on that. Didn't break the skin. Tell old Matty what's wrong."

I buried my face in Matty May's lap and rubbed the calluses on her hands over and over. "I want to be the Wicked Witch," is all that I was able to say. "I want to be the Wicked Witch."

"Well, we'll see 'bout that. Don't know—Lawd be—what Miz Jake and Mr. Lyle will say to your dressin' up like a girl agin. I remember hearin' tell 'bout that day your daddy had a hissy fit when your mama made you that little skirt. He near 'bout threw you in that garbage drum out yonder in the backyard, Miz Jake say, with that thang all ablaze. Say he near 'bout burnt you up with that skirt. But you just leave it up to old Matty. We'll make you a witch's costume ifen that'll make you happy. You hush up that cryin'. We'll see what we can do.

You just got too much woe for a child to ponder on, that's what's so. That's what's wrong. Woe's—ah-woe!—what makes a witch, sho'nuff. You come by it honest, I guess."

When Matty and I told my grandmother about our witch's costume idea, she quickly shot it down. "I won't allow it," she said. "I just won't do no such thing. How about you go as a cowboy or maybe John Glenn?" she asked too brightly. Appalled at those those ideas, I proceeded to throw the only tantrum of my childhood. I hit the floor with a full-body thud. I started kicking and screaming. It was behavior so unlike what my grandmother and Matty were used to from me that the two women stood startled watching me for a long minute, not knowing what to do. "I want to be a witch!" I screamed through my tears. "I want to be the Wicked Witch! I want to be wicked! I want to be a witch! The Wicked Witch!"

"Kevin, child! Lawd be! Kevin! Stop that! Don't you know yo' grandmama got enough to worry about!" Matty shouted over my screams, bending down to try and calm me, but afraid to step into my thrashing arms, frozen like that time an angry dirt dobber's nest exploded with a buzzing swarm toward our faces after we had poked a stick at it up in the corner of my grandfather's storage room behind the garage. We had been beside ourselves with boredom that day, after she had run the wash through my grandparents' antiquated hand-cranked wringer while I sat watching her do it, astonished at how flat the clothes were coming out piece by piece as she cranked and cranked and cranked, "as flat as Mr. Abe Hisself's face on that five-dollar bill Mr. Lyle give me on Sat'days," she had said. "Lawd, child!" she said now as I kept up my tantrum about wanting to be a witch. "Listen to your Matty. Hush up all this craziness. You ain't this crazy." She paused, amazement registering on her face as she felt she had to ask this next question: "Is you?"

My grandmother was wearing her crisp, light-blue nurse's aide uniform, her nametag and job title embossed on a pin attached to her breast like a medal a soldier might wear. She pushed Matty out of the way. I could hear the sharp rustle of her crispness coming closer to me. I could smell the white polish on her shoes, for they were the genuine article, bulky manlike brogues that all nurses wore, especially her idol, that chief R.N. at Lackey's, the big-boned boss woman my grandmother always referred to by her last name alone: the estimable Rogers. "Rogers says I should polish these shoes last thing before I hit the sack. That's what Rogers says—hit the sack. That's what she always does. Kills a couple of birds, Rogers says. Keeps you professional-looking. And helps you focus on what you have to do tomorrow at work. Me? I run my patients' names in my head while I'm putting this white polish on here so I won't forget 'em when I'm sleepy in the morning and make 'em feel less embarrassed when we got some bed-pan business to tend to first thing." She had told me this when I asked her why she polished her nursing shoes every night, shoes that were now standing right next to my reddening face where I was pressing it against the floor. With her uniform on, my grandmother became more officious, her presence less softhearted. She stomped one of those white nurse's shoes right in my face. "That's enough," she announced. "You hear me, Arlene? That's plenty 'nuff. Arlene! Stop it! *Arlene! Arlene!*"

That did the trick. I had been after my grandmother to call me Arlene for weeks. At least my tantrum had gotten that out of her. I stopped my thrashing. "Ah-woe! Miz Jake!" said Matty. "Don't go a'-callin' him no such thing as that. Don't go fannin' that notion in the boy. It ain't right. Boy's ain't supposed to be fancy like that. I'm tryin' to break him of all that nonsense. Arlene? I swuny. You just leave it to me. I'll break him of it yet."

"Well, too late, he done broke me first, Matty," said my grandmother, her voice completely exhausted. "I'm broke. Look at me." She settled into a chair. "I'm plumb broke." She sat at the modern black-and-white wrought-iron dining set my mother had moved in with us and ran her hand along the smooth flecked-marble top. The table sat juxtaposed to the old oak sideboard my grandmother refused to give up, the room too crowded now with different lives, different tastes. Other pieces of my mother's modern furniture in bright oranges and turquoise competed with the Shaker-like rockers and stools and beds in the rest of the house after we had upturned my grandparents' lives with our presence and our possessions. "What do you mean you are trying to break him of it anyway?" asked my grandmother. "You seem all for this witch idea. How do you explain that?"

"It's just Halloween," said Matty. "One night a year, Miz Jake. Not ever'day. A witch ain't nothing but fittin' for Halloween. And a hell of a sight better than goin' as Arlene Francis." Matty sat down next to my grandmother and put her arm around her shoulders as I dried my eyes all by myself. The two old women began to laugh softly in that conspiratorial way they had when, since they were girls growing up deep in the Mississippi countryside, swatting bugs off each other and swearing everlasting friendship, they found the same thing oddly amusing. "Maybe we should let the boy's mama have the final say 'bout this witch business," Matty suggested. "Might make her feel better bein' a mama for a while agin, bless her heart. She is—let's be God-honest here, Miz Jake—just yet the child's mama," said Matty.

My grandmother at first bucked at Matty's impertinence, her head jerking back with a start at the "just yet" Matty had used, the death of a daughter so implicit in the term. But then she calmed. She considered the suggestion. She continued to rub the marble tabletop, a gesture she would try to conjure after she had a stroke a couple of years later, when I'd watch her as she'd lift her right hand up there with her functioning left one and fight to feel the marble top once more, a memory of smoothness all that was left her. "Yes. Maybe we should leave it up to Nan," said my grandmother. "That's a good idea, Matty. I could use some cake and coffee about now. Did you make coconut or lemon today?"

"You was out of coconut and I couldn't find no more lemon extract in the pantry so I went with the Duncan Hines," Matty said. "Put pecans in the chocolate icin'. You want a piece, child? Put them pecans in there just for you. Matty knows how much you like to fancy stuff up with pecans. I'll cut you a extra big piece. You want one?"

I lifted myself into the chair next to them. I dried my eyes a little more. I nodded yes.

"Chocolate pecan cake it is, then," said Matty and kissed me on top of my head. She went into the kitchen.

My grandmother stared over at me. She continued to rub the marble tabletop. "What are we gonna do with you, Arlene?" she asked, shaking her head. "I pray about that all the time after I get through praying about your mama. But I ain't got no answer yet. I think the Lord is near 'bout puzzled by you as the rest of us are." She stopped rubbing at the table and took off her glasses so she could rub at her eyes. "Pour me just half a cup of coffee!" she shouted to Matty in the kitchen. "That's all I need right now. My nerves is jangly enough as it is."

———————

My mother gave her permission for me to go as a witch to the carnival. I knew she would once it was determined she would have the deciding vote. She was always encouraging my endeavors, no matter what they were, no matter how sissified. I could do no wrong in her eyes. Yet there had been one incident in which I was involved about which she did not approve at all. Only the month before, when I had started third grade in stern and staccato-voiced Mrs. Johnston's class, I had gotten in trouble for having a Little Miss Goldwater contest during recess. My grandparents were big Goldwater supporters; it was all they talked about leading up to the '64 election, when they weren't talking about my mother's health, her latest turn for the worse or turn for the better. I had even gone into my grandmother's closet and retrieved a big golden bow she had saved in her Christmas bow box and secretly taken it to school to use as a Little Miss Goldwater crown. I had also conducted a poll as to which candidate, Johnson or Goldwater, the teachers and students and janitors and maids were rooting for. The big vote-getter for Little Miss Goldwater was a blonde named Diane O'Bannon whom everybody, girls and boys alike, agreed was the prettiest girl in class. Goldwater also won in a landslide. In fact, Johnson got only one vote and it was from Flossy, the elementary school's tall black maid who regally swept the hallways each day while she hummed her favorite hymns to herself. "Tryin' t'rustle me up some peace a'mind," is how she put it when I had asked her why she was always humming.

Mrs. Johnston had overheard me that day asking Flossy about her choice of candidate and my subsequent berating of her for having the audacity to choose LBJ. Flossy, who up until that moment had always made a point of being nice to me, since everybody in town knew about my orphan-pending circumstances, flew into a rage at my questioning her vote. I thought she was going to hit me with her big push broom. Mrs. Johnston, hearing the overheated discussion, came out into the hallway and snatched my presidential survey from my hand and then marched me out to the playground to snatch the bow just as angrily off Diane O'Bannon's head where I had placed it with a flourish. Mrs. Johnston's accent wasn't soft and Southern like that of the rest of the adults I knew. My grandmother thought that her dead husband must have been a Yankee or Midwesterner and she adapted her cadence from him, it being "just a little too distant for my tastes," my grandmother had said upon meeting her when she took time off from the hospital to register me for school that year: "Don't act right friendly enough, but that might be the Presbyterian in her."

Mrs. Johnston, still clutching my Little Miss Goldwater bow in her fist, ominously told the class after we had settled in to our desks after recess that there was a "ticking time bomb waiting to go off around us here in Mississippi and you children had better start behaving yourselves, especially around the colored help. They are entitled to their opinions. They are entitled to vote for whomever they want," she said, staring right at me. "It's none of our business . . . and yet, well, it's everybody's business, I guess," she said, confusing the class with such circuitous reasoning. Mrs. Johnston, her usual staccato voice becoming shaky, barely audible, seemed scared to find herself in such a place, in such a time. She had only one son, Ray, who was the quarterback on the high school football team, and he was slated to graduate. Listening to her warn us about the world in which we all lived, there in Forest, Mississippi, circa 1964, I realized that she would soon be more alone than even I was. Instead of being mad at her for scolding me over my Goldwater behavior, I began to feel sorry for her. The year before, when President Kennedy was assassinated, the only two teachers who cried during the emergency assembly called by our principal, the brusque and Avon-deprived Miss Ishee, were my second-grade teacher, Miss Mills, too young to be an old maid but as yet unmarried, and Mrs. Johnston. I remember the other teachers pointing at them and whispering about their reactions. Eyebrows were cocked. Dry-eyed stares were curiously pointed their way. Within two years, no longer able to deal with the ostracism that began the day they had so openly displayed their grief at President Kennedy's death, both teachers moved away from Forest and headed for parts unknown in California, never to be heard from again. (Miss Mills added to the gossip by escaping with her widower next-door neighbor in the gleaming Airstream trailer parked in his drive.) "Some of your parents will tell you bad things about the civil rights movement," said Mrs. Johnston that day of my Goldwater escapade, summing up her thoughts. "But the civil rights movement is not bad. It is how we choose to react to it that can be bad. Don't be bad, children. Mississippi is already full of enough badness."

The next day Mrs. Johnston, asking me to follow her into the hallway, stopped Flossy after she had dropped off our pre-recess cartons of chocolate milk, the squeaking wheels on her milk cart always announcing her approach. She instructed me to apologize to Flossy. Miss Ishee witnessed what was going on and told me to hurry off to play before recess was through. Over my shoulder, I could hear her telling Mrs. Johnston that she had had some telephone calls from parents about her "little speech" the day before. I turned and saw her shaking her finger at Mrs. Johnston, who, we were told by Miss Ishee when she substituted for her the following week, "is home for a few days' rest. Remember that little speech she gave you boys and girls about colored folks? Well, whenever anybody talks about colored folks around you these days, you don't listen to them. It's nothing children should worry about. Colored folks don't have anything to do with reading and writing and arithmetic."

I raised my hand. "Is Flossy at home for a few days' rest, too?" I asked, having not seen her and her push broom that day.

"Flossy doesn't work here anymore," Miss Ishee said with her signature brusqueness.

If one Ishee weren't enough there was still another, the principal's look-alike younger sister who taught the requisite Mississippi History and Driver's Ed courses for the high school's incoming freshmen one building over, her own respective lesson plans full of Bilbos and turn signals and Choctaw chieftains. "Them two is sturdy women, them Ishee-or-ain't-she gals," my grandfather once said, nodding his head in greeting after they had passed him in lockstep, their gait prideful, puzzling me at his turn of phrase as he chuckled to himself. Neither Ishee had married at that point, nor seemed to put much store in the institution. The younger of the two did, however, like people to think she was dating our district's congressman, G. V. "Sonny" Montgomery. I'll never forget the afternoon when I was old enough to take her Driver's Ed course that she told me to floor the gas pedal in the Driver's Ed car and "blacktop the road" when an old African American man was crossing the street in front of me at the Rexall drugstore. "Go on, what you scared of, Sessums? Blacktop it," said that Ishee-or-ain't-she, nudging me in my ribs. The other two Driver's Ed students in the back seat laughed at her joke but I blanched at its crudeness. "What's the matter? You don't think that's funny?" she asked me, her lacquered and overly teased hair unmoved by the balmy wind blowing in from her opened window on the passenger side of the car. "I keep forgetting," she said, checking to make sure her hair wasn't moving. "You think you're better than the rest of us."

Word had gotten back to my grandparents about my Goldwater antics and Mrs. Johnston's scolding. It was the talk of the town that September of 1964. My grandparents had even bragged to my mother in the hospital about it, but she was quick to tell them that it was nothing to be proud of. It was the one time I felt she was disappointed in me, and my liberal politics were undoubtedly born in that moment I looked into her disappointed face. "You know I voted for Kennedy," she told my grandmother. "When will you face up to that? Seems like my cancer is easier for you to face than that."

"My gracious, Nan," said my grandmother.

"I told you I was going to vote for JFK when you kept sticking that Harry F'ing Bird and Strom Thurmond Dixiecrat literature under my nose. Can't believe you voted for those two awful fools. And I'm now an LBJ girl. If I'm still around come election day I'm checking off his name. You bet I am. 'Well, hello, Lyndon, yes, hello, Lyndon, it's so nice to have you right where you belong!'" she sang to the tune of "Hello, Dolly!," her love of show tunes and liberals combining into the ditty that Carol Channing was singing on the campaign trail in those days. My grandmother's face turned ashen above her light-blue nurse's aide uniform. My mother, satisfied by the response she had gotten, then turned her attention back to me. "Kevin, honey," she said. "You have to admit that Little Miss LBJ has a more ALLITERATIVE ring to it. Do you remember what ALLITERATIVE means?"

"It's when two words start with the same letter," I told her and watched her disappointment at my Goldwater antics at school disappear when I came up with the right answer. It wasn't just my love of liberalism that started that day at Lackey Memorial. Alliteration's allure also took hold.

―――――――

"You're not voting for LBJ are you, Matty May?" asked my grandmother when she and Matty were working on my witch's costume in the sewing room during those last few days before Halloween. "I couldn't stand the thought."

"Naw, now, Miz Jake, you know Matty ain't never voted a day in her life," said Matty May. "And ifen I could, ain't nobody I'd want to vote for 'cepten two folks—Sidney Poitier and Jesus Christ."

I sat under the Singer and tried to give my grandmother's foot an extra push in the ritualistic bit of sewing teamwork we had come up with over the years, but for the first time she kicked my hand away. Shocked, I stood next to the sewing machine waiting for the results of her work to be fitted on my ready body and watched as a raw fury overtook her. That foot of hers on the Singer's pedal became spastic with rage at her acquiescence in all this nonsense, at the continuing tragic turns of events in our shared life. Her right hand, always so steady when pushing the fabric through the slot where the needle did its woodpecker-like work, tremored with some sort of seismic knowledge that foretold how feeble it would one day become once a blood vessel broke inside her head and paralyzed her whole right side. I stared, in fact, at a blood vessel, which, in that moment, made its presence known on her flushing temple, a blueish worm that wiggled to the surface as if it were like the more earthly worms that my grandfather helped Kim and Karole dig up from our backyard soil and send sailing on their fishing hooks out into our pond. She finished the witch's dress and cape and tossed them both over to Matty May to try on me. The dress zipped up perfectly and the cape was an added touch I wasn't even expecting. Matty had fashioned a golden witch's hat just like the one described in *The Wonderful Wizard of Oz* on which she had drawn rubies and diamonds. She put it on me while my grandmother went into my father's foot locker, which contained his personal effects that my mother had saved after his accident, and retrieved his coach's whistle to put around my neck like the one that Matty mentioned was worn by the Wicked Witch of the West in the book I'd been reading to her. The whistle was attached to a long knotted shoestring from a discarded sneaker and it hung like a makeshift necklace toward my navel.

"Howard's gonna cuss so much with that filthy mouth of his once he looks down and sees you wearing this whistle with a dress that he'll have to leave heaven sure'nuff," my grandmother said. "Saint Peter Hisself'll give him a push."

Matty coughed up a laugh at such a comment and they shared one of their conspiratorial giggles, which seemed to calm my grandmother a bit. Matty next handed me an umbrella like the Wicked Witch had carried around in order to complete the outfit, but even at age eight I knew that the secret to accessorizing was knowing when to edit. Too much added flair could kill an outfit. I handed the umbrella back. "Suit yourself," said Matty. "All we need now is to go up to the Ben Franklin and get you a witch's wig and green face paint and you can use some of Miz Jake's leftover Avon to top it all off," she said, our having decided to forgo the one-eyed look since we couldn't figure out how to disguise my own two. "You gonna be—ah-woe!— one fine witch, boy. Gonna scare all them other chirren at that carnival so bad they gonna be wishing there weren't no such thing as Halloween."

"Can I still show Mommy before we go to the carnival?" I asked my grandmother.

"Of course, you can, honey," my grandmother said, then turned to Matty May. "I cleared it with Rogers. Visiting hours will be over but she's going to meet us at the Emergency Room entrance and sneak us in to see Nan so Kevin can show off his costume. I hope we're doing the right thing here."

"Oh, Miz Jake, look at the child's face," said Matty as they both watched me carefully running my hands down the black fabric that formed my ankle-length witch's dress. "Look how happy the child is. He ain't looked that happy in a long time. *Long time.*"

I'm not sure what Rogers was expecting that night when she met us at the Emergency Room's door, but the look on her face proved she certainly wasn't expecting me to come dressed as a witch. Her eyebrows, which had never had a tweezers' pincers anywhere near them, seemed to grow even bushier as they registered her astonishment at the sight of me, an astonishment that quickly led to an obvious unease in my presence. "You're a witch," she stated with not a little disgust, as if saying such a thing aloud confirmed the awful fact for her. Such unease pleased me. Witches were supposed to make people feel uneasy. I had witnessed Rogers doing her work for months now in my mother's hospital room. Nothing—not vomit, not shit-filled sheets, not the most wrenching pain—could throw her off her head nurse's stride. But I just had. It was a moment I cherished until I realized exactly where I was. I had not been in this part of the hospital since the day of my father's car accident when Kim and Karole and I had been babysat out on the bit of lawn by my father's great friend, mentor and prospective Black Angus cattle-ranching partner, Charlie "Chunkin'" Ward, an earlier Mississippi basketball legend himself. As soon as he was called about the accident, "Chunkin'" Charlie had sped to Lackey Memorial and brought along a football to pass back and forth with us to take our minds off what was going on inside. On one of my many fumbled attempts to catch the football, I heard my mother's terrible heart-tearing scream echo in the tiled hospital hallway. I had just crawled under a struggling hydrangea bush, its faded blossoms suffering in the Mississippi summer sun, to retrieve the ball where it had rolled away from me yet again, end over end over end. I turned to Charlie—his ruggedly handsome face as full of unease and astonished horror at my mother's scream as Rogers's ruggedly handsome one would be months later when she first caught sight of me in my witch's costume—and I said this to him, only this: "I know what that means."

"No, Kevinator," he said. "Everything's fine. Fine and dandy."

Then we heard my mother scream again and, as bad as her subsequent screams would sound when cancer later feasted on her, they would always be but faint echoes of those two that day, one right after the other, when she was told her husband was dead. Charlie put the football away. He huddled with Kim and Karole and me in what little shade the hydrangea offered. "Howard!" my mother called, her voice carrying out toward us in the blistering August heat. "My God! Howard!"

Charlie held us closer to him. "Hell," he said. "Dammit to hell."

My mother once more: "Howard! Howard!"

———

"It's Halloween," Rogers tersely stated, already regretting her decision to let me inside Lackey Memorial after visiting hours when the nurses under her supervision looked questionably at the little parade she was leading down the hallway toward my mother's room, my grandmother and me in tow, my grandfather and Kim and Karole having decided to wait out in the car for us. Could this really be that sad little Sessums boy? Is he really as odd as all this? Those seemed to be the two questions the nurses on duty that night were asking themselves when it dawned on them that it was I beneath the witch's cap and green makeup, my dress and cape flowing behind me as I swept toward my mother in Rogers's wake. My grandmother looked embarrassed for me, but I liked the attention. I had tired of all the pity that grownups constantly showered on me in those days, and this new sensation of disapproval was a heady antidote to that. "You've only got a minute or two before Dr. Bill and Dr. Jones start making their rounds, so hurry up. Doc Townsend's already made his. I don't want to get in any trouble. We've caused enough of a ruckus already," said Rogers when she opened my mother's door. "I just put a new drip in her," she whispered to my grandmother. "So I'm not sure if she'll even recognize the child, especially in that get-up."

My mother, already in morphined bliss, turned toward me when she heard the door open, ready to blather on like she did during those last days of her life when not only could I barely comprehend what she was talking about, but comprehend not at all the reason for such uncharacteristic blathering. I know now it was the result of all the morphine being pumped into her, but back then she was just my mother who was dying and not acting sad about it at all. She seemed giddy at the prospect. This tried my eight-year-old patience and, moreover, angered me. I was mad at her for not being as sad as I was at the prospect of her death. "Why is she talking to me like I'm Daddy? I'm not Daddy. He's dead already. Is she dead already, too?" I had previously asked my grandmother after the drip stand holding the morphine had been put in my mother's room at home and she was staring right at me and calling me Howard and how lovely it was for him to come visit her and how very sorry she was that she wouldn't move with him to New York City and how cute he looked in the Knicks uniform he was wearing.

"Now, Kevin, just humor her. It's the medicine she's taking," my grandmother had tried to explain. "She really thinks she's seeing your poor daddy. Don't disavow her of it. You just stand there and pretend that's who you are. You could do worse than pretend to be your daddy the rest of your life. He was a handsome fellow. A fine specimen. Look how she's a'looking at you, honey. She ain't never looked at you like that. Enjoy it, why don't you. When she calls you Howard you just answer up. The way I see it is, if you believe something, then it's the truth. Belief is the whole ball game as far as I'm concerned. If she sees your dead daddy standing there, then he's standing there. You standing there don't count none. Now behave."

I was not, however, called Howard the night of the Halloween carnival. "Double double, toil and trouble!" exclaimed my mother when she saw me. It was the first time I noticed that her skin—or what was left of it on her now bony cheeks—had grown as lightly green with illness and morphine as the pallor I had so carefully applied to my made-up witch's face, a color rather lovely next to the yellow of her nightgown. "Look at you!" she rasped. "You are the perfect little witch! Wonnerful wonnerful wonnerful," she said, sounding with her slurred speech like Lawrence Welk, who was never without his conductor's baton on the television, that fool my grandmother made me watch with her on Saturday nights. "Come over here so Mommy can get a better look at you," my mother said. "Come on. Do like I say."

My grandmother, pushing me forward, pursed her lips and stared on in a kind of half-hearted disgust, which helped disguise the full-hearted anguish that was becoming too much for her to bear as the death of her daughter was finally closing in on her inside that room so redolent of the medicinal that could no longer overpower the smell of rotting flesh that filled all our noses—hers, Rogers's, mine—a smell somehow sweetened when combined with the perfumy bath powder I had so often watched my grandmother tenderly apply around my mother's bedsores with the pink puff, mangy now with use, that came inside the powder's box. I climbed up on the stool by my mother's bed and whispered in her ear the question I had been planning to ask her all day, my voice mimicking her own overly excited whisper when she herself was about to do something unexpected. "Dare I?" I asked her, leaning in so close my mouth touched her hot ear. "Dare I? Dare I?"

My mother gasped with delight at the question, hearing her own secret voice now filtered through me. She queried me with her wallow-eyed look until I once again came into focus for her. "Yes," she whispered back. "Always. Always dare. That's my boy. You're Mommy's boy. Now you go out and scare you up some candy. Bring me back some of that awful Halloween kernel corn," she was barely able to say to me through her cracked lips. Then, her frantic energy a complete surprise, she began to ask the question herself. "Dare I?" she wanted to know, wanted to know it over and over, as she squirmed around in the bed before me. She no longer asked it playfully as she once had, when the question was posed as but the preamble to one of her behavioral examples on how to be naughty and fearless and feminine all at the same time, but asked it instead quite pointedly, her tone urgent, as if she were wondering aloud if she should just go ahead and die right there in front of me. "Dare I?" she kept up the refrain, her legs dancing about beneath the sheet like they could in the old days when we pretended we were stars of the stage. "Dare I? Dare I? Dare I?" she kept going.

I heard Rogers whisper to my grandmother, "I've seen it happen toward the end, when they get crazed with illness like this. It'll pass d'rectly. Don't worry, Jake. Just wait her out. The pain'll pass. Soon she'll pass right along with it. You'll be grateful. She'll be, too. Even that little booger there will, too, though he don't know it yet." I hated Rogers for making such sense. I wanted to disagree, but could not. I did not want to see my mother turn crazy. I tucked the hospital sheet about her body with a grim determination, in the hope that such busy work—I punched at the mattress, I punched at it over and over—would quiet her cries. Rogers went to help me but I pushed her away. I stared at my mother's breasts inside her yellow nightgown; they appeared to have shrunk to nothing but nipples still able to notice the cotton sheet as I kept punching it tighter and tighter around her. When she calmed, she calmed in an instant. But her eyes, the only movement left her, continued to wallow about. I picked up the glass of water kept on the bedside table and bent the straw to her mouth. She barely had the strength to suck a swallow past her dried-up lips. I put the glass down and touched them, her lips, with my fingers. They felt like Matty May's calloused palm. I dipped a finger into the opened jar of Vaseline now also always on the bedside table and rubbed a bit of it onto her lips like I had seen Rogers and my grandmother so often do when I sat in the corner and pretended to do my homework. My mother puckered up and I let her scrape her greasy lips against my green witch's cheek.

Then, the morphine really kicking in, she gasped, raised her needled arm in a giant sweeping motion and grabbed my wrist. Rogers, always quick on her feet beneath her fat ankles, checked to see that the needle from her drip had not come out, then backed up again against the wall with my grandmother, both women aghast now at the scene being played out in front of them. " 'Jarge!' " my mother shouted as best she could, sounding like Katharine Hepburn playing Martha Washington and calling out her husband's name in a fit of pique. What she was really doing was quoting from one of our favorite sections of *Pale Horse, Pale Rider*, in which the grizzled old copy editor of the newspaper where our beloved Miranda worked as a theater columnist bellowed the same sound. Yet my mother and I were never sure what exactly the word "Jarge" meant when the old man bellowed it. My mother at first surmised that it was, yes, the phonetic spelling for George, which might just be the name of the copyboy on duty for whom the old man was shouting, but, as my mother explained, "Porter, God bless her cynical soul, seldom resorts to being that cute, that's why I love her so. I hate cute writing. I hate cute anything—although I do like a nice pair of pedal-pushers from time to time. Wait!" she had said, her face reddening with pleasure when a new idea dawned on her. "Perhaps it's World War One–era jargon for just that—JARGON!" she reasoned, and made me look the word up with her in our big World Book dictionary when I told her I didn't know what that meant. "'Jarge!'" she hoarsely shouted again that Halloween night from where she lay in her hospital bed.

My grandmother and Rogers looked completely baffled by her outburst. But I knew exactly what she wanted from me. It was my cue. I took a breath, proud to be able to please her with my ability even then to recall words and scenes with a preternatural precision. "'Never say *people* when you mean *persons*,'" I told her, reciting the *Pale Horse, Pale Rider* section she had made me memorize when we closed the dictionary after having quickly dipped into the J's. "'Never say *practically*,'" I continued, "'say *virtually,* and don't for God's sake ever so long as I am at this desk use the . . .'" I froze. I could not remember what came next. It was the first time my memory had failed me when reciting these lines to her. I panicked. I stuttered, the very genesis of the stutter that would afflict me the rest of my life. "'Use the . . . use the . . . use the . . .'" I stared into my mother's dying face. I was stricken. Words would not form in my mouth.

My mother licked the Vaseline from her lips. "'Barbarism,'" she said so softly I could barely hear her. "It's 'barbarism.' Isn't it?"

I started again. "'And don't for God's sake ever so long as I am at this desk use the b-b-barbarism *inasmuch* under any circumstances whatsoever.'"

My mother smiled. I gave her another sip of water. I re-Vaselined her lips. "'Now you're educated. You may go,'" she quoted Porter. And I did.

It was my first Halloween in Forest and I was nervous wondering what everyone would think of my witch's costume. I knew enough to know

it was a rebellious and troubling choice. Although I can't remember
what Kim and Karole went costumed as that night to the carnival, I
do distinctly remember the crowd parting as we made our entrance
and the looks of puzzled appreciation on the faces belonging to the
other families, sleek with youth, who were there and all still intact,
mothers and fathers in their twenties showing off their first go at kids.
Suddenly, a disapproval even more pronounced than the kind I encountered from the nurses on duty at Lackey Memorial descended
upon the crowd as it dawned on them all that it was I who had come
dressed so convincingly as a witch. A bit of nervous laughter took
root. Then, as they saw how serious I was taking my role, an appalled
silence cast itself across them. What kind of creature was this that
had settled in their midst? "That's not right," came a whisper, the
judgment, once espoused, once passed, encouraging others to judge.
"If that boy's daddy was still alive—I hear tell his mama's not long for
this world neither, lingerin' like she's doin' up at Lackey's—he
wouldn't've showed up like that. Coach Sessums would've whupped
him good," came another whisper right at me. "What a sight," someone else said. Another: "We better pray for that young'un." Yet this—
"What a shame! What a awful shame!"—is the admonition that has
stuck with me above all others from that night, a whisper that
seemed to be honed among those gathered in the elementary
hallways—the Zorros and Casper the Friendly Ghosts and Robin
Hoods and Cinderellas and My Favorite Martians even greener than
my Wicked Witch—until it was shortened into the one-word con-
demnation that all little sissies must deal with at some point, the one
that reverberates in the echo chambers of our collective memory.
"Shame," came the utterance, "shame," the "sh" of it like the rustle
of that imagined petticoat Epiphany always longed for when she'd
slowly twist her hips back and forth and pretend she had one on,
"shame," that phantom sound now found. I swallowed hard and
sashayed through the crowd as if it were I who had on Epiphany's

make-believe clothes. I threw my bewigged head back in defiance. I made sure my "Dare I?" demeanor did not crack. This was for my mother. This was for myself. This was who I was. If death—my father's shocking one the year before, my mother's encroaching at any moment—was making me, back in that meanspirited Mississippi year of 1964, a pity-worthy spectacle for fellow Mississippians to focus on and feel less bad about the belligerence they were displaying in all its ugly glory for the rest of the country to behold, then I would take up its mantle and make the spectacle my own. No longer would I be the child for whom overweening sorrow was a parental replacement. No longer would I be a vessel for sympathy so that the sympathizers, through a sadness that was not even theirs, could cleanse themselves of their sinister culture and the sinister politics it bred. With a pride that confounded all who were in my path that night, I decided I'd go ahead and be the sissy everyone said I was. Let them whisper as I walked through them all. "Shame." "Shame." I would really give them something to fret about, to fight against. I might never be a woman. "Shame." I might never be a man. But I would always be a witch. The world could kill my parents, I reasoned, but I could kill it right back by being otherworldly. I would show them that a sissy could be just as sinister as they all were. I had had enough. "Shame." I felt like I was going to shit. "Shame." "Shame." I shuddered at my power.

My grandmother's hand grabbed my shoulder. "Want to go inside the haunted house?" she asked, sensing the stir we both were causing when it began to sink in that she had allowed me to come costumed better than any little girl at the school. Who was to blame here, some seemed to be thinking: the boy or the old lady who let him out of the house like that? My grandmother led me to the second-grade classroom where many of the mothers, dressed as ghosts and monsters and witches themselves, had created a scary environment full of fake cobwebs and skeletons. "Want to go on in?" she asked, pushing me forward so I would be out of sight and just maybe the whispers would stop. "I'll wait out here for you while Lyle takes Kim and Karole down yonder to bob for apples." I shrugged and headed inside the haunted house. Nothing could be as scary as the crowd we had just made our way through. As soon as I saw what awaited me, though, my arrogance abated. When one of the mothers, dressed like Frankenstein's bride, her towering green hairdo made from uncooked spaghetti, put my hand in a vat of eyeballs made from Jell-O, I began—uncontrollably—to scream. The other mothers tried to catch me and calm me down as I ran from their grasps, knocking over cardboard coffins and cauldrons full of dry ice. As I tried to find my way out of the darkened room, my screams grew even more bloodcurdling. My grandmother came rushing in and started shouting at the costumed mothers, "Call him Arlene! That'll slow him down! Arlene! Arlene!" She grabbed me by the shoestringed whistle around my neck but I shimmied free, continuing my rampage about the room and leaving her holding the whistle. I broke one mother's tackle. Then another's. One, costumed as a werewolf, grabbed me around the neck but I bit her hairy forearm and freed myself to run wildly in circles some more. By the time three of the fattest mothers ganged up on me and held me down to hand off to my grandmother, my witch's black dress was torn, my wig was askew, my makeup was ruined. When I finally emerged firmly in my grandmother's grasp, I discovered that all the carnival-goers had gathered around the door to the haunted house to find out what all the screaming was about. Again the crowd parted as I made my way back through it. They were even more appalled by me now.

"I think we should go home. This whole thing was a bad idea," my grandmother angrily whispered as we kept on walking straight for the exit. Now holding my father's coaching whistle in her hand, she wasn't quite sure what to do with it, so she hung it around her own neck. She jerked me forward. My grandfather and Kim and Karole, whose little worried faces were still wet from bobbing, arrived on the scene and followed us out to our car. "I don't know why I let your mama and Matty convince me this was okay," my grandmother said, once we had settled in for the ride home. Kim and Karole, more frightened of me by now than any of the crowd back at the carnival, huddled together on their side of the backseat. "She's not in her right mind, your mama," said my grandmother. My grandfather, his breathing always more pronounced through his hairy nostrils when he was upset, said nothing. He only wheezed in disapproval and gripped the steering wheel tighter before bumping up the headlights to high-beam when we got out on the country road where we lived. The eyes of the cows in the pastures we passed flickered, like fireflies pairing off, as they glowered at the sound of our family's Plymouth whining its way into second, my grandfather pushing harder at the gas pedal. "I ain't in my right mind, neither, these days," my grandmother continued. "Shoot. I barely have a mind left. But I tell you this—slow down, Lyle, you're gonna get us all kilt—I've never been so embarrassed in my life. I told your mama something like this might happen. But she wouldn't listen. She forgets where she lives half the time. Always did. This is Mississippi. We don't stand for no nonsense down here." She lifted the silent whistle around her neck and stared down at it. "Sometimes I think she'd'a been better off if she hadn't been pregnant with you, and her and Howard would've just went ahead and moved up yonder to New York City with all them heathens in them high-rises. You'd like it better, too, up yonder, I bet. Wouldn't you, Arlene?" she asked, her voice dribbling disdain atop the question like the sweet yet bitter sorghum syrup my grandfather liked to dribble on her biscuits. "I know Howard would have loved it. He loved to show off—you get that from him—and New York City is full of show-offs as far as I can figure from watching that Ed Sullivan mess. Next year, I tell you what, it's John Glenn for you. You'll look right cute in all that silver. You'll see, I'm as good at making spacesuits as I am a witch's dress. I bet aluminum foil would work right nice for a spacesuit. Cheaper, too, than that crepe wool you're wearing." I straightened my wig beneath my pointed hat and watched the night go by as we headed back into the pitch-black countryside. I counted by twos—up to sixteen—the eyes of the cattle when they caught the Plymouth's light. Why had the haunted house scared me so? It wasn't the monsters and the ghosts and the other witches with which I was confronted. I knew all that was fake. What was not fake were those mothers themselves who, unlike my own, were not dying. I know now it was that coven of the living that caused my screams, the rent in my dress. But back then I was just angry at myself for losing control. Somehow I knew that the appalled crowd had won a round. I vowed to myself never to lose control again. The rest of the rounds were mine. I pulled off my hat and wig and threw them on the seat between Kim and Karole and me. They huddled closer and scooted farther away. My grandfather turned into our gravel drive, that soft growl of home the sound we had all been waiting for.

4

James Brown, Jesus, and Jackie Susann

When I returned to school after the Halloween carnival I was even more ostracized than usual. "Witch Boy" became the newest moniker to be hurled at me at recess. I coped with all the meanspirited ribbing by pretending I really was a witch and could silently cast spells on my tormentors. After a couple of weeks of this, Miss Ishee's deeply timbred, disembodied voice, summoning me, issued from the intercom system's wooden box located above the chalkboard, the same box that slightly vibrated each morning at 8:15 when a specially picked student read a devotional from the *Upper Room* as well as an Ishee-chosen verse from the Bible before leading, too loudly, the whole public school in the Lord's Prayer. At first I thought I was being called to the principal's office because I had begun to spout my "Witch Boy" incantations right in the faces of my tormentors instead of suffering in silence. "Ep-pe pe-pe kak-ke ziz-zy zuz-zy zik!" spewed from my black-magic mouth as I warned them of the toads and other terrible things they would turn into during the night if they dared to fall asleep. Parents, I had heard, were beginning to complain that their sons and daughters were frightened to go to bed and they were blaming it on me, "that Sessums child, bless his heart, who's takin' out all his sufferin' on our young'uns. Them spells he's castin' at recess is takin' holt. That's why all them young'uns can't keep their heads off their desks. Toads, my foot. Stop that child. Stop him now or he's gonna be the only one awake enough to take a 'rithmetic test. Witch boys in school is near 'bout worse than a bunch'a coloreds."

The fear of being punished for my behavior quickly passed, however, for there was another fear, the one that filled my thoughts every school day. Each time I was summoned to the principal's office and made that slow walk from Mrs. Johnston's third-grade classroom, the very last one along the elementary school's hallway, I was afraid I was about to be told that my mother had died. Usually it was just a relative, most often Aunt Gladys, who had come to take Kim and me out of school early on a Friday afternoon so that, along with Karole, we could have a weekend visit far away from hospital rooms and frazzled grandparents. That day, however, I was certain it was not going to be Aunt Gladys. I prepared myself for what awaited me. The time had come to face the one fact I would have to face the rest of my life: My mother was dead. It was more than something I knew as I walked toward Miss Ishee's familiar office; it was something I felt. It imbedded itself in my Witch Boy body as her spirit, finally freed from her own body, swept me forward down the hallway, holding up my trembling chin with her still warm hands, hands that smelled, in that wondrous moment when they wafted by me, of the last bit of Jergens lotion my grandmother had but that morning massaged into the translucent flesh of her now translucent palms. My angry heart pounded faster. I focused on its pounding. "Dare I?" I heard my mother's voice, more disembodied even than Miss Ishee's over that loudspeaker, whisper in my ear one last time. "Dare I? Dare I?" I did not pretend I could not hear her, for if I were to be the Witch Boy I was accused of being by all those other children at recess—if, indeed, I were now to be an orphan—the only source of comfort left me would be just this: the supernatural.

When I rounded the corner to the principal's office, all was confirmed. There sat Charlie "Chunkin'" Ward. He was holding Kim, who had already been roused from Mrs. Stroud's first-grade classroom, in his lap. I stepped into the office. Ishee-or-ain't-she sat, a clump of efficiency, in the swivel leather chair behind her desk. I did not want to look at her or Charlie, scared that the badly camouflaged sadness that all adults seemed to have in their eyes whenever they looked at me would set me off and I'd start spouting my patented incantation right then and there in their carefully composed faces. I did not want to look at Kim, either. Every time I looked his way I longed to have his ease at being a child. I stared instead at the huge microphone on the intercom's console behind Miss Ishee and thought of the day I had been chosen to read from the Upper Room and how, the night before, my grandmother had written out the words to the Lord's Prayer for me so I wouldn't forget them. I began silently to say the prayer—as much of it as I could recall—while I stood there waiting for someone to speak. "Hey there, Kevinator," said Charlie, the fake cheer in his voice piercing right through the somber our-Father-who-art-in-heaven words filling my head.

I turned and said this to him, only this: "I know what this means."

He did not, as he had a year before outside the Emergency Room, disabuse me of the notion. Kim? He seemed only happy to see "Chunkin'" Charlie, for Charlie was, fake cheer aside, a truly jolly sort. Maybe that was why my grandparents had called him and asked him to be the bearer of such news.

Kim and I piled into the front seat of Charlie's Pontiac and he drove around our small town pretending he had some place to take us. Kim was beginning to look a bit puzzled as we instead circled about the residential streets and Charlie, choking up, turned back onto Marion Boulevard toward the elementary school from Highway 35. "Your mama has gone to sleep, boys," he said. "She's at peace. She's not in any more pain." He cleared his throat and nervously adjusted his rearview mirror. I looked up into it and saw Miss Ozella Weem's beauty shop down the hill behind us. I knew what was expected of me at that moment. I was expected to cry. And watching the tears surface in my eyes in the adjusted mirror, that's exactly what I did. It was but my latest bit of conjuring, something I had gotten good at since Epiphany left me to my own devices. (Yet Matty had called it something else. "You got the real thang in you since that Halloween carnival crybaby mess Miz Jake tolt me you got yo'self into," she had said when I wouldn't stop pouting post-Halloween about what had happened. "Miz Jake say she plumb vexed by you, child. But Matty ain't no such thang. I ain't vexed a'tall. I know voodoo when I see voodoo. Something's took a'holt' a'you. Devil's got you in his teeth. And the devil ain't nothing but a feist dog when it comes to a body's soul. We'd'bones all right. Nothing but a bag a'bones, that's what we is. Devil's'd'teeth.") Charlie reached out and patted my leg. Kim, confused, looked on. I concentrated on my face in the rearview mirror until another voodooed tear fell. I imagined myself in the devil's mouth.

It wasn't until the next day, when we arrived at Ott and Lee Funeral Home, that Kim figured out what had happened and he had a little meltdown when he saw our mother laid out in her open casket. He's told me in the years since that he can't remember it, but it is one of my most vivid memories, watching him wail in a way that was even more frightening than my own wailing inside that haunted house a few weeks earlier. It was in that moment—witnessing my little brother's unvarnished pain, a six-year-old's sobs full of the elemental alarm of being left alone in the world—that I realized what had happened had happened to *us*—to him and to Karole—not just to me. Vena Mae was sitting next to him—stoic, unstirred Vena Mae—and she put an armful of jangling bracelets around him. I wanted to pry him free and go get Karole, who was being watched by another batch of aunts back at my grandparents' house, and run away with the two of them. I fantasized about putting them on the back of my witch's broom and escaping high in the sky until we scraped that bit of heaven where our parents, we had been told, now resided. I wanted to protect them, Kim and Karole, wanted it with all that was left of my heart. But I knew I could not. "Go pay respects to your mama," Vena Mae told me as my grandmother knelt in front of Kim and the two women tried to calm him down.

I walked over to the casket and on tiptoe stared at my mother's overly rouged face. I hated the way she looked. She had been dolled up in death in a way she had never allowed herself to be in life. She had never worn that much makeup. Miss Ozella had been pressed into service to fix her hair in a crown of blond curls about her head, where it rested on the satin pillow. She wore her yellow nightgown. Kim continued to sob behind me. My grandfather came and put a hand on my head and then on my neck before resting it finally on my shoulder. He was crying, too. Everyone in the room was crying but me. All I could do was despise the way my mother looked. Her face, set in such lipsticked seriousness, seemed never to have shared a secret laugh with me, to have sung her Broadway tunes, to have moaned beneath my father, to have introduced me to Miranda. I looked at her plastic-like flesh and silently said my incantation, "Eppe pe-pe kak-ke ziz-zy zuz-zy zik," but it did not work. She did not rise. She did not issue one last "Dare I?" before climbing out of the casket to scare the mourners who milled about. All thoughts of my being a witch melted away right there in the funeral parlor standing on tiptoe in front of my mother's open casket. I pretended to put the incantation beneath her pillow inside the polished, satin-lined box where it would remain with her in her grave, not language exactly, but the sound of language, the music she had taught me to hear whenever letters were strung together. I would always believe in the power of that music—it was my inheritance from her—but I would never again believe in magic.

"How 'bout a moon pie?" I heard Vena Mae ask Kim, who continued to wail. "You like moon pies? Think I got half of one in my purse here that your Uncle Doots didn't eat all of on our drive down when I wouldn't let him stop for lunch. He wasn't none too thrilled with me making him eat a moon pie, let me tell you."

Karole, who was still in kindergarten, kept on playing at home during the subsequent days of Ott and Lee visits by everyone else. She continued her play during my mother's post-funeral wake, full of fried food and assorted pies crowned with golden-tipped meringue. Kim became even more of a big brother to her as she trailed him around and mimicked his butch demeanor after his tears had dried. When my grandparents sent me to my room for saying "fuck" one too many times as we sat beneath that backyard tree watching the flock of crows arrive that shoulder-chilling November afternoon, I shut the door and knew that the use of that one word (whatever "fuck" really meant) was the punctuation to my bedevilingly girlish bad-boy behavior. "Fuck," I said once more, loving the percussive sound of such a word, the music of language already taking on a harder edge in my life. I turned to Miranda and read some Porter passages while my mother's voice was still so clear inside my head, the sound of it cutting through the hushed hubbub of the wake's stragglers in the dining room across the hall. I knew even then that my mother's voice—that soft, smart, and artful tone—would not always be inside me but would morph into my own voice someday, the one that now tells my story, that tells hers, as I transcribe it for others to decipher its fealty to the truth, to the facts, the former something that is forged from the latter, a different object altogether, cleaner, purer, or, according to the talents of the forger, more ornate.

I shut *Pale Horse, Pale Rider*—shut it for many years to come—and hid the book in my closet next to Cecil the Seasick Sea Serpent. I climbed onto my bed and felt the nub of one of my grandmother's prized chenille spreads that had been placed on it during the wake in case any of our company came in my room. I sat completely still. I kicked off my freshly polished Sunday-goin'-to-meetin' shoes, as my grandfather called them. My eight-year-old feet dangled down from the bed and rubbed those soft nubby raised lines of the chenille's pattern with the soles of my socks. In my stillness, I remembered the secret (I always had to be completely still to remember it) that I shared with my father. I bowed my legs a bit like they bowed around his neck that day. Our secret—like my mother's voice still being able to read to me inside my head—was a way to keep him alive. Finished steeping myself in my parents' presence—a kind of trance I could put myself in throughout my childhood to calm my nerves—I jumped down from the bed. I stood, not knowing what came next. What is the next thing you do when both your parents die? Do you comb your hair? Do you take a piss? Do you fly away with the crows outside? This is what I did: I opened the curtain on my bedroom's window and watched my grandparents, forevermore now Mom and Pop, holding hands as they walked slowly back toward the house, their heads hanging downward side by side, nothing left to say, the clouds behind them just as gray as they were. This is what I thought: Yes, I have to straighten up for a while and not be a burden to those two old folks out there; tomorrow I will start being good no matter what, no more tantrums, no more bad costume ideas, no more sissy nonsense, no more longing to be Arlene. Mom and Pop looked up and caught me studying them. They dropped each other's hand. I shut the curtain. I lay on my stomach atop the chenille. I listened haplessly for Epiphany. I held my breath, but breathed again when I could not kill myself that way.

I got through the rest of the third grade without incident. My good-little-boy days were deemed a success by all those who were in a position to deem them as such. Teachers. Mom and Pop. Grace Speed. Even old Venomous Mae mentioned to Uncle Doots how much I'd changed. During my fourth-grade year, though, the good-boy act became a bit more difficult when I was the first to begin among my classmates to experience puberty. Pubic hair sprouted. My upper lip became shadowed. Hormones harrumphed inside me. An older cousin even taught me about the birds-and-bees by demonstrating on Karole's stripped-down Chatty Cathy doll, a difficult feat, as the only holes in her plastic body were arranged in a tiny square on her chest where the voice box was located, from which she spoke her limited number of sentences every time you pulled the string behind her neck. The cousin and I had locked ourselves in the back bathroom, which is what we all called the one located in the drafty wooden addition quickly added to my grandparents' brick home by Uncle Benny and his lackadaisical construction crew when Kim and Karole and I moved in. The addition consisted of a short hallway connected to my grandmother's sewing room. To one side of the hall was the large bedroom where bunk beds held Kim and me; to the other side was the smaller bedroom where a queen-size bed held Karole and Mom, who had moved out of Pop's room to hold my little sister during the night instead of her lonely, fuming husband who snored more loudly to spite us all in his now emptier bed down at the other end of the house, his sleepwear consisting of his tight white Hanes briefs pulled up as high as they would go on his old stomach and his wife-beater T-shirt tucked much too neatly into the briefs' elastic band.

It was in that back bathroom where, also during my fourth-grade year, I began to masturbate. I didn't exactly know what masturbation was at that point. I just knew I felt compelled to play with myself when I thought about Bobby Thompson, who was still the prettiest boy in my class. During my first ejaculation, I had no idea what had just happened. It wasn't until I was sitting at the school cafeteria table with Bobby and his best friend, Dave Marler, that I figured out what I had done and put a name to it. We were being served hamburgers and shared the hamburger-day-joke we always told each other before we choked down the leather-like patties: that the hair-netted, big-hipped cafeteria workers made the hamburgers by flattening the meat beneath their smelly armpits. Laughing yet again at how vulgar we could be, we passed around the condiments that were placed on the table in water glasses. "M-may I have the m-mayonnaise?" I asked, my stutter having worsened in the year since my mother's death.

When it was passed my way, Dave said, "Looks like jack-off. Kevin's eatin' jack-off."

Bobby laughed. I loved him even more when he laughed. He had a tarnished silver crown on one of his front teeth and I longed to touch it with my tongue. I laughed too, anytime he laughed, but I had no idea what this newest joke was about. Bobby and Dave then proceeded to let me in on what the older boys from their neighborhood did in the woods behind Hillsboro Drive where they both lived, something called "jack-off contests." They said that one older boy, whose father had John Birch Society signs stuck all over their front yard on Hillsboro, was the frequent winner and used a more succinct word that the older guys used for jack-off: cum. "He's got the biggest wiener," said Bobby, utilizing the appropriate cafeteria lingo and making us all laugh even more. "And he's always got a heap'a jack-off at the ready. Cum. Whatever you call it." Dave giggled with a mouthful of hamburger, sputtering bits of bun on the table.

"Cum, cum, cum," I teased Bobby as I pushed the glass of mayonnaise toward him and said the word for the first time, attempting to be one of the boys.

"More'n' that mayonnaise there comes outta him," Bobby said and pushed the glass full of the stuff right back at me.

I spent the next few days fantasizing about being part of those contests and beating the John Bircher's son to the punch. I can't eat a hamburger today without thinking of those horny Hillsboro boys. The taste of Hellman's has had a hold on me ever since.

This was also around the time that I picked my first cotton. Aunt Lola, Pop's sister who lived down the road, had been making one of her afternoon visits with Mom so they could gossip and go over what all they had cooked that day and planned to cook the next, as well as the latest news from their respective "growd-up kids." As I hung on their every word, Aunt Lola asked if I might want to help "the niggers pick cotton this Saturday. Just may be what he needs to get some of the girl out of him," she told Mom.

"Didn't do no good for Jim, now did it?" asked Mom, rather pointedly, mentioning Aunt Lola's younger son, on whom Lola doted. Jim had gone to art school in Florida and become an interior decorator in Los Angeles and Charlotte and Dallas, and always brought young men home with him who were just as prissy and preppy and well-creased as he. One Christmas, he gave Kim and me our first pairs of 501 Levis, and each subsequent December brought a new pair with him as he drove up in his Mercedes and unpacked his trunk full of presents, which always contained the biggest bottle of Chivas Regal he could smuggle into Mississippi—Scott County, where Forest was located, being one of the state's many dry counties. I loved making Jim laugh—a sound exactly like Lola's raspy chortle—by putting a lawn chair in our yard, and making him sit there as if he were an audience member while he watched me do my impersonation of Zsa Zsa Gabor, mincing about as the Derricks' cattle mooed in the background. On one occasion, I showed him some poems I had written—one titled "A Mouth and Its Uses," another that rhymed "Miranda" and "veranda"—and he, not knowing exactly who Miranda was, was nevertheless impressed enough to be the first person ever to tell me that I was a writer, a real one. "Seems to me, Benny had Jim up around them cotton bolls come pickin' time as much as he could, but Jim just ended up bein' Jim, which ain't nothin' bad, just something that's so," Mom told Lola, then nodded over at me. "I tell you what, though—this'un's got more Jim in him than Jim does."

Lola chortled in her raspy way. "You got a point there, Jake. But like I told Lyle when he was a'likenin' y'all's troubles with this'un to mine and Benny's with Jim—all you can humanly do is love your young'uns. You can't cut 'em out like a McCall's pattern you picked special 'cause you like the way it looks on you," she said and took a sip of coffee. She brushed some pie crust crumbs from one of the softly flowered beltless housedresses she always wore on her big-boned body, the lone McCall's pattern she seemed to allow herself. "Benny don't see it, but Jim's just as ornery as he is. Jim just goes about it another way." The two women fell quiet and contemplated the rest of the pie on their plates. They sipped at their coffee. I looked over at Lola. She never once put a rinse in her hair, as Mom and Aunt Vena Mae and all the other old gray-haired women who surrounded me in my childhood did, turning their permanents into preferred shades of periwinkle. Lola's pageboy bob retained its natural color, a tawny combination of grays and browns and saffrons that decades of the Mississippi sun had woven together. It was something Jim insisted on. "He don't never want me to put nothing out of a Clairol box on my hair," she once said when Mom had suggested she might want to try such a thing. "Don't know why he's got such a bee in his bonnet about it. But when he calls up he makes a point of asking me about it each and ever' time. One Christmas, he even talked me into lettin' him cut off some of it with my pinkin' shears. Said he wanted a swatch of it. That's one of them words he's always a'usin'—swatch. Said he was tryin' to find a carpet with just that blend in it for some fancy woman who wanted him to make her house pretty like only he can. You ever hear tell of nothin' like that?"

"Can't say I ever did," said Mom. She studied her plate. "Honest now, Lola, you think I'm a'losin' my pie crust touch? This'un don't seem near 'bout flaky enough. I'm faultin' the Crisco. I think they're makin' it different. Ever'thing else is changin' in this world, don't know why Crisco should be no different."

"I don't know," said Lola, pricking the crust on her own plate with her fork. "I figure Crisco's one of the last things we can count on. This pie crust is just fine, Jake. Don't be so hard on yourself. Long as Lyle and these kids ain't complainin', you shouldn't neither. If I could make a crust like this I'd be right satisfied. A'course I was never no Betty Crocker like you," said Lola, who knew when to lavish my grandmother with just enough praise to keep her content. She'd been doing it since they were teenagers, when her little brother had first started courting the high-strung girl who starred in so many of their agricultural high school's musical revues.

My grandmother's favorite memory from those times was her solo of "Alice Blue Gown," a song written for President Teddy Roosevelt's young daughter, she had once explained to me. When I'd wash the dishes with her—just the two of us alone in the kitchen—she'd often sing the song softly to herself, each word of the lyric still as fresh for her as when she was a girl. Her face would gladden as she sang the song, once remarking when she had finished its refrain yet again that "your Pop first fell in love with me when he saw me in that little blue dress I wore for that number. It was as pretty as I've ever been in my life. He'd been cast as my dance partner. We did a little waltz durin' the musical interlude. We were the hit of the show. Ever'body for the rest of the school year called me Alice Blue Gown as a nickname. I loved it. Really loved it. Alice Blue Gown," she quietly said the name, almost singing it again, summoning above the dying suds in the dishpan an image of herself as someone who was once young and hopeful. "It was the first time Pop ever held me in his arms. Lord, that was another life altogether. Lyle was a looker back then. We both were. To this day, when I wear somethin' blue I can see by the way he cuts his eyes at me he's rememberin' the first time he ever touched me around my waist and held me to him and how I looked when folks kept a'braggin' on me sayin' I had the sweetest soprano ever in Scott County where we all had to board back then if we wanted any book learning."

She paused, looking down at her gnarled hands submerged in those dirty suds. "Never grow old, Kevin. Or if you do, make sure you've got at least one good thing you can ponder on like that. It's the only ponderin' your Mom's got that's still a pleasure. But it's such a right fine thing to ponder it beats havin' a heap a'stuff stuck in my old brain to choose from. I just go straight to that. No dawdlin'." Mom had no way of knowing it at the time—neither had I, for that matter—but standing there with her as I dried the last of the dishes she handed me and heard her recall such a time in her life remains for me just such a "right fine thing to ponder" in my own. In my darkest moments—and there have been dark ones—I find myself humming, like her, the tune to "Alice Blue Gown," the lyrics still as fresh to me at the beginning of this sorry century as they were when my grandmother first learned them at the beginning of her sorry one. "I once had a gown almost new," I can sing, hearing her voice and the bit of happiness she could barely still wring from it, "Oh, the daintiest thing, it was sweet Alice blue, With little forget-me-nots placed here and there. When I had it on, how I walked on the air. And it wore and it wore and it wore, 'Til it went, and it wasn't no more . . ."

I looked over at Lola's open face. I was grateful she knew what to say to my grandmother to alleviate, if only momentarily, a bit of the sadness that overtook her when Alice Blue Gown ceased to be her nickname and life became harder for her to deal with than any lyric could describe. Lola winked at me in a way she had that let me know she was aware of what she was up to. Durable old Aunt Lola. She hardly ever wore makeup or perfume. She instead smelled of her cooking ingredients and, when cold weather came, the red brick hearth of her fireplace. She and Uncle Benny never went to church, but instead gassed up their newest Chevrolet and headed out to "Singin's" each Sunday to meet a bunch of like-minded backwoods Mississippi sorts who gathered in designated spots all over the state to have dinner-on-the-ground (which meant basically a pot-luck picnic lunch) and sing in unison or in groups the twangy gospel music white folks kept time to that was so different from the gospel of their black counterparts. They took me with them sometimes and I reveled in the raucous toe-tapping rhythms of those Singin's. White gospel consists of music based on precision, its tunes sung at an earthly clip, more like a canter than the Holy Ghosted gallop of black gospel. Yet even on those Singin' Sundays Lola only looked more scrubbed clean, not dolled up, her housedresses maybe a little more flowery. In fact, if you didn't know better you'd swear she was a Mississippi country version of a beautiful unadorned lesbian, butch but never loutish.

Nothing, however, could have been further from the truth. Mom even confided to me once, two years later when I was in sixth grade and finally a little taller than she (which wasn't such a big deal, as she was about the same size as Matty May, both barely five feet) that Lola had stolen Benny from his first wife. Sharing such a salacious confidence with me seemed for my grandmother to be her way of accepting the fact that I was growing up way too fast; there was nothing she could do about it, so she might as well tag along.

My two years of good-boy behavior were coming to an end by the time I reached sixth grade. I couldn't shunt my true self over to the side any longer and had intercepted my grandmother's Book-of-the-Month Club order form—I had been the one who insisted she join—

and replaced her order of Catherine Marshall's *Christie* with my own for Jacqueline Susann's *Valley of the Dolls*. There had been much consternation when Susann's book arrived in our house, but I had convinced my sixth-grade teacher, Mrs. Fikes, to let me do my second-semester book report on the "scandalous tome," as Mrs. Fikes kept calling it. My grandmother had not only been appalled by my hijacking her order form but also by Mrs. Fikes's allowing me to read such a book. ("He's a precocious child, Jake. If we don't guide him in his precociousness, he's going to get into some real trouble, that's the way I see it. We'll just keep this a secret from Dot Ishee. She'll have a fit if he's not reading something on the approved list. And, God knows, this is not approved. I bet he won't even understand half of what's in that book." My grandmother, against her better judgment, had acquiesced. "I guess it's okay," she said. "Bless his heart, the only valley he's been an expert on up until now has been that yea-though-I-walk-through-the-valley-of-the-shadow-of-death one. Guess he's earned him a walk through this'un.")

So it came to be, with her knowing how I'd had my nose stuck in that Jackie Susann book for days on end as I sunned myself on a chaise longue lawn chair out back, that she turned to let me in on this Lola piece of family gossip. "Yep, she was Benny's mistress before she was his wife," Mom whispered that day. We were washing the dishes together yet again and we saw my aunt through the kitchen window lumbering down the road in one of those flowered house-dresses for another of her visits with us. The diminutive sounding term "mistress" seemed so ill-fitting for such a formidable woman as Lola, who carried what femininity she had as if she were a locomotive and it were the cargo she was delivering to the man who wanted it. He was nothing but the depot, as far as she was concerned, where she had to slow down and chug to a scheduled halt. "When Benny's first wife found out about him sleepin' round with Lola," Mom kept talking and scrubbing at our cast iron cornbread skillet, "she sprinkled

some of her homemade pepper sauce on the outside of one of his rub-
bers." She cut her eyes over at me, the way Pop would, I assumed,
when he wanted to get a quick gander of her when she was wearing
something blue. "Oh, don't look so shocked," she said. "Ain't you
readin' 'bout stuff like that in that book about dolls? Even as a littler
boy you was always findin' a way to play with a doll. Stealin' your sister's Chatty Cathy. Beggin' for a Barbie come that Christmas after
your daddy was kilt in his car wreck. Guess this is just you fancyin' a
doll again," she reasoned out loud. I was so startled by this piece of
Lola news that I didn't even have the presence of mind to let Mom
know that the "dolls" in the book's title was a slang word for amphet-
amine pills. It wasn't only this piece of family gossip that was shocking me so, but also the fact that she was its bearer. It seemed as if my
dead father had possessed my grandmother in that moment and she
were channeling him, for this sounded exactly like a story he would
tell to make my mother blush before they shut the bedroom door behind them. My grandmother checked the skillet for any greasy
residue, then waved at my aunt who was turning toward us at the end
of our gravel drive, that tawny-haired head of hers bobbing a bit as it
always did atop her body as she trudged along. "Lola burned for a
week from that peppered-up rubber," Mom whispered.

I loved going up to Aunt Lola's and Uncle Benny's farm over in
Harperville and hanging out at their fishing cabin next to their pond,
or donning long sleeves in the summer heat to pick okra so its vines
wouldn't sting my arms or, at the first nip of fall in the air, helping
make syrup from the harvested sugarcane crop which had been
hauled to one particular ridge where it was ground for its juice by a
rigged-up combine, its clear sluice running down chutes toward the
fishing pond and emptying into vats that sat atop roaring fires. I loved
stoking the combine with those sugarcane stalks, but loved it even
more when it was my turn to lead one of the plow mules that Uncle
Benny had specially chosen that year for the syrup-making task. He

pretended it was a reward for the mule who had plowed the straightest row that year. He'd yoke a pole to the mule's back, which would then be attached to the combine and, by leading the animal round and round, it ground the gears in the most rudimentary fashion while expertly mashing the cane, the animal snorting out of dizziness or boredom or perhaps even equine pride while Benny grabbed a stalk or two of the cane to cut with his pocket knife into bite-size bits and hand around so we all could put them in our mouths like chaws of sweet tobacco. The gurgling vats would be skimmed of the cane scum that covered the cooked juice, and after the remains would be jarred and divvied up, we'd have the kind of syrup for our upcoming winter biscuits "that'll have such a kick to it it'll put hair on your chest," Benny always promised.

One of my favorite things to do at their farm was to hang out on a shanty stoop with two of Benny's sharecroppers, Sister and Brother, who, despite such incestuously generic names, were not related except by marriage. At the end of the syrup-making day, Sister always had some biscuits ready down at her shanty so we could have the first taste of what our hard work had wrought. Sister was an African-American version of Aunt Lola—large and lovely, with bobbed hair and a troublingly enticing butch demeanor that attracted men to her "like white on rice," which was one of her favorite expressions. Sister taught me how to shell Crowder Hull peas with my thumb alone and the right size a butterbean pod had to be before one should pull it from its vine. "Sister and Brother'll watch after him, if he can't take the work," Lola said that afternoon back when I was still in fourth grade and she fixated on how her cotton-picking idea would rough out my smooth edges. "You think you're man enough to pick you a sack'a cotton, boy?" she asked me.

I have to admit, the idea intrigued me on many levels. I knew even then it had the makings of a story I could always recall to shock the friends I planned to have in New York City when I grew up. I also knew that it would probably be one of my last chances to participate in such a Southern tradition because manual labor for such back-breaking work was being phased out. Uncle Benny's farm was one of the few that still relied on human hands instead of machinery to pick his cotton. And by the looks of the dilapidated old cotton gin we always passed on our weekly visits to my parents' graves in the Harperville Cemetery, I knew King Cotton was about to abdicate its throne in my world. Most important, however, I knew I'd get to see Matty May once more. She had quit working as our maid soon after my wicked-witch Halloween fiasco and after having not been invited to my mother's wake. I'm not sure if either or both of those factors were the reasons she and my grandmother had what appeared to be a falling out. All I knew is that I missed her desperately and that she and her husband, June, were part of the crew who picked cotton for Uncle Benny. Matty had once told me the stoop in her shoulders was caused by all the years she had worked those rows. "I'm m-man enough to pick me some cotton," I told Lola, squaring her in my sissy sights. "Will M-Matty M-May be there?"

Lola looked over at my grandmother, who continued to inspect her pie crust. "Yeah. Matty'll be there. She ain't never missed a pickin' long as I've known her. I think she can forget about Martin Luther King and that crowd long enough to chop a row or two."

"Do her good," said Mom. "Do him some good, too," she said, nodding over at me.

"Want m-me to tell her hi for you?" I asked my grandmother.

"I reckon you can do that," said Mom. "Go ahead on and tell her hi all you want."

My grandmother at first seemed nonplussed by the idea of my picking cotton. But as soon as she started sewing me a cotton sack to wear, fitting the lone strap attached to the sack across my chest so the sack's mouth would hang along the side of my waist in order for me to more easily deposit the picked cotton into it, she seemed even more excited about the prospect than I did. It sure made her happier to whip me up a "pickin' sack" than that witch's ensemble the year before. The day I was to accompany Uncle Benny in his green pickup to his farm, I rose early and put on a white shirt and my favorite clip-on necktie. I had put on a tie because part of the family legend I had heard while listening to the grownups talk was about Uncle W. F. when he was Benny's overseer. W. F. was Pop's and Lola's baby brother. He had run Benny's cotton operation "back in the day," according to Pop, "and he'd make them nigger men all wear shirts and ties to pick cotton. You talk about a bunch of mad niggers. But W. F. said they should dress like they was goin' to work, just like white folks. He wore him a necktie, too. Dangdest thing you ever saw when you looked out in them fields. High noon and neckties and niggers as far as the eye could see. Women in Sunday dresses. Some of 'em in their Sunday hats. All of 'em singin' that nigger church music cause they was dressed in their Sunday-goin'-to-meetin' clothes anyway. W. F. didn't last long in that overseer job."

W. F. didn't last as long as Lola and Pop, either. He ended up committing suicide after moving from Neshoba County into a trailer between Lola and Pop so he could be closer to them when they all grew even older and alone, Mom having died of pancreatic cancer, Benny of "hardening of the arteries." After getting divorced from a woman named Peggy with short-cropped bright red hair—he doted on the two stepdaughters he had with her—W. F. had lost all sense of direction. He always bragged to anybody who would listen that he knew exactly who killed Chaney, Schwerner, and Goodman, those three civil rights workers whose names everybody around me had memorized and could spout with seemingly the same urgency as "God, the Father, and Holy Ghost," though that former trinity of names was spoken as if they encompassed the evil against which the latter could be invoked. The earthen dam into which the civil-righters' bodies had been buried was close to W. F.'s house. For a few seasons he farmed a plot of land out there close to the dam, with black plastic spread over the ground and holes punched into the plastic where, he insisted, the shoots would sprout after he targeted the fertilizer there. He'd walk Pop around all that plastic and Pop would just shake his head and hold his tongue. Lola found W. F. with a gunshot wound through his temple, lying in his blood-splattered bathtub in that tiny trailer he parked, divorced and despondent, between Pop and her. "I know what I can do if I can't take it no more," Pop would say years later. "I'm a diabetic," he'd remind me. "I know how to give myself the wrong amount of insulin. I know how to do myself in. Just like W. F." More than once I listened as he told me how he knew how to kill himself, yet, when he got tired enough, he died suddenly at an old folks' home. He keeled right over in his wheelchair by the reception desk. I've always wondered if his last thought was of W. F. Or Mom. Or me.

Benny laughed when I showed up at his house wearing that clip-on tie which I had carefully chosen to match the beige "pickin' sack" Mom had made for me. I ignored his laughter; ridicule was, after all, the first rite of passage any Mississippi sissy had to master. We climbed into his pickup truck and I put on the seat between us the paper sack with the baloney sandwich and Fritos Mom had prepared for me. I placed my thermos full of iced Tang between my legs. Lola had made Benny some fried chicken and wrapped it up in aluminum foil. His thermos was full of Barq's root beer, he informed me after I told him what I had in mine. "Tang?" he repeated, the word itself tickling him. "Ain't that what them astronauts drink up in space where they don't belong?" he asked as he cranked up the truck and we headed for his farm.

Uncle Benny considered cotton a business and wasn't so sure he wanted his fields to be used as some sort of family playground. But he was by nature a deeply bemused man—more than Tang tickled him in some private way—and shrugged off any concern he might have of my making his field hands less productive with my distracting presence. On the drive out to Harperville he warned me not to leave any of the cotton behind in their bolls so he'd have to send one of the hands back around to re-pick what I had left. He told me of the few times Jim had unsuccessfully attempted to pick cotton, all the while gently patting me on my leg like "Chunkin'" Charlie had patted me that day when, speaking in code, he told me my mother had died. Benny's leg-patting, however, was habitual and it always ended up with his grabbing at your knee and saying, "That there's how the horse bites the apple." When we pulled up to the cotton field he reached up from my appled knee and snatched that tie from my neck. "Give that thing here," he said, wadding it up and stuffing it into one of the pockets on his overalls. "Them niggers out there is gonna be put off by a little upstart like you anyhow takin' cotton out of their sacks and money out of their pockets. Don't want 'em laughin' at you, too, do you? Ain't nothin' worse than bein' laughed at by a nigger."

We had pulled up next to a big flatbed truck into which all the cotton would be dumped at the end of the day. A scale was attached to the side of the truck where each sack full of cotton would be weighed and the pickers would be paid according to how much of the crop they had managed to pack into them. Uncle Benny's going rate was twenty-five cents a pound. I looked out in the cotton fields that lay down the hill from where he and I were parked. The workers were already busy bending over and moving along all those rows of bulging white bolls. A low hum filled my ears. At first it sounded as if the pickup's engine were idling, but I knew Benny had just turned off the ignition. I had watched him do it after pocketing my tie. So where was that hum coming from? Then it dawned on me: It was the murmur of the field hands out there—hymns sung in a kind of fevered cacophony from their collective past, conversations filled with the patois of their collective pain, an eked-out chuckle or two at their collective lot in life—a sound low and concentrated, keeping them all focused at the task literally at hand as they reached over and over and over into those bolls and snatched the cotton free, gathering it up into huge black fistfuls of white fluff until it looked like what they were harvesting was not cotton at all, but something cumulous, heavenly, something God meant for man to reach for but not to carry around here on this earth. A wave of nausea rippled through me. What I was seeing was as beautiful as it was horrible. I was suddenly frightened to get out of the pickup. This was now the latest world in which I did not belong. What had I been thinking when I agreed to such an outlandish idea as this? Up until that point I had been proud of my "pickin' sack," considering it the newest addition to my wardrobe. But staring out at the workers I realized how puny my little sack was. Theirs, even those belonging to children as young as I, lay as long as dragon tails down the many dusty rows. The very size of my sack proved I was not serious about this cotton-picking idea. Uncle Benny was right: This was just a lark to me and not, as it was for those out there in the already searing morning heat, a livelihood. I wanted him to re-crank his truck and take me back home.

And then I spotted Matty.

I jumped from the pickup and ran straight for her, my little sack flapping behind me like the one wing left on a wounded bird who still believed it could fly. Her stooped shoulders bent low toward the bolls as she muttered to herself those three syllables that had once been an incantation all her own but now seemed nothing but a curse as she, bending farther downward to the lower bolls, thrust it up from deep within her throat, each syllable accompanying the motion of her hands as they picked two bolls at a time. "Poi-ti-er Poi-ti-er Poi-ti-er," she'd grunt and pick, keeping time to each grasp-twist-pull grasp-twist-pull grasp-twist-pull of the cotton until her hands could hold no more and she stuffed it all back behind her in her sack. I stood in the row waiting for her to look up at me. Her face was glistening. She glowered down at each boll that needed her attention. "Poi-ti-er Poi-ti-er Poi-ti-er," she continued to grunt. She was bent over so far now I could see down into her dress and noticed that she wore, as was her wont on such summer days, no bra, her breasts dangling before me. "My—ah-woe!—skinny ninnies," she called them when she caught me staring at them one August morning as she bent down to get the newly washed laundry from the basket to hang out on the line in my grandparents' backyard. I handed her the clothespins and hurried her along so we could head into the kitchen and discuss not only her cake-making wisdom but also the importance of Martin Luther King and Rosa Parks. This was a conversation she made sure was whispered in case we were ever overheard, an intimacy much more profound than my having caught a glimpse of her nipples, so pointy and black they looked like the sharpened lead in my prized Berol Mirado No. 2 pencils.

I continued to watch her work the cotton. Her plaited hair was grayer than I remembered, strands of it almost as white now as the bolls she hadn't yet gotten to, the morning sun beaming down onto her scalp and causing rivulets of sweat to run down between the plaited rows into her eyes. She stood to wipe her brow and take a breath. She spotted me but she did not speak. Her eyes looked a little yellow in their hollowed-out sockets and reminded me—I had been too excited to eat breakfast that morning and my stomach now ached with hunger—of the last bits of banana pudding she would let me lick from the spoon after she would empty the mixing bowl full of the thickened concoction into the vanilla wafer crust. I longed to be back in that kitchen with her and not standing here in a dusty cotton row. I unbuttoned the top button of my shirt where it remained fastened because the tie had been clipped there beneath my collar. I could see Matty's tongue getting ready to say something, that busy way it had of running itself along her gums and the inside of her cheeks until it looked like "a critter, June say, tied up in a sack and about to git drownt." She straightened her stooped shoulders as best she could and held me in her gaze. Her tongue continued to try and free itself there inside her mouth but still nothing was said. I decided I would have to be the first to speak. "So, how y'dwine?" I asked, mimicking her old greeting, the dialect tripping off my tongue with a practiced ease since I had begun to use just such expressions when I wanted to make Mom laugh as we washed dishes together and kept watch out that window to see if Lola was coming our way.

It was the first time I had ever seen Matty May's old stooped shoulders straighten all the way up. She had never heard me use my dialectal expertise, and the authentic sound of it—a child's taunt, but a taunt nonetheless—seemed to strike her right in her sternum. She took a step back. "How you think I'm a'dwine?" she asked, her tone as pointed as the one she had summoned that morning when I had asked her in my bedroom if she'd seen Sidney Poitier win his Oscar and proceeded to use the N-word in her weary presence. "I'm a'pickin' cotton, ain't I?" she said, wearier than ever. "When a soul's a'pickin' cotton, child, it ain't got no time to think about *how* it's a'dwine. It's only got time to think about *what* it's a'dwine. *How's* a luxury out here in all this heat. A cotton field ain't no place a'tall for no *how*. Lawd be. How'm I dwine . . . hmmph," she said and grunted in disgust at the affront of such a question. Her yellowed eyes looked up the hill at Uncle Benny leaning against the front of his pickup. He was staring down at us. His hand was feeling around inside that pocket where he had put my tie. I was certain he was wrinkling it and I would never be able to wear it again to church. The thought of him touching my tie disquieted me, just as Matty's next question did. "So how *you* dwine, Arlene?" she asked.

Matty May had been dead set against anyone calling me that when she worked for my grandparents. What was she doing calling me that name now? "I ain't Arlene no m-m-more," I said and straightened the strap on my empty cotton sack as if, incongruously considering my protestation, it were attached to a gown Arlene herself might be wearing on *What's My Line?* "I don't like folks calling me that," I said, sticking to the lie I had chosen to tell my grandparents to make them feel better. "I ain't Arlene."

"You never wuz, child," Matty said, shaking her head. "You never wuz. What'chu got on there? That's a sorry excuse for a cotton sack. That thang won't hold but two bits' worth'a cotton ifen you lucky. What'chu up to out here? You gonna help old Matty pick cotton to-day? I swuny. I done seen it all now. Little sissy thang like you wantin' to get out here in this sun and chop cotton. What's the world a'comin' to? Was this Mr. Benny up yonder's idea?"

"It was Aunt Lola's and M-Mom's," I said.

"Hmmph," she grunted again and ruffled her sack back behind her, evening out the cotton already in it. I wanted to go lie down on it like the toddlers several rows over who used their mama's sack as a makeshift bed and were dragged along behind her on top of it while they napped. "Wonder what them womens was a'thinkin'—ah-woe!—comin' up with something like that—you pickin' cotton," said Matty. "Can't rightly figure on that." She wiped her brow again.

"They said it would cure me of the girl in me," I told her.

Matty studied me for another moment. "Well, they be right 'bout that," she said. "I was fo' year old when I chopped my first cotton. Got the girl out of me f'sho. Weren't no little girl a'tall left in Matty at the end of that day. Naw, sir. Not enough to speak of no mo'."

I reached for my first boll of cotton, but Matty May shouted for me to stop before I could yank it free. "You leave that alone, child. That's cotton for my sack, nobody else's, not even yo' no-count one," she said. "You git on out of Matty's way. Don't you be takin' no cotton out of these rows right'chia," she said, spreading her arms toward the ten or so rows around us. "These here rows is mine. Always is. Ever' year. These rows line up real good with them two oaks down yonder. Come 'bout an hour from now I can catch me some shade down toward them limbs. I need all d'quarters I can get from Mr. Benny today. June's birthday gonna be here d'rectly. You go on over yonder to Sister's rows. Or Brother's. Or some of them folks that showed up from Homewood I never seen hide-nor-hair of befo'. Mr. Benny keep lookin' down here at the two of us. Git. I got work t'do."

Sister had overheard my conversation with Matty and motioned for me to come join her over in her section of the field. "Forget about Matty, baby. She's done got like that old mule Mr. Benny had that turned too mean t'plow. Don't know what got into that mule. Whatever it was is the same somethin' that done got into Matty. I wouldn't go standin' behind her, that's f'sho. Might get kicked."

I turned and watched Matty May over in her rows huffing and puffing "Poi-ti-er" over and over, then started saying it myself as I tried to pick the cotton as best I could. "Poi-ti-er Poi-ti-er Poi-ti-er," I said in Matty's rhythm, trying to approximate her very voice, as I pulled at the bolls. The cotton clenched inside them didn't want to budge.

"Harder than it look, huh, baby," said Sister, who could pull five or six bolls free of cotton before I could empty out one.

After about an hour of the strenuous work I walked up the hill and asked Uncle Benny if I could take a break. He looked at me up and down and didn't appear bemused at all. "I'm gonna tell you the same thing I told Jim when he pulled this same shit on me back when he tried to pick. You can stop, but if you stop you ain't goin' back down in them fields. If you pick cotton with the niggers then you pick it just as same as them. Nigger rules is your rules. No stoppin' till lunch. Then no stoppin' till them sacks is full. Quicker you fill 'em up, quicker you stop. Your choice. You near 'bout had enough?"

I stared right back at him. My shirt was drenched with sweat. Must everything be a choice? I thought. Why do grownups make everything a choice? I wanted my tie back but was afraid to ask him for it. "Hmmph," I said, trying some of Matty's indignation on for size. I headed back down the hill toward the fields. "Fooled me, boy," I

could hear Benny back behind me. "Nigger rules, then, it is for you.
But best be careful," he said. "Jim did the same thing. Turned on his
little Miss Priss heels just like you did. Far as I can tell, he's been
playin' by nigger rules ever since."

By lunch I had barely filled up half my sack. I was surprised at how
easily the cotton scrunched down on itself and how tightly it could
be packed, so tightly that it seemed I could never get it to reach the
top. Benny would walk through the rows and use a blunt-headed instrument to stick down into the sacks of the field hands who didn't
even break a stride or miss a yank as he made sure the cotton was
stuffed deep down into those already seemingly overstuffed sacks,
making room for even more. After his third trip through the rows
with that cotton-packing stick, he called a lunch break. I looked over
and saw Matty slowly heading toward the shade those twin oaks offered her. From one of her pockets she handed June something
wrapped in a napkin—his lunch, I surmised—as he passed her and
walked on over to the row where all the men had gathered around
Brother. The women, except for Matty May, made their way to sit in
circles around Sister. They called their children to them. Matty,
alone, unstrapped her cotton sack and sat down atop it under the
oaks to gnaw at a stringy fried chicken wing she unwrapped from another napkin she had stuffed into the other pocket of her dress. I
went to Benny's truck and got my sack lunch and thermos and decided I'd try and join her for a bit. "W-w-want some Tang?" I asked,
knowing she couldn't turn down such an offer. I unscrewed my thermos and handed it to her. She took a giant swig and wiped her
mouth. "Good, huh," I said. "Can I sit d-down?"

"Suit yourself," said Matty as I plopped down on the sack next to
her. "What'ch yo' Mom make you to eat? Bet she can't make no sandwich as good as Matty. 'Member them musdadine and peanut butter'uns I'd make us both on Sunbeam, us both fightin' for d'heel bread
on d'loaf 'cause we both crust folks, like our bread to chew right back,

you and me. Mmmmm, tell you what, wish I had one them now instead of this nasty wang. And—ah-woe!—when we'd put that peanut butter on some Ritz crackers—'member that?—and stick a marshmallow on 'em and put 'em in Miz Jake's little toaster oven till them marshmallows was golden brown. Almost brings tears to my eyes thinkin' of them toasted Ritzes sittin' up under them marshmallows like that." I showed her my baloney sandwich. She hated baloney and made a face at it. I shared my Fritos with her. We passed my Tang back and forth. "So. You got enough of this cotton pickin' yet? Can't figure how nobody would want to pick no cotton ifen they didn't have to," she said, eating my last Frito.

"I come to see you, M-Matty," I said. "That's why I come today. Cotton ain't got nothing to do with it. M-Mom told me to tell you hi."

"Hmmph," Matty huffed.

"I m-miss you, Matty M-May. M-Mom misses you, too. She d-don't say it but she does."

"Hmmph."

"How come you left us? W-was it because of Halloween? Was it b-because the voodoo d-done took a'holt of me? D-devil ain't got me in his teeth no m-more. I'm a good b-boy now. D-devil ain't got no taste for m-me. He d-done spit me out. Is it because you wasn't invited to my m-mama's w-wake? Was it M-mom and Pop saying n-n-n-nig . . . you, know . . . that w-w-word all the time? Why d-d-did you leave?"

Matty crunched the last bit of Frito in her old black jaw. She deeply sighed. "It weren't none of that, child. It weren't none of that," she said, and wiped her mouth with her greasy napkin. "You got any more Tang in there? Matty do miss that Tang in yo' house," she said. The baloney and my share of the Fritos, combined with the heat and work I'd done that morning, caused me to suffer from a thirst I had never known before, but I made yet another choice: I gave Matty that last sip I had in my thermos. I licked my parched lips and watched the Tang ripple down her skinny throat. She smoothed out some of the cotton stuffed into the sack between us. "I was snappin' beans with Miz Jake oncet in the carport when you and Kim and Karole and them filthy Derrick boys—big eaters them nasty two thangs—was about t'play hide'n'seek out in d'yard. Ya'll was doin' that eeny-meeny-miny-mo nonsense, tryin' to come up with who was a'goin' to be d'one t'do the lookin'. Miz Jake went inside to answer the phone and left me a'sittin' there with nothing t'do but listen to you chirren play. I heard you bein' d'boss out there and doin' that eeny-meeny-miny-mo. I hear you go: eeny-meeny-miny-mo-catch-a-nigger-by-his-toe-if-he-hollers-make-him-pay-fifty-dollars-every-day-my-mama-told-me-to-pick-this-little-nigger-but-I-pick-this-very-best-one. That did it. Child, you d'one that made Matty leave. Wasn't no Miz Jake or Mr. Lyle. Wasn't no Halloween. No wake. Wasn't no devil. You d'one that done it. You, child. I'll pick cotton out there—a soul's gotta eat better from time to time than what I can scare up in my own patch of earth, plus it's June's sixtieth soon and he wants hisself some of that Old Spice Mr. Lyle let him slap on oncet when he come to pick me up from work. But I don't have to sit in no poor white folks' carport and pretend I can't hear what I can hear. Miz Jake and Mr. Lyle sayin' nigger don't bother me so much. They don't know no better. They's the way they is. They ain't like Mr. Benny up yonder gettin' out of his pickup, that mean lunch almost over. Mr. Benny's niggerin' gets him mo' money. Miz Jake and Mr. Lyle ain't much better'n a couple of niggers theyselves. They know it too and that's why they use d'word so much. Nigger from they mouth almost like nigger from mine. But outta yo' mouth—hmmph," she said, finding one last bite of chicken on her wing before throwing it over in the bushes. "Little sissy thang like you, child, is smarter than most folks in these parts. You know better. God put some kind of— Lawd be—Yankee sense in you. We both know that. Nigger out of yo' mouth cut Matty to d'quick. I told you that when you called Sidney

Poitier a nigger that mornin' in your room and I be d'one—ah-woe!—that give d'Tang to you. Tables turn, don't they now. Tables turn." She smoothed the cotton in her sack. I could not look at her. Again, we fell silent. "Matty wouldn't have her heart broke no more by the likes of you," she finally said. "When listenin' breaks yo' heart, time sho'nuff t'stop listenin'."

We watched Uncle Benny walk up and down the rows checking to see if all the bolls had been denuded to his satisfaction. "You miss yo' mama and daddy?" Matty asked, sensing she should change the subject.

"I m-miss Epiphany," I said. I had been stunned by Matty May's soliloquy. What would have been Epiphany's response to it? What would be mine? I gathered the courage to look back over at Matty. Her tongue had started working away at the inside of her mouth. She stood, akimbo, and tilted her head to the side, watching Benny inspect her rows. "I l-love you, M-M-Matty," I said.

She sighed. "Child, love ain't enough in a place like Mississippi," she said, her shoulders relaxing a bit once Benny had made his way, satisfied, through the rows she'd picked. She shooed me off her cotton sack. She made me lift it for her and restrap it to her stooped old body. Her shoulders sagged even lower from the sack's weight. "You'll see, the more growd you get, what Matty be talkin' 'bout," she said, and searched my eyes with her tired old yellowed ones. "Love ain't enough for the likes of us. We standin' on the same ground but we folks from different lands. Like them fools outta d'Bible, we is. Love? Hmmph. It ain't never 'nuff in a crooked-letter state like this."

I watched Matty drag that cotton sack back toward the field, but did not follow her with mine. I stayed right where I was in the shade. I would never pick another boll of cotton after that morning. I climbed the hill and told Uncle Benny I was tired, but he wouldn't take me home. He told me I had to stay till the weighing and get paid when everybody else did. I went back down under the oaks and watched Matty pick the rest of her cotton. "Poi-ti-er Poi-ti-er Poi-ti-er," I heard her muttering to herself when she'd get close enough to me. I thought about offering her the cotton I had picked to put in her sack, but decided I wanted some quarters for myself. I had earned them fair and square, I reasoned. At the weighing, Benny threw me four quarters when all I had picked was two pounds worth. The field hands stared at me with anger on their sweat-drenched faces when they saw I was getting paid more than I was entitled. Sister had finished early—she was the strongest and best cotton picker—and had gone into her shanty to make everybody some iced tea and lemonade. I skipped over to her and helped her hand it out to each person as soon as they got "weighed and paid," as Uncle Benny liked to put it, so they wouldn't be so mad at me. Sister gave me a glass of iced tea for Matty and whispered to me to go give it to her where she had gone back down under the oaks to count her quarters. She had them all gathered together in the upturned skirt of her dress. I helped her empty them onto the ground and counted them out with her. She had picked twenty-five pounds' worth of cotton and there were twenty-five quarters. Benny hadn't cheated her. She stared down at the silver stacked in the dust. "How much is that now, child, ifen it was green?" she asked.

"Six d-dollars and twenty-five cents," I said.

"That'll get me a right nice little bottle of Old Spice and a bit of pork at Paul Chambers," she said. "That'll do."

"I'm sorry I m-made you leave, M-m-matty," I said, then abruptly changed my mind about keeping my four quarters. I offered them to her.

She studied the money in my outstretched hand. "I know you's sorry, child," she finally said. "I know you is. You keep them quarters, though, they's yours. Go to the movies with them quarters. I know how much you love them movies up at the Town Theater. Save them quarters for a special Sat'dy-afternoon movie and you think about the day Matty made you keep 'em. When that Sat'dy-afternoon movie get real good you think about Matty May."

I watched her walk away that day. June met her and put his arm around her as they disappeared over the hill. In the years to come my grandparents would have other maids—the dignified and beautiful Emma Dee who couldn't make a coconut pie if her life depended on it, the custard always tasting as if she'd put perfume in it instead of vanilla extract, and the belligerent and always terse Bell who bossed me around way too much—but none would change my life the way Matty did. I realize now, I never knew much about her. I only knew her within the parameters of my own life. To be honest, I wasn't sure back then if she had kids of her own. (She did: Flozell, Odell, and Ruby Nell.) Or what church she went to. Or what losses and sorrow she suffered. I knew her only from the perspective of a lonely boy from a crooked-letter state but I sure cried when she walked over that hill that day on Uncle Benny's farm, for I recognized something had ended yet again in my life.

———————

I saw Matty May again only one other time. I had returned home from New York for a visit with my grandfather before we moved him into the convalescent home, as the senior-citizen living facility was called by the locals. The convalescent home remained a private institution, even while Pop resided there into the late 1980s, so that it could also remain whites-only. Medical facilities around Forest had always been the last to integrate. Even after our school system came up with an integration plan of its own the year I entered seventh grade, the doctors' and dentists' offices around town maintained their separate waiting rooms, each with the receptionists' stations located in a closed-off middle area with a window for the white patients and one for the black ones. When I was taken in for a doctor's visit, I would always look into the reception area and through the "colored" window, trying maybe to catch a glimpse of Matty. I never did.

My grandmother had died a year before my return home from New York to visit Pop, who had been left alone to ramble around our old house. Kim was attending the University of Mississippi Medical School after a brief sojourn at Tulane's. Karole was about to attend nursing school there also after graduating from college. Both of them were living in Jackson, and Pop had gotten another Chihuahua to keep him company and named it Jingles. Lola helped him out with food. W. F. hadn't yet pointed a gun to his head. Pop and I had always had a strained relationship resulting from what I had once found hidden in his closet. The first boy I had ever physically loved (Bobby Thompson would remain unattainable) was the son of a renowned liberal editor of a small-town newspaper in Mississippi. The boy had become my pen pal after our meeting at a high school drama festival at the University of Southern Mississippi at which I, a sophomore, had won the Best Actor Award for my performance in a one-act called *Impromptu*. The boy went on to volunteer for the Peace Corps and later to work in politics and serve in the State Department.

Everyone at that drama festival at Southern was commenting on how I had looked like a young Nureyev onstage—Frank Hains had not been the first to tell me that—and this boy, who had come with his own school as the photographer for his father's paper as well as the school's, asked to photograph me. We were at a party in a hotel room with others from our schools. We went into the bathroom and shut the door. He closed the toilet's lid and told me to sit on it and look over at him. He pushed back the shower curtain and stood in the empty tub. When he looked at me through his lens he whispered rather matter-of-factly, "You're beautiful." He saw, through that lens, the look in my eyes and knew I had been waiting almost sixteen years to hear a boy say that with just such matter-of-fact normalcy. He put the camera down. We kissed. My life changed.

When we returned to our respective little Mississippi towns we took turns calling each other long-distance every night. When the telephone bill came Pop hit the roof, not only because of the amount of the charges I had incurred, but also because it was a boy on the other end of the line. We fought loudly about it while my grandmother sat on a stool before his nasty diabetic feet and attempted to tend to his rotting toenails. Pop and I shouted back and forth above her head. "Please, stop, both of you," she begged, digging into my grandfather's caked cuticles. After the fight, my friend and I began to correspond, many of the missives unabashed love letters. I would go to the letters after school each day—I had hidden them inside my old copy of *Valley of the Dolls*—and reread them before I'd watch *The Dating Game* and *The Newlywed Game* back-to-back while I ate some freshly made popcorn and drank some Tang poured over crushed ice. It had become my ritual: reading a love letter, downing the icy cold Tang, deciding which male contestant on *The Dating Game* was the cutest, and trying to see the outline of their penises as the contestants thrust their crotches toward the camera as they sat in their high stools and tried out double entendres on the giggling female who asked them questions. One day, after I had emptied the kernels and oil into the popcorn maker, I went to retrieve my favorite letter, in which the boy had written the word LOVE for the first time—right there in ink as indelible as the ink my mother had used when she sat up that night with me after my father's funeral and wrote her thank-you notes, handing them to me to put in each of the envelopes I had stamped for her. When I opened my copy of Jackie Susann, however, I discovered the whole stash of correspondence had disappeared. I knew instantly my grandfather had stolen it. He always looked on disdainfully whenever my grandmother handed me the latest letter I had received in the mail from the boy. He was out back, my grandfather, tending to his garden when I went blazing into his bedroom. I rifled through his drawers and lifted his mattress trying to find the letters. I stared at the shotguns on the rack above his bed and for the first time since my mother's funeral willed Witch Boy into existence. The popcorn began to pop. My head was filled with that one word, no ink needed for its indelibility: Pop Pop Pop. Those letters would be found. I closed my eyes. I concentrated. I opened my eyes when the popcorn had stopped its popping and all I could hear was *Dating Game* host Jim Lange telling the giggler to make her decision. I walked over to the smaller of the closets in my grandfather's room. "Bachelor Number Two," I heard the giggler say. *The Dating Game*'s music started. The smell of the popcorn filled the house. I lifted the blankets folded on the top shelf. My Witch Boy powers were intact. The letters were right there beneath those blankets. I grabbed the stash, still wrapped up in the rubber band I had circled around them, and went back into my room.

I got out a piece of notebook paper and started writing my grandfather a note. "Dear Pop," I wrote. "I cannot believe you would stoop so low as to steal my letters. These are my most personal property. You want me to say it, I'll say it: They are love letters. I will not confront you about this. I don't want Mom to have to get upset. She's never been herself after her stroke and she cries too much already. Our fighting makes her cry even more. I hate you for stealing these letters, but I love you because you're my grandfather. I forgive you." I put the note in a envelope and addressed it TO: POP FROM: ARLENE then crossed out ARLENE and wrote KEVIN then crossed out KEVIN and wrote ARLENE once more. I put it under the blankets where he had hidden the letters. I walked back into my room and retrieved the stash and walked out to the backyard where the old oil drum was, in which we burned pine straw and garbage and in which my father had so long ago burned the little dress my mother had convinced my grandmother to make for me. Pop looked up from his tomato vines and watched what I was doing. I unwrapped the rubber band from around the wad of correspondence. I put a match to one letter, then another, then another, dropping them all, one by one, into the drum where the flames grew and they turned to ash. I strode back into the house. I clawed around inside my own closet and found *Pale Horse, Pale Rider*. I needed a little Miranda. I needed a lot of my mama. I was determined not to cry. I concentrated on Katherine Anne Porter's syntax, her heightened common sense, the music to be found in those letters of a different sort, aligned along Porter's oft-read pages, letters that did not have to be stolen, that did not have to be burned. I am certain my grandfather that same day found the note I had left him under his blankets, but neither of us ever spoke of it. Not even all those years later, when I returned home from New York for an early springtime visit after my grandmother had died and we sat saying nothing as we took turns petting Jingles.

"Want to drive out to the cemetery?" I finally asked him, the question that could fill so many conversations around that old house when there was nothing left to say. Even Jingles seemed to have figured out the meaning of such words, jumping down from Pop's lap and heading toward the backdoor for a trip out to Harperville. We all climbed into my grandfather's old Plymouth and silently headed toward my parents' graves, toward Mom's now. The cemetery was across the way from Harperville's Methodist church. A dirt drive circled through it and my parents' grave site abutted it. We parked and got out of the car. "Jingles, don't," Pop said as the Chihuahua headed straight for my parents' double-sided gravestone and cocked his leg to relieve himself upon it. Pop took out an already soiled handkerchief from his pocket and wiped the dog's urine from the gravestone's granite, then folded it and walked to the double-sided gravestone next to my parents', which now contained Mom's name and dates of birth and death. He wiped dried bits of bird shit off of it and stood back to stare at his name already carved on the other side awaiting the date of his death. The plastic poinsettias he'd placed at both graves at Christmas were still there, their color not as sturdy as their petals, the months of sun fading their red dye to a color now closer to pink. I looked around the cemetery and recalled the many weekend afternoons Kim and Karole and I had frolicked through the place playing tag and reading all the names and long-ago dates of births and deaths, many as far back as the early 1800s. I turned back to my parents' gravestone and, after I ritualistically did the math in my head, subtracting their dates of birth from the dates of their deaths, once again felt the familiar shock at how young they were when they died. "These poinsettias are lookin' mighty poor," said Pop as he bent down to wipe them with his handkerchief. We watched Jingles running about the many neighboring graves. "That little thang almost likes it as much out here as you young'uns did when you'd whoop and holler and play when Mom and me'd make ya'll come with us to tend to your mama and daddy."

"Are Matty May and June still alive?" I asked, surprising us both with the question.

"I ain't heard tell of 'em dyin'," Pop said. "Far as I know they're still around. Why you askin'?"

"I was just thinking about Matty on the flight down and wondered if we might swing by and see her," I said. "It's been a long time."

"Lord, I don't even know if they still live out yonder past Benny's old farm. But we could, yeah, swing by and see. Ain't got nothin' else to do," Pop said. He cranked up his Plymouth and we headed out that way. Sure enough, when we drove up to their old shanty June was sitting out on the porch. Two mangy feist dogs ran up barking at the car as we came to a stop and I thought of Matty's long-ago admonition about the devil being just such an animal with a taste for me, my bones, my very body. June was sitting in a rocker but the only movement from him were his eyes taking us in as we got out of the car. Pop held Jingles who shook and barked back at the dogs that circled around us.

"Mr. Lyle, that you?" June, still not moving, called out over all the barking. "Is my eyes deceivin' me? Mr. Lyle? Lawd, you dogs hush. That ain't no squirrel Mr. Lyle be holdin'. Sorry 'bout this. They actin' like they treein' a squirrel. Them's good squirrel dogs but they anxious critters. Ifen they didn't put such good eatin' on the table I'd haul off and shoot 'em, sho'nuff. Hush!"

Pop chuckled at all the canine fuss going on. "Yep, June. It's me, Lyle Britt," he said.

June finally moved: He reached down and took off one of his shoes and threw it at the dogs. They yelped and ran under the shanty's front porch. "That'll keep 'em for a spell. Onliest thang that'll hush 'em up sometime," he said and hobbled down the steps to greet us.

Pop chuckled some more. He handed June his shoe. The old men hugged each other and Jingles licked June on his gray whiskered face. "This thang ain't never hunted no squirrels," June said, allowing the licking to continue. "Onliest thang this thang ever sniffed for was somethin' to eat outta yo' pocket, I bet that's so, ain't it, Mr. Lyle?"

"You right about that," Pop said as June began to look me up and down. "You recognize this boy?" Pop asked him.

"Can't rightly say I do," said June.

"This here is Kevin. You remember Nan and Howard's oldest, don't you? He's a Yankee now. Hightailed it to New York City a few years ago. He wanted to come by and give a hello to you and Matty. She around?"

June rubbed his hands together and stared down at the ground. He slipped his foot back inside his laceless shoe. "Yassir. Her body be around, but she don't. She don't know she's in this world, Mr. Lyle. She ain't been in her right mind for a while now. Been some kinda burden but I guess d'Lawd know what he doin'. I heard tell up at Paul Chambers 'bout Miz Jake takin' ill with d'cancer and takin' her leave.

Cancer got a end to it. But this business with Matty don't look like it got one. I just hope I don't take my leave before she do."

"Sounds like hardenin' of the arteries," said Pop. "Is that what it is?"

"That's what some say. Good a name as any, I guess," said June. "Some days she's sharp as a tack, Mr. Lyle. Other days she ain't. This is one of her tackless days, this'un. Sometimes I think she's just a'playin' with me. Matty could always pout. 'Bout trip on her bottom lip, she could pout so much. Sometimes when I'm sittin' up there figurin' on it, I figure this is just some serious poutin' on her part. Lord knows, us colored folks got reason enough to pout, that's fo'sho."

"Is she inside?" I asked.

"She be where she always be, sitting in there at the kitchen table. Onliest place that don't seem to upset her. For a while there she'd only sit in front of the TV set and ifen I went to touch it she'd have a hissy. Matty always loved her TV shows. She even got to saying there for a while that that's where she come from—outta d'TV—instead of out there around Ringold where she was bornt. Can you 'magine that? Thinkin' a soul was bornt in the TV? But now she just sit there in d'kitchen all day. When d'TV broke last year d'rest of her spirit broke right along with it. Didn't have 'nuff money t'fix it. Sho' not have 'nuff money to fix her. So she just sit in d'kitchen till I spoon some Campbell's in her and tuck her in. Sometimes she'll take to the Jell-O, but mostly it's just d'Campbell's," he said, still eyeing me. "So you growd right up, boy. Matty used to talk 'bout you all d'time. She'd come home and tell me all kinda stories 'bout you and what a mess you was. You took up a might big place in her heart. She always say you'd turn into a Yankee someday."

"Would it be okay if I went in to say hello?" I asked him.

June considered the request. "Don't see why not. Sho'nuff. Go on ahead inside. But don't go 'spectin' her to know who you is. She don't even know who she is no mo'. Mr. Lyle, you want to go in with him?"

"No. That's okay. Me and Jingles'll stay out and visit with you a spell, June."

The two old men began to reminisce. Pop put his Jingles-free hand down into the waistband of his slacks and leaned up against the Plymouth. June pulled out a pocketknife to clean his fingernails. I climbed the steps and walked into the darkened hallway that led back to the kitchen where Matty sat with her back to the door. She hummed a tune I did not recognize. The plaited hair on her head was now completely white and had thinned out to such an extent that it appeared to be one of those bolls I could not free entirely of its cotton, no matter how hard I tried, all those years before. The whole house smelled as if a fire must have been extinguished recently, the aroma pungent, smoky. The kitchen had not been cleaned in a while. Dishes were stacked in the sink. Boxes of Jell-O, all cherry flavored, lined one of the shelves of the doorless cabinets. A sack of sugar sat opened on another shelf next to several cans of Campbell's tomato and chicken noodle and cream of mushoom soup. Ants marched across the counter. On the window sill a dusty unopened bottle of Old Spice with a tattered bow still wrapped around it was propped up against a dirty pane of glass. "Matty M-may," I softly said, my stutter surfacing at such moments when my childhood intruded on my life. She did not respond. Her hum continued. I walked around the table and stood in front of her. "Matty, it's m-me—Kevin." She stared at me. She stopped her humming. "It's Kevin," I said. Her tongue—this much remained true to who she was—still seemed to be trying to free itself inside her mouth. I watched it poking at the inside of her cheeks, then run itself along her gums.

"Chiiiild!" she suddenly blurted, startling me with the strangely familiar outburst, not her voice but another's, the rather drawn-out Swahili-tinged lilt filling the room. I should have expected the sound of such a voice after June's remarks about her belief in her television heritage, but it shocked me nonetheless, shocked me to my very core. "Chi*iii*ild!" she blurted again, slinging the word right at me. Such dialectal expertise—an old woman's taunt, but a taunt nonetheless—hit me in my sternum. I took a step back. This is what had happened to Matty. This is what had happened to Epiphany. This is what had happened to me. None of us said anything for the next few moments until a look of satisfaction—so like Epiphany's when she got the better of me—settled across Matty May's face. Again, she began to hum. I didn't know what else to do, so I turned and washed June's dirty dishes in the sink until I also started to hum my own tune, "Alice Blue Gown." Matty, who must have at some point heard Mom's rendition of the song, amended her own tune and followed, haltingly, along with me, our memories disjointed but undying. Our humming, for a few notes somewhere there in the middle, approximated a rough-hewn harmony until Matty May's silence imposed itself once more. I again followed her lead. I watched the ants nudge a few crumbs across the countertop, and then, as she so often did to me when I was a sad little boy, I kissed her on the top of her head.

I made my way back outside and Pop and I said our good-byes to June. "Did she know who you was?" he asked.

"She did, June," I told him. "Yes. She did. For a moment there, I think she really did."

"Well, I'll be," he said. "Don't that beat all. She ain't knowd nobody in a long time. She still don't know who she be, I bet. That's what the sad story is. Sometimes she thinks she's somebody else when she thinkin' a'tall. Say she know Tarzan. Ain't that tacky? A colored woman sayin' she know Tarzan like she ain't nothin' but a savage. Say she know somebody named Alice and Trixie, too. That's got me stumped. We oncet had a preacher whose wife went by the name'a Alice but I ain't never met me no colored woman called Trixie. That's not no colored woman's name. White folks can get away with callin' they womens something like Trixie. But not us coloreds. We'd near 'bout call some sorta pet that maybe we let come in d'house. Maybe we would—*here, Trixie!* Naw. That don't sit right in d'mouth either. But she knowd you, huh? Guess that part of her heart is still a'workin'. Did y'get a 'ah-woe!' out of her?" I shook my head. "That's what I been waitin' fer for all this time. I sho' would like to hear my Matty say 'ah-woe!' just one mo' time befo' I die. That be right pleasant to my old ears. Hear my Matty be Matty just one mo' time."

The feist dogs emerged from under the porch. They did not bark but bared their teeth at me. Jingles whimpered. Pop cranked the Plymouth. I buckled myself into the passenger side of the car. I looked back over my shoulder as Pop and I pulled away. I saw June climbing back onto the porch. He folded up his pocketknife. He shook his head at all our plights.

I don't remember much about being eleven, but I do recall Mrs. Thompson's fifth-grade class. For a Mississippi elementary school teacher, she possessed a sophisticated edge. Her full mouth was never without its dark smear of deep red lipstick. During her many pop quizzes, she'd sit at her desk waiting for us to finish, eyeing us all to make sure we didn't cheat, and take out her tube of lipstick and smear a fresh bit of color on her mouth. Next, she'd pull a fresh Kleenex out the box she always kept in her top drawer and blot her lips on it, her trash can full of discarded tissues precisely stained with the imprinted outline of her mouth. The luxuriant flair of her nostrils made her nose seem even flatter and she wore her hair in a chignon. There was a beauty mark on her cheek like the one I admired on the right cheek of *Gunsmoke*'s Miss Kitty, played by Amanda Blake. Mrs. Thompson was my own Amanda Blake. She liked to wear tight belted dresses to show off her tall lithe figure and she was infamous among the students for making us all memorize the poems "Winken, Blinken, and Nod" and "Annabel Lee" as well as all the bones of the body.

Mrs. Thompson was a baseball fanatic and got Miss Ishee's approval to suspend all her classes when the World Series was on. That year's first game between the St. Louis Cardinals and Mrs. Thompson's favorite team, the Boston Red Sox, was on a Wednesday afternoon and my pulse started racing when she and Miss Ishee wheeled in a television so we could watch it. Mrs. Thompson had told us that the Red Sox had finished ninth in their division the year before and it was "a bless-ed miracle" that they were in the World Series, that they hadn't won their division that year till the final day of the season, and that they hadn't won a pennant race since 1946. As much as I loved Mrs. Thompson, I had been rooting for the Cardinals since the December before, when the Yankees had traded Roger Maris to them. I was, in honor of my dead father, a Maris man, and when Maris got two big hits in that first game I screamed louder than anybody else in the room. Miss Ishee had walked back down the hall at game time to stand in the doorway and watch a few innings with us. When I screamed at Maris's hits she told me each time to pipe down. "That's right," said Mrs. Thompson. "You keep that up, I'm gonna give you an F on your test Friday no matter how many bones you get right on that mimeographed skeleton. Bob Gibson keeps up this kind of pitchin' I've a good mind to break some bones in his leg myself all over again. Come on, Yaz!" she shouted at the image of Carl Yastrzemski striding to the plate and smoothed her chignon in anticipation of a Red Sox hit. Miss Ishee couldn't take her eyes off her.

I played a little baseball on a Little League team, believe it or not, peer pressure proving less a prod than that of the pneumatic paternal kind. The team was sponsored by Tower Loan Association and our colors were maroon and gray. Though I was still kidded about being a sissy by my meaner teammates, I had also inherited an innate athletic ability from my father. A speed demon, I could run faster around the bases than any of the other kids my age. My grounding needed some improvement and I had to concentrate in order not to throw like a girl, but I still started every game at first base. The manager of the local Tower Loan company was a big hale-and-hearty fellow named James Moore, who volunteered to coach our team. His wife Yvette taught Special Education for those too academically slow to be put in regular classes at the elementary school. I hit a home run once, way over center field where the cars were parked between the Little League field and the one used by the girls for their softball games. The high school football coach, Ken Bramlett, who was calling the game, announced over the loud speaker that I had hit a "humdinger" as the crowd began to cheer in astonishment that I of all people had done such a thing. It was the first time I felt like a real boy, when Dave Marler's fast ball connected with the middle of the fattest part of the end of my bat, my hands completely relaxing, letting go of the wood where I had slightly choked up on the handle after they had felt no sting at all at the hit, only the perfection of the ball landing against the bat's sweetest spot. As I rounded second base, I thought of my father only a few years earlier being hit by that throw as he slid into second at Battlefield Park, and that white plastic neck brace he subsequently had to wear, the secret cool firmness of it against my legs when he told me to let go then "run like hell for home," like the way I was running at that very moment to that plate with the same name where my teammates waited. I loved hitting that home run as much as I loved carrying around that awful secret my father and I shared. Both made me feel powerful in ways I could not quite understand. My amazed teammates swarmed around me at home plate. I looked over at Coach Moore, expecting his approval, wanting to see his own look of amazement on his jowly face. But he was still looking out beyond center field, his eyes focused on that spot of the fence over which my ball had sailed, yet also, seemingly, seeing something else farther away, something none of the rest of us could see. He turned and looked into my eyes and what I saw was not amazement at all. A thought passed through me at that very moment, a slight shiver going through me—whether at the thought or the continued touching of my body by my swarming teammates, I'm not quite sure—but the shiver is as much a part of the memory as the perfect feel of that bat in my hand when I hit the pitch. The thought was the same one I had when another coach had looked into my eyes in that lounge at the Pelahatchie gym, a lounge that reeked of cold fried chicken and aftershave and my puked-up bits of popcorn. *He is sadder than I am*, I thought once more. After the game, Coach Moore bought me a congratulatory vanilla milkshake at the Tasty Freeze. He shook my hand. "Your daddy would be proud of what you done today, boy," he said. Several Fridays later he was found outside of town behind a bulldozed mound of earth at a construction site, a hunting rifle beside his body. He had been missing for several days. "Shot hisself in the chest. Must have pulled that trigger with a toe. They found him with one shoe off," said Pop, describing what had happened without explaining it.

———————

By the time I reached sixth grade, my nickname among my male classmates was "BD" for "Big Dick." I was bigger than many of the boys around me and they had noticed how hair had begun to sprout under my arms and on my legs. When I pulled out my penis in the bathroom on the elementary school's sixth-grade wing, many of the boys looked over my shoulder to get a look. I only liked it, however, when Ricky Crimm dared Bobby Thompson to see it for himself, for I longed to look at Bobby's dick no matter what its size but could not summon the courage it would take to do such a thing.

Yet I had by that school year developed enough sassy sissy smarts (perhaps my budding confidence came from that nickname bestowed upon me) not only to convince my teacher, Mrs. Fikes, to let me write about *Valley of the Dolls* for my second-semester book report, but also to let me try and direct my class in my own abridged version of the play *A Man for All Seasons*, a film version of which had won the Oscar for Best Picture the year before but had only recently been shown at a Saturday matinee at the Town Theatre in Forest. I had trouble following the story of Sir Thomas More's fight with Henry VIII, but reveled in the pageantry and accents and fierce debates that roiled the characters' lives, as well as the love they had for the power of their well-spoken words. Paul Scofield, who starred as More and won an Oscar of his own, fascinated me with his bemused demeanor, a more dignified Uncle Benny without the overalls but with that same cast to his eyes—knowing, wary, always lying in wait. I sat through the movie twice and made sure to buy a paperback copy of Robert Bolt's play when I was visiting Aunt Gladys in Jackson over the next weekend. I got as far as casting the play—writing the names of my classmates next to their character's names on the blackboard—but rehearsals fell apart when most of the cast preferred recess to rehearsing and complained that they could not comprehend what they had to read aloud. Some of their parents complained also when it became clear to them that Sir Thomas More was not a Baptist, a Methodist, or a Presbyterian but a Catholic, something slightly not Christian enough in those parts. There was a tiny local Catholic church in Forest but it was peopled with a Lebanese clan from the Delta who ran the town's department store, Thomas Great M, and the upper-level management of the Sunbeam plant, men and their families who had immigrated from up north. Once again, Miss Ishee had to step in and run interference for me when parents began to call her up about my latest endeavor.

I think Mrs. Fikes's allowing me to write that book report about *Valley of the Dolls* had a lot to do with how obviously disappointed I was at having to cancel my plans for *A Man for All Seasons*. "I liked *The Russians Are Coming! The Russians Are Coming!* better anyway," she said, naming a film that had lost out to *A Man for All Seasons* at the Oscars.

"But I am glad that *Who's Afraid of That Big Bad Virginia Woolf* one lost. I certainly didn't drive all the way to Jackson to see Elizabeth Taylor look like that," she said. "And why must Hollywood always take the Lord's name in vain?" she asked, reminding me of those earlier years when she had also been my Sunday-school teacher, at Trinity Methodist. Trinity, before it moved into its modern A-framed linoleum-floored sanctuary where my mother had sung her solos and duets with Ozella Weems, had held its services in the offices of the old Farmers and Merchants Bank on Main Street. Mrs. Fikes's Sunday-school class had been in the bank's walk-in vault, its round entrance big enough for children but small enough that Mrs. Fikes had to duck to enter. "*Valley of the Dolls* can't be any worse than that Elizabeth Taylor movie. Virginia Woolf, poor thing, is probably still turning over in her grave even if Liz did win her an Academy Award for looking ugly and cussing a blue streak. Plus that movie was in black and white. I think movies should all be in color nowadays. No call for black and white—except, of course, in the school system starting next year," she said, clucking her tongue at the prospect of teaching African-American children over at E. T. Hawkins. "I'm going to miss this place. I love our little sixth-grade wing all to ourselves here. Go ahead and do your book report on *Valley of the Dolls*, Kevin. I'll deal with your grandmama."

The novel had been out for a couple of years by then, and I had seen its author, Jackie Susann, on all the talk shows. I loved her throaty, Pucci-wearing glamour and yet, always aware of my own audience, knew that I was going to have to do a hatchet job on the book if I wanted an A on the report. Don't get me wrong. I loved reading every word of it. Jackie Susann was no Robert Bolt. She was easier to figure out. I'd lie out in one of my grandparents' green-and-white chaise longue lawn chairs in the backyard and read the chapters of the bitchy show biz saga, filled with pill popping and hot sex, while Kim and Karole played basketball at our goal attached to a creosote pole next to the Derricks' cow pasture. During the last week in March, on the day after my birthday, Dave Marler (who later became an all-SEC quarterback at Mississippi State and a star of the Canadian football league with the Hamilton Tiger-Cats) and Bobby Thompson, both invited by Kim, came walking by me to fish in our pond as I was sunning in my bathing suit and finishing up the Susann. I was lying on my stomach feeling my hard-on, a perpetual one in those days, pressing against the lawn chair's plastic meshing. The combination of Susann's prose and Bobby's shirtless presence out by the pond, where he was casting his rod and reel, racked my body with a rush of hormones I had not known was humanly possible. When Bobby whooped at catching his second bass, I ejaculated without even touching myself, my fingers pressing down on the last of Susann's pages as I also pressed my body more forcefully against the mesh. I remember reading these two words as it happened—*civil war*—and, once I was over the pleasant shock of it all, grinning to myself (overly aware even then of my surroundings) at how appropriately Southern it all was: those words, the algae-scummed bass pond, my Mississippi backyard, the feelings that could get me lynched if I let on to why more than my heart leapt at that shirtless sight of a blond-haired boy named Bobby. As I contemplated writing this book, I looked up those two words again in Susann's novel when that memory came washing back over me. Could I have made them up, during all the times I recalled that moment when falling asleep at night and trying to lull myself into a dream state with thoughts of times in my life—some only as long as seconds—when happiness seemed possible? Sure enough, there they were—"civil" and "war"—two words that every Southern boy, whether a sissy or not, is confronted with more than any others as he matures and takes on a more modern world. "'It's like a civil war with her emotions against her talent and physical strength,'" Susann wrote. "'One side had to give. Something had to be destroyed.'" It was her character Anne speaking of another character, Neely. But she could have just as easily been describing that sixth-grade boy who somehow sensed he be-longed in that book and not in a place that still suffered from a hundred-year-old defeat, a place that had not matured, had not be-come, not really, more modern. Except for gasoline-powered vehicles and cathode-ray tubes, the Mississippi of the 1960s could have just as easily been the same as the one that existed in the 1860s, slavery no longer a "necessary evil," as it was so often described by my history teachers, but the attitudes of slave owners still so deeply inculcated within the culture that I half-expected to see Scarlett O'Hara shop-ping at Thomas Great M or Jefferson Davis serving on a jury up at the county court house that anchored Forest's town square.

My book report on *Valley of the Dolls* was due on April 5th. I re-member that date so precisely because I was putting the finishing touches on it the night before while I was watching Chet Huntley and David Brinkley talk about Martin Luther King being killed only a few hundred miles north of us in Memphis. The next day, when I arrived for Mrs. Fikes's class, my fellow students, parroting their par-ents, no doubt, were giddy with the news of King's death. Mrs. Fikes told me to shut the door because the school's maid, Flossy's more cir-cumspect successor, might hear the celebration going on around us. It was in front of a room full of all that repressed redneck delight—more obscene than any prurience Jackie Susann could come up with—that I read to them about Jennifer and Neely and Anne. I saved my most inspired prose, however, for that battle-ax, Helen Lawson, who could belt out a Broadway tune. As an example of what a Broadway tune was, I belted out bits of "Comedy Tonight." I then held up a container of one of my grandmother's prescription medi-cines, which I had pocketed on the way out the door that morning, and explained to the class that "dolls" were pills. A girl in the back row interrupted my recitation: "Well, that's just dumb." The last lines of my book report? "God forgive m-m-me. I have sinned. I have read V-Valley of the D-D-Dolls." Mrs. Fikes gave me an A.

King's assassination, followed by Robert Kennedy's a couple of months later, and the reactions of those around me to both, hastened my desire to escape Mississippi. It is hard to describe the fear and disgust I felt when witnessing others' elation over the deaths of those two men. I was not yet thirteen but grew up immeasurably during the spring and summer of 1968. If my parents' own deaths had deepened my perception of the serendipitous nature of life, the deaths of King and Kennedy expanded it to include a concept of cruelty much greater than that needed for the utterance of the sissy epithets that I had had to suffer up until that point. Kim and Karole and I were visiting Aunt Gladys and my father's extended clan when RFK was shot. My father's brother, J. D. (short for Joy David), was visiting from Augusta, Georgia, with his wife, Pauline, and their two children, Janice Kay and a lanky son called Little Joy. Aunt Gladys's husband, Dallas, reeking as usual of liquor, was home from working on another oil rig in the Gulf of Mexico and their teenage daughter Glenda, a Hinds Hi-Stepper, was pouting in her room listening to an album by the Mamas and the Papas.

Aunt Drucy, my father's mother's sister and a honky-tonk proprietress from way back, was sitting sharing her Lucky Strikes with J. D. and watching the news of the RFK shooting on television. Their cigarette smoke filled the living room as Uncle Dallas whooped with delight at the announcement that Kennedy was officially dead. The others began to clap, but they all became surly when ABC cancelled plans to air some baseball game they had hoped to watch. "Both nigger-lovin' Kennedys and that bastard Martin Luther King!" Uncle Dallas hollered and scooted to the edge of his recliner to get a closer look at the television, one of the few times I ever saw him rouse himself to sit straight up. "We're gettin' 'em all. Them Yankees may have whupped us back yonder all them years ago, but we showin' 'em now. Hot damn!"

Aunt Drucy pulled on her Lucky Strike and wanted to know if anybody still wanted to go with her to the VFW hall to play bingo as Glenda turned up her stereo to drown out all the commotion, Mama Cass singing "Dream a Little Dream of Me." Kim and Karole divvied up the butterscotch candy Aunt Drucy had given them after she dug around to find it in the big purse she always kept sitting in her lap, her elbows propped on it as if she were protecting whatever was in it besides the butterscotch. I saw a pearl-handled pistol in there once when I went snooping for some candy of my own. "This don't change nothin'," Aunt Drucy said, staring at the television and motioning with her cigarette lighter for Dallas to turn it down. "Y'all all crazy if y'all think this does. I even found out the other day that Louella is a member of the NAACP," she said, referring to her cook up at the latest honky-tonk café she owned on Terry Road in a rough section of Jackson. "Had a good mind to fire her on the spot, but that's the times we live in. NAACP or not, she can still make the best breaded veal cutlet I ever put in my mouth and veal cutlets is my bread-and-butter at the café. That, along with that shuffleboard table I put in when Toy told me to. He said our cut of the silver it took to play the thing would add up. He was right. That's my bingo money tonight."

Toy was Drucy's husband, who had one glass eye and scared the daylights out of me when he stared at me with his one good one. Like Dallas, he always smelled as if someone had doused him with something cheaper than Dewar's. He married Drucy when she was fourteen and, childless, they had spent their lives around jukeboxes and blue plate specials. A story they liked to tell was about the time they owned a café at 313 West Capital Street back during World War II, when a soldier on leave and bivouacked at the old Jackson airport was shot dead at the place during a drunken scuffle. Drucy didn't want the police to be called so she had some customers dump the body in a barrel of discarded cooking grease in the alleyway, to be found in the morning by the garbage collectors. "No need to interrupt business," she had said. "We're having a good night." For years she and Toy had a big old rambling boardinghouse down West Capital from that lethally boisterous juke joint and one of their favorite boarders was a man named "Crooked Joe," not because of any dishonesty on his part but because he had broken his back in his youth and walked around completely bent at the waist so that his torso was parallel to the ground. "But if you put him up behind a steerin' wheel, it was a right nice fit," said Drucy, who enlisted Joe to chauffeur Toy and her to Vegas on several occasions when they wanted to gamble on bigger games of chance than bingo. "Come on, y'all. I want to get a good table close to the caller and pick out my cards before the VFW gets too crowded," she told the rest of the clan who still sat transfixed by the RFK news, having quickly forgotten about the cancelled baseball game. "Them folks at the VFW is gonna be all worked up with this latest Kennedy rigmarole same as y'all. I can snag my favorite cards while they're all a'goin' on about it. Gonna win me that final blackout card jackpot and buy them two over there some more butterscotch."

Pauline sipped some iced tea out of one of the Dixie cups she always brought with her on her family's visits from Augusta. She was a secretary at the Dixie cup factory there and she made sure to keep Gladys supplied in boxes of the product. She touched her overly teased hair. "Janice and J. D. want to go with you, Aunt Drucy. But I'll stay here with Little Joy in case the baseball game comes on," she said.

I stole a butterscotch from Karole's pile. She complained but I put it in my mouth before she could snatch it back.

Mama Cass, muffled now behind Glenda's slammed door, continued to sing.

"Hot damn!" said Dallas once more at the television set.

Drucy lit another Lucky.

The deaths of Martin Luther King and Robert Kennedy politicized me even more than my mother's look of disapointment at my Little Miss Goldwater shenanigans four years earlier. That summer I stayed glued to the television during coverage of Nixon's nomination at the Republican convention in Miami and the riots that overtook the Democratic convention in Chicago, when "Chessy Cat" Humphrey, as my grandmother liked to deride him, won his party's nod. I couldn't get enough of the fiery speeches and the newscasters' commentary during both events. (Mom and Pop were, of course, George Wallace fanatics during the presidential campaign, having mourned his wife Lurleen's death from cancer that May with almost the same intensity that they had my mother's.) Those political conventions— Mom kept shaking her head at my interest in them—were even more entertaining to me than the Barbra Streisand concert in Central Park that aired after Labor Day, and, let me tell you, that was a transfixing experience of another sort for a sissy child who was busying himself with making cultural choices all his own.

The year that followed was filled with images from a rock festival in a place called Woodstock and a landing on the moon by a preppy-looking guy named Armstrong on whom I had another of my secret crushes. Hurricane Camille hit the Gulf Coast. *Easy Rider* opened. *Hee Haw* began, and *The Brady Bunch* and *Marcus Welby, M.D.* Jack Kerouac died. So did John Kennedy Toole. I'd sit on the pot every morning before heading off to school and think about my draft number. I'd wait to wipe my ass and read about Vietnam in the *Clarion-Ledger*, Jackson's morning daily thrown onto our gravel drive at dawn, and wonder if I were old enough, what I would do if that draft number were called. On the bottom right-hand page of the *Clarion-Ledger/Jackson Daily News* one Sunday morning, I read the same story about the Stonewall riots over and over and over and over, though Judy Garland (the story said she had died) was still just Dorothy to me in *The Wizard of Oz*. In eighth grade a whole new decade started and everyone around me was glad to see the sixties disappear completely. I played football and ran back kickoffs and interceptions for touchdowns and played first-string guard on the basketball team and hated every minute of it, especially when I made a great play and was cheered from the stands. I felt like an impostor. I did not want cheers. I wanted recognition of a different sort. I wanted respect of a deeper kind. I continued to watch *Ironside* with Mom on Thursday nights and let her go on about how wonderful Raymond Burr was (a sexual fellow traveler of mine, I would discover later in life). I saw *Patton* and *M.A.S.H.* at Saturday matinees at the Town Theater but not *Midnight Cowboy*. I grieved for the students killed at Kent State and, a week later in Mississippi, at Jackson State, while I listened to Simon and Garfunkel sing "Bridge over Troubled Water" and next put the needle down on Neil Young's nasal plaint of "oh" and "lonesome" and "me." Most important, back in 1970, I read two first books by women I would come close to worshiping. Maya Angelou's *I Know Why the Caged Bird Sings* spoke to me in a voice that took what I heard out of the mouth of Matty May and molded it into poetry, into magnificence. And Toni Morrison's *The Bluest Eye* I found myself reading aloud in my backyard under that tree where my grandparents and I had sat after my mother's funeral. As I heard my voice reading Morrison's words, I hoped my dead mother could hear me and understand how someone had rightly replaced Katherine Anne Porter in my life. "Pecola," I'd mutter over and over the name of the book's main character to myself, just as Matty muttered "Poitier," both names metered with the same rhythm and weighted, for me, with the same aural wonder, the same importance, each imbued, as a word, with a noble mien, ever nuanced, never simple. "Pecola Pecola Pecola . . ."

But none of these things proved as significant to me as Billy Graham and his crusades. In 1969 and 1970, they were televised, respectively, from New York and London. I had reached a point in my life around the seventh and eighth grades, as my teenage years approached, when the difference I was feeling had become oppressive.

My grandmother knew I was struggling. Her solution? More church. More prayer. More preaching. The Billy Graham crusades broadcast over Channel 12 fit right into this remedy of hers, which, with Graham's presence, had become a rather homemade one since he was right there in our living room. My deep-seated differences—sexual, political, cultural—were no longer ways for me secretly to revel in my superiority. They had begun instead to chafe at my soul. I was primed therefore to answer Graham's altar call one night from New York's Madison Square Garden when he turned to the camera as if speaking directly to me, though it was Ethel Waters, yet another black woman demanding attention be paid, singing "His Eye Is on the Sparrow" at that same crusade who first convinced me to believe that His eye was also on me and that I was finally truly seen. "Every word that you speak," Graham intoned after Waters's wobbly yet piercingly beautiful solo, every one of her syllables carefully pronounced as she approximated their every note, "every thought, every intent," continued Graham, "everything that you ever did in the dark, everything that you swept under the rug, everything that you thought *had been hidden*, will be brought to light . . ." That night, I listened as his North Carolina drawl—so much more soothing, more proper, than the hick-encrusted accents I had grown up around in Mississippi—told the congregation at the close of his sermon to "come now, don't *lingah*, you up at the top sections—*come*, your friends and family will wait, we will pray with you and give you some *lit-tra-toor*, come now, come, come, *come*." Cliff Barrows, Graham's musical director, began to lead the choir in the invitational hymn, "Just As I Am." If I had been in New York in those top sections I would have gotten out of my seat, just as I was, and headed down toward the makeshift altar. I would not have lingered. But there in my house in the Mississippi countryside I did not move from the couch where Mom sat beside me as she sang every lyric of "Just As I Am" from memory, a miracle in itself, I remember thinking, because she had only recently suffered her stroke and was more than forgetful. She was enfeebled. I reached out and held her newly crippled hand. "Come, come, come," Graham intoned. I continued to sit completely still and listened to my grandmother making her way through every verse of that hymn, her voice in its post-stroke state even more wobbly than Miss Waters's. Graham insisted: "Come." Though I did not move from my seat, I did silently pledge to live a better life. But was I giving that better life to Christ, as Reverend Graham insisted I must? Was I, in that moment, being born again? Was such a thing even possible? Or was it all just spiritual claptrap? Mom's crippled hand grasped mine as best it could, as if I were the paraffin the physical therapist had so often poured into her palm, so she could try to shape me now inside that fist she could not quite yet form. "Just as I am, though tossed about with many a conflict, many a doubt," she sang, finding the words somewhere within her. "Fightings and fears within, without. O, Lamb of God, I come. I . . ." "Come," said Graham. "Come, come."

I let go of Mom's hand and rushed into the kitchen. I grabbed onto the counter and took deep breaths. "Honey, you all right?" I heard her voice ask behind me once she had made it to the door. "Is it the Holy Ghost? Is it something you ate?"

I turned and hugged her, hugged her as tightly as I could without hurting her. "N-nobody loves me," I said, trying not to sob. It was the meanest thing I now know I could have possibly said to her. "N-nobody loves me, Mom. N-nobody."

She fashioned again something that resembled a fist and hit me over and over with it on my back where she held on to me and would not let me go. Unlike me, she was glad to have an excuse to cry. "Oh, honey. Don't you say no such thing. Don't you dare," she said. "You ain't nothin' but loved. You just have t'learn how t'feel it. There's somethin' inside you that's always fought bein' loved. I ain't never understood it. I just know it's a fact as true as anything Billy Graham can quote letter-perfect from the Bible. Don't fight it so. It's a fine thing: to be loved.

You go on and feel it. No more fightin' it off." Her fist pounded me. "You listen t'Mom. Stop a'cryin'. Stop it now. Shshsh . . ."

Billy Graham had disappeared from the television in the other room and I heard Carol Burnett now answering questions from her studio audience. Mom hummed "Just As I Am" and rocked me in her unsteady arms. The audience laughed at an answer.

———————

Billy Graham has continued to play a part in my family's life long after those nights when Mom and I would watch his crusades and try not to cry when the Holy Ghost moved through yet another stadium full of families with histories no doubt just as troubled, just as tragic as our own, families who also sought solace and sometimes, as we did, found it when all that was left them was faith. Religion's consoling presence in our lives cannot be discounted while my brother and sister and I were growing up, but its hold on Kim and Karole has remained steadier, its grasp more secure, than it has in my own life. Maybe it's because they still live in Mississippi and churchgoing is not so much a choice one makes there; it is a social obligation. That is not to say their deeply held religious beliefs are not sincere. I'm sure such beliefs have enabled them to heal from our shared past in ways I have been unable to heal. It has molded them into good and decent people, though very dissimilar in their grown-up lives. Karole, just as devoutly Christian as Kim, is a lesbian who has been in the same relationship now for almost twenty years. Her politics are as liberal as mine. Kim, who married his childhood sweetheart just as my parents married theirs, is the father of four children and his politics are rock-ribbed red-state Republican. And yet, such early trauma in our lives has caused a bond among the three of us that is undeniable. Early trauma can also lead—this is my own most devoutly held belief—to a creative spirit in those who somehow gracefully survive it. In fact, Karole and her partner, H. C. Porter, own an arts studio in Vicksburg called just that, Creative Spirit, and travel around the country selling Porter's art, which is based largely on images of African-American life in the state. And the only thing that has come close to equaling Kim's Christianity in importance—other than his wife and kids, certainly more than his medical practice—is his own artistic bent, which has finally manifested itself in his sculpture. All creative spirits are Godlike in our belief that we can imbue life with the shape of art. It is what initially led me to make sense of our shared childhoods. It led Kim to Billy Graham himself.

After sculpting his busts of Eudora Welty and Andrew Wyeth—both having posed for him—Kim headed up to Montreat, North Carolina, to meet with Reverend Graham at the mountaintop home he shares with his wife, Ruth, in order to put the finishing touches on the bust of Graham he had been working on for almost a year. The Wyeth bust had already been cast in bronze and was in the trunk of Kim's car as he drove up the steep mountainside. Miss Welty's head, however, had not yet been cast and, like Graham's, was still formed in clay. Her head and the reverend's sat side by side secured on a platform Kim had rigged up on the car's backseat. He was careful not to speed around any mountain curves as he headed up to the Grahams' homestead, in case the heads shifted and all his work came to naught in two massive smashed-together clumps of sculpting clay.

Kim had been introduced to Ruth Graham by a mutual Mississippi friend and she had commissioned the work without even telling her husband about it. Kim's arrival would be an early Saturday morning surprise for him. "This will definitely be a case of outwitting and not submitting," she had told Kim over the phone a few months before. "But it is an idea whose time has come. We simply must find a way."

Kim had expected her to tell Reverend Graham about the sculpture at some point before he made his pilgrimage to the mountaintop, but Ruth had wisely reneged on informing her husband beforehand.

She said she knew him better than anybody and this was the best way to go about it. Kim was simply told to show up and she'd summon her husband, who would be too polite to back out at that point. Kim had his doubts about such a plan, but went along with her. He trusted her instincts for they had been honed by more than fifty years of marriage to the man. Though Billy Graham belonged, profoundly so, to God and to the millions who had heard him preach, he also belonged, more intimately, tenaciously so, to this strong-willed woman blessed not only with the patience of Job, not to put too fine a Biblical point on it, but also a movie star's beauty.

Nervous at what awaited him, Kim arrived that morning at the gates of Little Piney Cove, the 150-acre compound that Ruth, in an earlier secretive maneuver, had bought for $4,300 in 1954 while her husband was away behind yet another pulpit. The gates parted at Kim's prearranged two-honks-of-the-car-horn signal and he drove up the steep winding drive where he was met by a small bulldog of a man named Bill, the groundskeeper, who emerged from a garden house to welcome him to the property. "See you found your way up here to Piney Cove without a hitch," Bill said, shaking Kim's hand. "Miss Ruth's expecting you." They both walked up the stone steps of the elegant home, an elongated log cabin. The front door was opened by Mrs. Graham before they had a chance to knock. She was still in her ankle-length housecoat and slippers. Her white hair was swept back from her face and that beauty of hers was highlighted in the early-morning mountain light where it still lay pentimento, such beauty, beneath the many finely layered lines stroked into her flesh by age and experience and that very light—warming, Southern—that filtered through the towering trees on her beloved mountainside.

Ruth Graham's sister was visiting from California and the two women were finishing up their morning cups of coffee in the kitchen. After a bit of small talk, Kim unloaded the car and placed the two busts of Wyeth and Welty on the kitchen table. The one of her husband he placed on a sculpting stand he'd brought along on which to do some work if Reverend Graham agreed to pose for him for a few hours. He positioned the stand next to a large comfortable wingback chair that sat in front of the kitchen's stone fireplace so that the bust would be staring right back at Reverend Graham when he came into the room. He then made one more trip to the car to get his sculpting tools. When he returned he found Ruth standing close to the stand and studying her husband's clay face. "I think it's marvelous," she said. "I think he'll like it." She turned to Bill, who was warming his hands at the stone hearth. "Why don't you see if he'll come up here to the kitchen?" she asked. "He's back in the bedroom." She turned again to Kim, her voice apologetic. "He's not moving very well this morning—his Parkinson's, you know. But I think he'll be surprised and delighted when he gets in here," she said.

Kim nervously fingered his tools. "So he still doesn't know about this?" he asked.

Ruth grinned a rather devilish grin for someone who had lived so long next to a man of God. "He will in a minute," she said, snickering to herself, and went over to the kitchen sink to wash out her coffee cup.

Her sister came over to the stand to get a better look at the bust of her brother-in-law. She stared into the eyes. "It's uncanny, Ruth," she said. "I think he's going to speak."

At that, Kim heard the shuffle of feet easing down the planked floor in the hall adjacent to the kitchen. He went over to the bust and repositioned it one more time to make sure those eyes he'd fashioned so diligently in the clay were staring at the flesh-and-blood ones when the man entered the room. He turned and there stood the Reverend Graham in the doorway, all six feet and four inches of him, slightly stooped now, his long white hair, like his wife's, swept back from his face, his own movie star looks undiminished. He wore eyeglasses "tinted like Mom's ice tea in the summer when the ice cubes always melted too quickly," Kim told me later. He wore a pair of blue jeans and a jean jacket that once belonged to Johnny Cash, he bragged when Kim complimented him on it. Graham stopped staring at the bust of himself and turned his attention to this strange young man in his kitchen. Ruth dried her hands on a dish towel and snickered once more at her husband's disconcerted expression. Kim walked over to shake the man's hand and said, "Before you say anything, I want you to know this is really not about you or me. It's for your lovely wife. She sort of put this together, though I realize this all must be a little bit of a shock."

A slight smile crossed Reverend Graham's lips as he shuffled closer to the bust. "Well, son, she's shocked me a few times before," he said. A silence fell over the room as Graham inspected his likeness, then settled into his comfortable chair there by the fire. "How did you do this?" he asked Kim.

"Well, it's taken quite a bit of research," my brother told him. "I watched a lot of your sermons on video. You're not a bad preacher, by the way." The sisters chuckled, quieting themselves as Kim then explained to them all the process of building an armature and applying the clay as well as how the tools he was still holding in his hands worked.

"So, what now?" Graham interrupted him.

Kim nervously cleared his throat and moved toward him. "Well, to really get it right I need some measurements using these calipers," he said.

Graham eyed the aluminum prongs suspiciously. "How does that contraption work?" Graham asked. "Those cali-*puhs*?"

Kim moved even closer. "Well, if you don't mind, I'll show you," he said. He opened the calipers and carefully measured the center of Graham's right pupil to the center of his left one. He then measured the pupils of the sculpture. It was Kim's turn now to chuckle. "It's a perfect match," he said, shaking his head in the only bit of disbelief allowed on the property. "Your eyes are the right distance apart."

Graham shifted in his chair. "Aren't they supposed to be?" he asked, slightly bewildered by what was going on in his kitchen. Kim continued his measurements and found that he had placed Graham's ears too far forward on the sculpture. He took out a carving knife and sliced them off to move them back a few millimeters. Graham covered his real ears with his hands. The kitchen filled with laughter as the backdoor opened.

"Dr. G, how you feeling this morning?" asked Maury Scobee, Graham's longtime best friend and factotum, though a highfalutin' one, as he entered the increasingly crowded room. "Miss Ruth, you're up early," Scobee said, stopping when he saw Kim and the three busts in the room, his eyes coming to rest on Graham's next to the fire. "Miss Ruth, what have you been up to?" he asked, instinctively knowing that she had surprised her husband once again. Scobee, after introducing himself to my brother, inspected the bust more closely, backing up to get a longer view of it before turning his attention to the ones of Welty and Wyeth. "Look at these, Dr. G," he said. "Have you seen these?"

Kim walked over to the table. "I brought the Wyeth to show what a finished bronze looks like," he told them. "The Eudora Welty I just thought Miss Ruth might enjoy seeing. I plan to take it to the foundry with this new piece of Dr. Graham for casting at the same time."

Scobee kept looking at the Welty. "What do you think, Dr. G?" he asked, pointing at her.

Graham shrugged. "I thought it was Eleanor Roosevelt," he said from his wingbacked chair, and warmed his hands at the fire's hearth.

"You know, I hadn't thought of that," Kim said. "But I can sort of see it now. I'll tell you this, though. When I drove up here yesterday from Mississippi, I kept noticing these cars passing, even truckers, and staring over at me. I kept wondering if there was something wrong with the car. Then it hit me. They were looking at you and

Eudora riding on that back platform looking out the windows. I know there've been no scandals in your ministry, sir, but I can see the headlines now—BILLY GRAHAM SPOTTED IN ALABAMA WITH ANOTHER WOMAN."

A snicker, Ruth's loudest yet, shot through the room and mingled with her husband's smile. With a wire hoop, Kim went back to work and scored a thin layer of clay from the contour of the left ear on Graham's bust. He then palpated the man's real one. He went back to the clay. Back to the flesh. Clay. Flesh. Clay. Flesh. Graham patiently let him do his tactile work until Kim asked if he might take a few photographs out on the back steps in the natural light now filtering with greater authority through Piney Cove's abundant trees. Graham agreed. Kim and Scobee helped him from his chair as Bill held the door open. Once they were outside, Kim began to click away with his old Canon AT-1 at every crag and angle of Graham's face, his massive head, his shock of hair. Ruth stood at the kitchen window and, like Mom while washing dishes back in that mountainless Mississippi of my sorrow-filled youth, she seemed with her knowing gaze to be watching not only all the life that passed in front of her but also all that had not. Kim squatted down low on the ground to get a shot from beneath Graham's prominent chin and felt a large mass of something furry pressing against his back. He knew it had to be an animal from the mountainside—a growl erupted somewhere in the vicinity of his own left ear—but why hadn't Reverend Graham warned him of its approach? Was it a wolf? A bear? Was Graham scared his famous voice would rile the creature even more?

"That's a real German shep-*uhd*," Reverend Graham finally said as the giant canine nudged my little brother all the way to the ground. Kim protected his Canon from the dog and continued to click away. The old man there in his lens—his famous profile proffered for yet another stranger—turned and peered up past the Smokies. He smoothed his white hair back with one quick, tremored sweep of his flattened palm, then gathered Johnny Cash's old jean jacket more snugly about his infirm body. The shepherd continued its close watch as Kim saw a grin quickly flicker across Graham's face—a click captured it—with the same devilish glee that his wife had displayed earlier when he walked into the kitchen. "That dog there sniffing at you only *seems* tame," he said. "He's really a trained kill-*ah* who could tear your throat out on command. We had to get guard dogs and increase security back in the sixties when things got bad up here. Death threats and all. Especially after Dr. King's assassination."

The devilishness, though not the glee, just as quickly vanished from Reverend Graham's face and he once more silently peered up past those Smokies to a place he'd been peering at his whole life. The shepherd was finally satisfied the old man was safe. Ruth, satisfied also, remained at the window, now watching neither the life passing in front of her nor the life that had not, but beginning to see more clearly (the commissioning of that bust by Kim over by the hearth was perhaps her acceptance of this) the life that would never be. Her husband turned to her and smiled at how she still was able to surprise him. She smiled back. What passed between them—tearless, eternal—could not be sculpted.

———

Dr. Graham. Dr. King. RFK. Maya Angelou. Arlene Francis. Toni Morrison. Eudora Welty. Katherine Anne Porter. All of them played significant roles in my growing up in Mississippi. But there was another person, Dr. Andrew F. Gallman, who was not as famous as they, not as accomplished, but who played an even more important role in my life. Once a Methodist minister in Mississippi, he had become the director of development for Asbury College when I met him. Asbury is a conservative "Christ-centered" school in Wilmore, Kentucky, that states in its "mission purpose" that the school is guided "by the classical tradition of orthodox Christian thought. Central to this endeavor is a clear affirmation of the scriptures of the Old and New Testaments as God's infallible and authoritative word." Dr. Gallman's job at the college back then—this would have been during my seventh- and eighth-grade years—entailed his traveling to states throughout the South and raising the college's endowment by visiting churches (mostly Methodist) as well as rich business leaders with the same "Christ-centered" bent who might want to donate to the school's coffers.

Some in Mississippi insisted that Dr. Gallman was as good a stemwinder as Billy Graham, and he still preached from time to time when called upon. One of his sons, a brainy sort who was a linguist who had been called by God to interpret the Bible into languages as yet to be transcribed, had asked a first cousin of mine to marry him, and after their wedding they were headed off to the jungles of the Philippines and later Brazil to be linguistic missionaries, the two of them turning newfound yet ancient tongues into the numbered chapters and verses of Deuteronomy and Acts and Leviticus. My grandmother was thrilled not only because her eldest grandchild was getting married, but because she was entering into such a God-fearing and dedicatedly Christian family. Always a fervent Methodist, Mom had heard Dr. Gallman preach at several churches around the state before he took up his bureaucratic position at Asbury. The idea that her granddaughter was marrying his son "uplifts my soul," she told me when making sure to pass on to me her deep respect for the man. Ever since she had witnessed my counter-grabbing conversion in our kitchen, or whatever it was that had happened there during that Billy Graham crusade, Mom had taken a keen interest in my spiritual well-being. She passed along her *Guidepost* magazines to me and pointed out verses in the Bible that meant the most to her. "Jesus has got a plan up his sleeve for you, honey," she said more than once. "I can sense it. Them solos you used to sing with Grace Speed when you was a boy soprano at Trinity was just the beginnin'. We get that stutter of yours cured—time we claimed a healin' for that anyway—I bet you could near 'bout preach as good as Dr. Gallman. Shoot! Billy Graham hisself better watch out, I'm tellin' you. That's one thing this family could use, seein' as all the funerals that keep a'comin' our way—a readymade preacher. Somebody we could have on call, like Doc Townsend."

When Mom heard that Dr. Gallman himself was going to officiate at her granddaughter's wedding she was beside herself with joy that she would get to know the man in a more personal way. Then, when word came that he had accepted an invitation to preach, in the days before the wedding, at a revival meeting at her old Methodist church out in Harperville, across from the family cemetery, all the physical aftershocks of her recent stroke seemed to lift. She was newly energized and made sure we were there for his inaugural sermon, making a pit stop at my parents' graves and saying our first prayer of the evening before settling into a pew. I was nervous about attending the revival. With Mom's build-up of the man, I began to believe that Dr. Gallman, once he met me, would see right through me. Though I had been living as godly a life as I could after Billy Graham's Madison Square Garden altar call, I still wasn't sure about the whole born-again experience those around me presumed I had had. But instead of focusing on that, or perhaps because of such doubts, I busied myself with helping start a Christian youth coffee house in the rambling old antebellum mansion that had sat vacant for years next to Trinity Methodist Church's sanctuary. Some had suggested that the almost dilapidated dwelling was haunted but I had long ago gotten over my fear of such places. I had come to accept, after all that had happened to me, including a bit of prompting from Matty May I could never quite shake, that "haunted" was, in fact, the best way to describe my life. "Lawd be, child. Why you carry on like you done at that carnival?" Matty had asked me after Mom told her what had happened that night. "Witches ain't supposed to carry on like that around folkses. Folkses is supposed to carry on like that around witches. When you comes right down to it—Matty be right about dis—yo' mama'n'-daddy is haints. A boy with haints for his mama'n'daddy ain't got no right to such foolishness. Haints is what loves ya. You shouldn't—ah-woe!—boo-hoo at nothin' that says boo at ya, child. Might be Miz Nan and that fine husband a'hern just a'sayin' hello."

Haints or not, I was excited about fixing up the old mansion and even came up with a name for the place: House of the Rising Son. We hosted visiting youth choirs there and served refreshments and had group discussions about what sorts of things kids my age might be unduly influenced by during those days—Vietnam protesters, *Bob and Carol and Ted and Alice*, tabs of LSD, Boone's Farm wine. One Saturday night a duo called the Two Lynns arrived from Jackson and entertained us, one of them, the Liza Minnelli look-alike, catching my eye and engaging me in whispered conversation in one of the house's corners. We joked about our matching shag haircuts and confided to each other that we really wanted to go into show business, a different kind of missionary field but one that held us in its thrall. I loved hanging out there and singing Christian folk songs. My favorite was "Pass It On." Its first lyric, "It only takes a spark to get a fire going," was appropriate, for the House of the Rising Son lasted only a matter of months before it burned to the ground. "Faulty wiring is as good a guess as any, is what the fire chief said," my grandfather told me when he broke the news to me. "The good Lord's too busy these days with all that's going on in the world to stoop to electrical work, I guess." He drove me up to the remains of the place the next morning, parking our old blue square-fendered Plymouth Fury III beneath the oak that towered over the front lawn. The smoldering sight broke my healing heart. When we got out of the car, Pop put his hand on my shoulder like he had done when I stood at my mother's open casket. It did seem like something had died. And, like at that casket, I felt the stirrings of the Witch Boy well up inside me, for I did not feel sorrow but anger at what I was seeing. I did not want to pray. I wanted to incant, to retrieve those black-magic sounds I had placed beneath my mother's pillow in her coffin now buried out there in Harperville, and sling them into the smoke that still stubbornly billowed in isolated pockets of scorched lumber. A bluejay, a scavenger's sense of tragedy no doubt guiding its wings, alighted on the hood of our Plymouth. I wondered if it were a sign and decided it was just a bird.

Dr. Gallman had a rather avian look himself that first night of the revival at Harperville Methodist where he sat perched in the high-backed chair behind the pulpit waiting to start his sermon. I tried not to stare at him but every time he turned his head in front of the choir loft my heart jumped a bit, like some frightened field mouse, at his hawklike profile. Though not as handsome as Billy Graham, Dr. Gallman still possessed the magnetism that all great preachers possess. They hold you, such preachers, in their physical sway even as they appeal to your spiritual hunger. I watched him—gray-haired, a little over sixty years old, I estimated, that beaklike nose of his seeming to be sniffing the very air in the church now for lost souls—as he surveyed this little country congregation to whom he was about to preach. I did not so much sense condescension as I did some profound recognition on his part. At that very moment, his eyes came to rest on me and did not move on to anybody else. Just as I had thought. He was seeing right into me, spotting the vestiges of my witchery. Yet he did not seem bothered by what he was seeing. A grin—a bit more devilish than the one that years later would flicker across Billy Graham's face when that German shepherd found Kim's shoulder—parted almost imperceptibly the somber set of his lips. Had he just nodded my way? I blushed at the thought of his acknowledgment.

A hymn was announced and we all stood to sing it before he took his place behind the pulpit. Once there, he asked us all to bow our heads in prayer. I always kept my head bowed in church back then until I heard the requisite amen, but this one time I opened my eyes early, thinking I could steal a glance at him. When I looked up he was still staring right at me as the rote words of his prayer were rounding their preacher-like bend to his pronouncement of "in God's name we pray; amen." Heads lifted and he, in turn, lifted a huge notebook into the air over his head and slammed it to the floor. I jumped at the sound of the thing hitting the platform where he stood, a sharp purposeful report like that of the starting gun brandished by my junior high track coach. Dr. Gallman's voice, full-throated, thrilling in its sonorous reaches, took off at full sprint toward its own finish line. "I was prepared to preach a whole other sermon," he said. "Had it written out right there in that book," he thundered, pointing to the leather-bound holder, its pages having come undone from the ringed binder and now spread in disarray all over the floor around him. "But the Holy Ghost is moving me tonight to talk about a whole other subject. I hope you'll bear with me and humor an old preacher glad to be home in Mississippi, back where he belongs. Being here at this little country church has brought back memories of my own orphaned childhood, when I was raised by a grandmama who would bring me to a church just like this one, where I first accepted Jesus Christ as my Lord and Savior." Sweat was already appearing on his forehead. The energy he was emitting that night, as he improvised his way through his sermon, was that of a much younger man. I sat there mesmerized by how similar our stories were, how he had once felt as lost as I was feeling, how he had gone through the motions of "being the good boy that everyone expected me to be but knew deep down that all that goodness was just something I could keep pouring into that empty bottomless hole in my soul," which was a pretty good description, as far as I could tell, for my "Jesus-freakiness." It was as if the sermon were being tailored especially for me. By the end of it, when he made the invitation to "come and accept Jesus as your Lord and Savior, let Him fill up that empty hole in your soul with grace, not goodness," I was the first one up and moving down the aisle. My heart had not pounded so since that day I made my way to Miss Ishee's office to hear the news I knew awaited me of my mother's death. I knelt at the altar that night and wept with relief. This, I was certain now, was what being born again felt like. Dr. Gallman kicked those pages on the floor out of his way and crouched before me on the other side of the altar. He held me in his arms, held me like he knew he was going to hold me since that first moment he saw me sitting on that pew. He had targeted my soul that night. No doubt about it. He whispered over and over in my ear as I continued to weep, "Let it out, son, let Jesus love you, let it out, Jesus loves you, let Him love you, let it out, let Him in, let it out, let Him in." He rocked me to and fro. I was saved. I had never been surer of anything in my life.

In the months that followed, Dr. Gallman and I carried on a stilted though heartfelt correspondence. He would write me from bucolic retreats he referred to as "Christian ashrams" on his many postcards from the Smoky Mountains. He told me such retreats were filled with young boys like me who lived in tents for a few days and became one with nature as well as with God. As the correspondence continued, he wrote in even more detail in sealed letters about how alike we two were, based on our life stories, how he understood me in ways that most adults could not, how he knew in the deepest part of his own soul what I was going through because he had once gone through it also, how we could always trust one another, no matter what, how I was not to show those letters to another person, not even my grandmother. "The postcards are for both you and her, but the letters are just between you and me. And God," he wrote. He sent me Bible verses to study. He loved the book of Proverbs. Two of his favorite verses were from the eighteenth chapter. "Death and life are in the power of the tongue" was one. The other: "A fool hath no delight in understanding, but that his heart may discover itself." After he wrote the latter one to me, he signed the letter: Your foolish, Dr. Gallman (Andy). I studied the letters every night, reading them over and over, then turned to the Bible and read his recommended sections. In so doing, I felt closer to God. And him.

One of his letters informed me he was making a return trip to Mississippi for some fundraising in Jackson. In it, he asked if I thought that my grandmother would let me come visit him for the night. His letters and postcards had been interspersed with regular phone calls, making sure I passed the receiver over to Mom so the two of them could carry on a bit of conversation. She was growing close to him also and was delighted that he had taken such an interest in me. She could see how happy it was making me, how I had no longer seemed so lost or felt so unloved. A few weeks later, after giving her consent and convincing a reluctant Pop of the idea, she and I were both happy to see Dr. Gallman turn into our gravel drive in his Mercedes sedan. I had packed an overnight bag and climbed in the car with him. Though I was newly thirteen and not exactly sure what I would be doing in Jackson with a man of Dr. Gallman's age, I was still excited about the trip. I loved being a reborn Christian, but, if I were being honest with myself, I did not want to spend all night reading Bible verses from Proverbs or listening to him talk to me as if he were delivering a sermon. When we got onto the Interstate, he pulled his Mercedes over on the side of the road and asked if I might want to get behind the wheel for the forty miles it took to get to Jackson. I had ridden before in my cousin Jim's Mercedes, but not even Jim had been nice enough to me to let me drive it. I climbed behind the wheel as Dr. Gallman slid over to the passenger's side of the front seat. I started back out onto the Interstate as he, yes, coached me through it, patting my leg for reassurance much like "Chunkin'" Charlie had done when he broke the news about my mother's death, like Uncle Benny did right before he'd show me how the horse bit the apple. But it was different, too. Gentler? No. Stronger? Slightly. What it was was soothing, but strangely so. I wanted him to stop touching my leg but I didn't want to tell him to.

Dr. Gallman had no plans lined up after we arrived at the Downtowner Hotel in the middle of Capital Street in Jackson. His only plan, in fact, seemed to be to hang out with me and see what transpired. As he had already checked into his room a day earlier, we went on up. His Bible was opened on the bedside table and I put my bag onto the one queen-size bed that was there beside it. He opened up the newspaper to check to see what movies were playing at the Paramount Theater a few blocks down on Capital Street, or at the Lamar on another downtown street close by us. *Five Easy Pieces* was at the Paramount and *Women in Love* at the Lamar. "Don't think that Jack Nicholson movie is quite right for a boy your age, by what I've read about it," he said. "And I'm certain nothing based on anything by D. H. Lawrence would be suitable." He put the paper down and stared at me for a long moment where I sat on the edge of the bed. It didn't seem like he wanted to leave the room but thought he had to entertain me in some way. "Why don't we just take a walk?" he finally asked. I shrugged and followed him out. We meandered around the deserted downtown streets and talked about God and Jesus and how forgiving They both were. We walked by the old Capitol building and the big white governor's mansion where then-governor John Bell Williams resided. Mom had been a big supporter of his because, though a Democrat congressman from the state, he had raised money for Barry Goldwater in 1964 and been stripped of his seniority in the House of Representatives for such an act. He came home to Mississippi a hero and was quickly elected governor. He had been a strict segregationist since he was twenty-seven and first elected to congress in 1946, the youngest man ever to serve in the House of Reprsentatives from Mississippi. After the Supreme Court handed down its

Brown v. Board of Education decision, doing away with the concept of separate-but-equal, he took to the House floor and denounced the day of the decision as "Black Monday." Dr. Gallman listened intently as I told him all of this. "How do you know so much about Governor Williams?" he asked after it all came nervously rushing out of me as we stood staring at the mansion. I told him that Mom and I discussed politics as much as we discussed Jesus Christ and though we agreed about the latter, we increasingly disagreed about the former. "Mom's love of Jesus just makes her more conservative and mine makes me more liberal. How's that possible?" I asked him, trying to get him to talk to me instead of just staring my way.

"Everything, son, is possible in Christ," was his answer as he rubbed my back a bit between my shoulder blades. "Christ is all-encompassing," he continued. "He's brought us together, has He not? And look at us—an ugly old man like me and a beautiful boy like you. There is no age, though, where believers are concerned. We are all the same age in Christ. You getting hungry? I saw a Krystal hamburger place back there on Capital. How many Krystals can you eat at one time?" he asked.

"Most I've ever eaten is four," I told him, Krystals being the Southern equivalent of White Castles, little, square, onion-topped burgers that melted in your mouth. "I've got an Aunt Drucy who calls 'em Kryschal's," I said, coming up with more conversation, but he didn't know what to make of that.

"I think I'd like something more substantial," he said. "Why don't we just eat at the restaurant in the Downtowner?"

"That's okay," I told him, and we walked back to the hotel.

For most of the dinner we sat in silence until he asked me if I read many books. I told him about my sixth-grade book report on *Valley of the Dolls.* "Well then, maybe D. H. Lawrence isn't out of your league after all," he said, that devilish grin of his parting, more perceptibly this time, the somber set of his lips. "Have you read any Faulkner yet?" his asked. "Or that local woman everybody goes on about down here, the one that wrote about why somebody lives somewhere."

"Eudora Welty," I told him. "Yeah, I've just started reading her. You're talking about 'Why I Live at the P.O.' That's a good story. I've read that one. Faulkner's too hard. I don't know if I'm old enough for him."

"I'm not sure any of us are old enough for Faulkner," Dr. Gallman said, and took a bite of his steak. As he chewed, he contemplated that last remark. "But I must say that if you're old enough for Jacqueline Susann then I think you might be able to handle William Faulkner. I don't read much anymore myself except for financial reports and the Bible and the morning newspaper," he said. "In seminary I read a lot of John Wesley, of course."

When we arrived back at the room Dr. Gallman immediately stripped down to his boxer shorts. His body looked a lot like Pop's and I was glad he didn't wear tight white briefs pulled up on his old stomach like my grandfather did. Boxer shorts made more sense for men of their age. I went into the bathroom and put on the gym shorts I slept in and took off my shirt. I checked my hair in the mirror, shaking my shag into place. When I came back into the room Dr. Gallman was leafing through his Bible. Without looking up from the text, he asked me if I had a girlfriend. I told him I did not. He nodded, seemingly pleased by the news, and ran his finger along a few verses he was focused on. "I think we should turn in early. Never much on television, and the trip to pick you up on top of all my other recent travels wore me out today. Ready for bed?" he asked.

"Should I sleep on the couch?" I wanted to know.

"I think there's enough room for both of us here," he said, patting the bed beside him. "Do you say a prayer before you turn in at night like I suggested in one of my letters?" he asked.

"Yes, sir. You're right, too. It helps me sleep better sometimes."

"Not all the time?"

"No, sir."

"I'll make sure you sleep tonight. I have a few tricks. Let's pray first, though," he said and knelt before me. "I spend too many nights alone kneeling by hotel beds," he confessed, motioning for me to join him by his side. I hesitated—I always said my bedtime prayers silently, with my head already on the pillow—but since I was his guest I went along with his routine. I thought it the polite thing to do and Mom had warned me about my manners before he had come to pick me up that day. I knelt beside him and we both bowed our heads. His voice took on that sonorous tone, though a quieter version of it, the one it could take on when he was behind a pulpit. I flinched—rudely so? would Mom be mad at such a flinch?—when he reached out during his prayer and again rubbed my back between my shoulder blades. "Amen," he said and tousled my shag, touching my bangs where they fell down into my eyes and pushing them back a bit. "Amen," I said, too.

Before we climbed into bed he took some papers out of his brief-case to read by the lamp on his side of the bed. I picked up his Bible and read the passages he had chosen to highlight, flattered that he trusted me enough to let me do it. I remember being perplexed, as I held his personal Bible and perused it, at how something so sacred could also feel almost illicit. After a while, he put his papers down and took the Bible from me and, reaching across my body, placed it, still open, on the bedside table there beside me. "You seemed tense between your shoulders when I was touching your back. Maybe it was all that driving you did today," he said, and I felt flattered by the reason he had come up with for my tension. It made me sound like I was a real teenager and not someone who had just left twelve behind. "Here. Let's try something," he said and stood. He told me to get out of bed and lean back against his body as he wrapped his arms around me from behind and succeeded in cracking my back several times. "Did you hear your spine give way? You needed that.

You're more tense than I thought. Has no one ever cracked your back before?"

"No, sir. That was a first," I said.

"Lie down. Go on. Do as I say," he commanded, summoning once more his sonorous voice, yet the tone this time was slightly different, breathier perhaps, a little anxious. "Let me give you a massage." I lay on my stomach atop the bed. He began to touch me. His fingers, pressing firmly against my flesh, couldn't stop trembling. Was it his encroaching old age? Was it the result of the room's air conditioning? Was he suddenly as oddly nervous as I was feeling? "We used to do this to each other in seminary," he said. "Seminary can be quite stressful. Really hard subjects. Maybe you'll find out one day," he said as he continued to knead my back muscles, daring to let his fingers find the ones right there above my buttocks. "Have you ever thought about attending seminary, Kevin? You'd make a fine preacher. You are certainly charismatic. But you really are tense. I think you might need a pill to sleep." He abruptly stopped the massage and went into the bathroom. He came out with a glass of water and a pill in his out-stretched hand. I wondered if it were like one of those dolls Neely liked to down. "Take this," he said. "You'll sleep like a baby. Better than a prayer, I have to admit." I took the glass of water from him and stared at the pill now in my own hand. I hesitated. "Swallow it," he told me. "Do as I say." I did and fell fast asleep.

Late the next morning I was awakened by one of the hotel's maids trying to get into the room in order to clean it, but the chain latch still attached to the door stopped her from entering. "God! We'll be out in a minute," Dr. Gallman said with an angry groan where he lay close behind me, his breath rancid and hot against my ear. He had his hand down my gym shorts and was masturbating me. The inside of his fist, tightening about my erection, felt oddly smooth for a man. I had not noticed such smoothness the night before when he massaged my back. I thought I might be dreaming. But as he continued to grab my cock I realized it was not a dream, not at all. I focused on the smoothness of his palm as he pulled on my foreskin, a palm much smoother than Matty's callused one that could calm me so when I rubbed those calluses over and over as I fell asleep with my head in her lap. It was as smooth, the inside of his fist, as Mom's enfeebled one after it had been dipped in paraffin and she let me run my fingers along it before I peeled it off for her after she had done her rehabilitative exercises the physical therapist had taught me how to talk her through. It was the smoothness of his touch as much as the masturbation itself which I found so alarming. It sickened me. I felt as if I were going to throw up right there in the bed. What else had this smooth-palmed old man done to me during the night? Should I stall until he removed his hand before I got up? He had to know I was awakened by the maid at the door and his response to her, the smell of his rapid breath increasingly repellent on the back of my neck. I said a silent prayer for him to stop. But he would not. He would not stop even when he heard me trying not to cry as I stared at the upside-down verses from Proverbs in his opened Bible on the bedside table where he had placed it the night before, after reaching across me and brushing my stomach with his hairy arm. I could not help it—tears were now coming—and I thought of that night I tried not to cry in the kitchen when Mom held me after Billy Graham's crusade and told me I had to find a way to let myself be loved.

I ejaculated.

Fear. Anger. Utter sadness. They all surfaced to mix forever with my emerging sexuality, the same sexuality that Dr. Gallman had no doubt spotted that first time he saw me in my pew at Harperville Methodist church, the same fear, the same anger, the same utter sadness I felt that night when I begged my toga-clad mother not to tell my daddy about my naked exploits with my tomboy neighbor in that baseball dugout back in Pelahatchie. I felt as confused and oddly powerful lying there in that hotel bed with Dr. Gallman's hand down my gym shorts that morning as I did that night so many years before, when my father finally got home and everything erupted around me before I, safe in the knowledge that I was the repository of family secrets, could tell my mother the one I shared with my father, the one I never even told her—though "Dare I?" I thought, "Dare I?"—on her death bed. I lay there in Dr. Gallman's grip and blocked out any thoughts of what the old man was doing to me with only those of my father and what he told me never to tell another soul. All through my childhood I could put myself in a comforting trance—as I had done the day of my mother's funeral when I sat on the chenille bedspread—if I made myself concentrate on those few secret moments my father and I alone shared. Dr. Gallman continued to squeeze at the head of my cock for any last drops of sperm he could coax to the surface. I closed my eyes. I became completely still. The trance commenced.

———————

I spotted my father crawling in the bushes behind the Simpson Lady's house next door when my mother had taken Kim and Karole for an overnight visit to Forest. There had been yet another spat between my parents. It was only a few days after my father's baseball accident sliding into second and my mother had wanted him to quit the team. He refused. She took Kim and Karole and fled to my grandparents' house, leaving me behind, knowing how my sissy presence irritated him. Usually I would have hated being abandoned by her and left in his strict clutches, but I had become fascinated by the sight of that white plastic whiplash collar attached to his neck. Also, since he had been taking the painkillers that came with the collar he had been much nicer to me. I liked him better when he took those pills—my first exposure to dolls, I see now—because he liked me better, too. My girlishness amused him when he was high on those pills instead of, as it usually did, leaving him fearful, angry, utterly sad. He even let me pretend we were having a tea party at the kitchen table that night, getting down some of my mother's good china to use as props. I watched his temples pulse as he chewed the imaginary cake I served him, though he had begun to fidget with his silverware. "You go on serving yourself this make-believe Betty Crocker shit," he suddenly said. "Daddy's got something he's gotta do. You stay here," he said and fled outside. I put a chair next to the backdoor after he carefully closed it and climbed up to pull the curtain back a bit and peek out at what he was up to. I caught a glimpse of the whiplash collar's white plastic glinting in the the moonlight as it moved along down low, there next door in the Simpson Lady's bushes. I put the chair back, took one more sip of the tea I pretended was in my cup, and snuck outside. I tiptoed over to watch him crawling in the dark on his hands and knees in the flower bed in the back of the Simpson Lady's house. I silently watched as he reached her bathroom window. He started to stand, careful not to make any noise himself, and I shocked him by pulling on his pants leg where I, following his example, had crawled up behind him. For a moment he did not know what to do, but decided he should make a game out of it all. "Want to see, Kev-inator?" he whispered, putting his fingers to his lips to make sure I continued to make no noise. He lifted me on his shoulders and I wrapped my legs around that cool white plastic that encased his neck, so soothing in the humid nighttime heat. I peeked in the window. I saw the Simpson Lady's son sitting on the toilet. I saw him wipe his ass. His naked mother was taking a bath in the sudsy water before him, her breasts as white as the collar around my father's neck. She asked her son if he wanted to sing in the church choir. I shifted on my father's neck trying to get a better angle at what I was seeing and he let out a loud groan of pain. The Simpson Lady heard us at the window and screamed for her husband. My father dropped me to the ground. He hissed, "Run like hell for home!" a bit of advice that's kept me running ever since. He let me scamper in front of him at first but scooped me up when I wasn't escaping fast enough. Coco barked wildly at us as we ran past her pen. In a matter of seconds we were sitting back down at the kitchen table, both of us out of breath. I started right up again, pretending I was serving my father tea. He reached out and fiercely grabbed me. I thought I was about to be hit. Instead he held me closely to his chest. "Don't breathe a word of this to another soul," he said. "We're on the same team now, you and me, Kevinator. This is our secret. Don't you never tell nobody. This is between you and me. We're teammates, you and me, *teammates*." His heart was beating wildly where my ear was pressed next to his chest, as wildly as my own heart was beating as Dr. Gallman gripped me tightly one last time before he let me go.

I opened my eyes.

Dr. Gallman's palm lingered over my sperm. I stared again at his opened Bible. He sighed against my neck—relieved, ashamed, unsure how exactly to deal with me now—like my father sighed against it, all those years before when he held me at the kitchen table and we finished drinking our imaginary tea. Was he, my father, the Peeping Tom, or was I? Dr. Gallman took his hand away. Proverbs, upside down, remained unreadable.

Nothing was said as Dr. Gallman and I readied ourselves for breakfast that morning. He finished showering and got dressed in front of me. After perfectly knotting his necktie without even looking in the mirror, he said, "I'm going to go down to buy a newspaper and get us a table at that restaurant off the lobby. Want me to order you eggs or pancakes?"

I shrugged.

The mention of food made me feel even sicker. "Let's say pancakes," he decided. When he shut the door I ran to the bathroom. I knelt at the toilet. I tried to vomit but could not. The maid entered. She wet a washcloth and put it to my head. "You okay?" she asked, yet another gentle black woman coming to my rescue. "What was a'goin' on in here this mo'nin'?"

I shrugged.

When I arrived at the restaurant downstairs it was filled with African Americans of a different sort dressed in their hippest show-biz finery even though it wasn't yet noon. The neon colors of their big-collared shirts shone under the restaurant's lights. "I asked the waitress about all these people," Dr. Gallman said when he saw me looking around at our fellow diners. "Some famous Negro singer was down the street last night performing at the Mississippi Coliseum. This is his retinue. If I had known about it we could have gotten tickets. Would you have liked that?"

I shrugged yet again. I could not look Dr. Gallman in the face. I looked down at the floor instead and saw a pair of platform shoes coming my way. I gazed up past the tight red bell-bottom pants and saw that it was James Brown walking by to sit at the table next to us. Dr. Gallman did not recognize him. He spoke instead about some headline in the morning's *Clarion-Ledger* that concerned Spiro Agnew. He then asked me if we could see each other again the next time he came to Mississippi.

"Sure," I softly said.

I watched James Brown eat his scrambled eggs.

5

Audrey Whatshername

I lied. I do remember more than just watching the World Series in Mrs. Thompson's class when I was in fifth grade. I wish I didn't. But I do. I tried to ignore it, but it is a memory that inserts itself into my life at the oddest of moments just as it inserts itself here into this, the heightened narrative of my life. It is the secret I have always kept paired with the one I shared with my father. They are the tandem essentials of all residual secrets. I apologize to my father. I vowed to him never to reveal what happened at that bathroom window. It is a vow I had always kept until now. But breaking that one has freed me to go ahead and break another. What was it my little tomboy neighbor said to me in that dugout when we were naked and nobody then yet knew what we had done? "We just kids. We just do stuff. It's *tellin'* that makes it bad," she said. I've heard her wrongheaded voice inside my own head my whole life. No more. I've told. I'm telling. I'll tell.

During that fifth-grade year, my fascination with Arlene Francis gave way to a more refined crush on Audrey Whatshername, as I always liked to refer to Audrey Hepburn in deference to the memory of my father regaling his cracker-ass cronies about his love of "little-titted" women. My own little-titted mama loved Whatshername as well. One of my favorite things in all the world was to accompany my mother to the movies over in Jackson and she likewise loved to take me along, even paying for an extra ticket during the reserved-seat engagement of *Cleopatra* at the Paramount. However, it was at the Lamar where I had noticed posters announcing an upcoming Audrey Whatshername movie when my mother and Miz Kirby had gone there to see a Gig Young picture. My mother agreed to bring me back with her to see Audrey when I begged her to, nonstop, at the snack bar, so fascinated was I by the images of such a creature in the stills and poster from the upcoming film. The big black sunglasses Whatshername wore in a few of the stills added to the confused yearning I felt for her, because my father wore similar big black sunglasses himself when he was coaching or playing any outdoor sport. My mother agreed to bring me back to see Audrey Whatshername just to shut me up. "Yes, for godsake, we'll come back to see *Breakfast at Tiffany's*," she had said. "Stop tugging at me so."

My adoration of Audrey grew later on, when I saw her in *My Fair Lady*. That performance confirmed my crush on her and banished Arlene Francis for good from my fevered daydreams. I saw the film soon after my parents' successive deaths, and her transformation in it made me believe I could transform myself, too, once I escaped Mississippi—the very lusciousness of the film helping alleviate the bare-bones mourning from which I suffered back then. I began to watch for Whatshername's chic image—and her chic image alone—

in every movie magazine Aunt Gladys bought for me when I went to visit her in Van Winkle.

By the time *Wait Until Dark* made its way to the Town Theater in Forest, I was besotted. I knew the movie was going to be a scary experience because all the kids in school were talking about the poster that Old Lady Jacobs, the harridan who owned and ran the Town Theater, had put up for a whole month before the film's arrival. On it, Warner Bros. had printed a warning: "During the last eight minutes of this picture the theater will be darkened to the legal limit to heighten the terror of the breathtaking climax, which takes place in total darkness on the screen. In those sections where smoking is permitted those patrons are respectfully requested not to jar the effect by lighting up during this sequence. And, of course, no one will be seated at this time."

Mom told me she wasn't sure that the movie was appropriate for me, as I had enough nightmares on my own, but I convinced her to let me go if I could come up with the money myself, knowing, of course, I could. I went into my closet and opened *Pale Horse, Pale Rider*. The year before I had taken the four quarters I earned picking cotton up at Uncle Benny's farm and Scotch-taped them into the inside cover of the book. I had honored Matty's wishes and saved them for a special Saturday matinee. There was not going to be a more special one than this.

It was a warm early-December day as matinee time approached, so I was allowed—if I wore the heavy sweater Mom laid out for me on my bed—to ride my Western Auto Western Flyer bike the few miles it took to get to the theater, which sat across from the county jail up in town. I had just enough money (Pop slipped me an extra quarter) to buy a ticket, a box of Milk Duds, and a small mixed drink, which was all the varieties of soda in the fountain—Coca-Cola, Mountain Dew, Dr. Pepper, and 7-Up—pressed into one cup full of crushed ice.

Old Lady Jacobs had hung a couple of new posters of coming attractions in the lobby. One was for *Thoroughly Modern Millie* starring Julie Andrews. The other was for *Hillbillys in a Haunted House* starring Ferlin Husky, Joi Lansing, and Lon Chaney Jr., the follow-up of one of the biggest hits the Town had screened the year before, *Las Vegas Hillbillies*, in which Ferlin had costarred with Jayne Mansfield and Mamie Van Doren, two women too big-titted, I concluded while downing an earlier box of Milk Duds, for my dead daddy's taste.

I had misjudged the time it would take to ride my bike into town. When I walked inside the theater with my Milk Duds and mixed drink the place was already packed. Having always had a phobia about sitting in any seat in a movie theater that is not on an aisle, I tried to find one in the section where all the school kids sat, over to the left side, but I was unable to. Mad at myself for getting to the matinee late, I circled back through the lobby. I went to the other side of the theater. I found an aisle seat in the middle section where the adults always sat. Pouting, I plopped down and waited for Whatshername's image to flicker to life up in front of me.

A man hurried into the darkened theater and sat down beside me right before the movie started. He quickly began to frighten me more than anything up there onscreen. The story concerned a doll—yet another one in my life—that Audrey accidentally had in her possession and the villain who wanted it back because it contained a stash of heroin. The plot was convoluted and circumstantial, but I was mesmerized by Audrey's beauty and "mosquito-bite" breasts, as my father liked to describe them. I also have to admit I was equally mesmerized by the outline—there is no other way to put this—of her pussy so visible in her tight beige pants. It disconcerted me that I noticed that. She's the only woman to this day who ever made me glad to notice such a thing. By the time Audrey Whatshername's character had figured out what was going on up on the screen, I had figured out that the man sitting next to me wanted to touch my cock. I had been hard for most of the movie, especially every time Whatsher-name's outlined pussy came into view. It had taken the man next to me over an hour but he had finally gotten up the nerve to drop his hand into my lap. I had removed my heavy sweater soon after I sat down and it now covered his determination as he undid my pants and maneuvered his hand inside.

I had had to pee for most of the movie, but was afraid I'd miss something if I went to the bathroom. I had also been waiting for my erection to subside, so I could pee more easily. But there was no holding it in any longer, especially with what was going on beneath my sweater. I pushed the man's hand away and buttoned my pants. I headed for the bathroom. It was the moment in the movie when Audrey discovered that her phone wire had been cut and she couldn't call the police. Her face was pressed against the railing of the stairs that led down to her basement apartment on St. Luke's Place, a block in Greenwich Village that I often went out of my way to meander along when I first moved to New York City, remembering each and every time I found myself on the bend of that lovely block the day in the Town Theater when I had first been touched by a stranger.

At the lobby door, about to open it, I turned back to look at Audrey. Instead, I saw the man get up to follow me. I hurried into the bathroom's stall. Before I could lock the stall's door—had I hesitated?—he pushed in behind me. I had to make a snap decision between heading back out to a victimized Audrey or staying inside the bathroom's stall and allowing my own victimization to begin that day, a victimization—I hate that word but there is no other for it—that led me right to Dr. Gallman two years later. When he was sitting in that church before his sermon out in Harperville and I thought he was sniffing out souls to save, he was instead, I am certain of it, sniffing at the stench of that bathroom stall that still adhered to me, that adheres still. The man locked the stall door. He knelt before me. I put my penis inside his roughly whiskered mouth. I bent down trying to find his own penis. "Don't touch that," he warned me. He straightened me up and touched my hips. He pulled me deeper into his throat and guided my body until it instinctively began to pump him back and forth. I couldn't hold it any longer: I pissed a little inside his mouth. He pulled away and reached up and grabbed me by the neck. He spit my bit of piss in my face. "You stupid little *fuck*," he whispered that word that had worked so well after my mother's funeral. "I've heard tell of you," he said, putting his mouth right next to me. Was he going to kiss me? Was he going to make me kiss him back? He tightened his grip on my neck. "You that boy that ain't got no mama," he said. "Daddy kilt in a car wreck. Front page of the *Scott Fucking County Times*. But it don't stop people from talkin' bout you and the way you act. You know that? I seen you walk in here this afternoon, you fuckin' sissy piece of shit. I followed you in. I knew you'd do this. *I knew it*." He smelled like he'd eaten bacon that morning for breakfast and washed it down with a beer. He banged my head against the stall and continued to strangle me. I assumed I must be turning blue, as blue as I was the moment I was born and Mom ran from the delivery room thinking I was a stillbirth. I wondered if I would die right there. I wondered if my parents would recognize me when I died. I wondered if the man was going to press a little harder against my neck. I wondered if I would like that. Abruptly, he let me go and fled from the stall. I sat on the pot. I pushed my still hard penis between my legs and pissed some more. "That's the way girls piss, Kevinator," my father had told me once when he caught me peeing that way. "Stand up," he had demanded and pulled me toward him in mid-piss, my spraying urine running down both our legs. I blew my nose on some toilet tissue inside the stall. I wiped the bit of piss and spittle from my face. I masturbated the rest of the way. I sponged the sperm from the top of my penis with more tissue. I tried to conjure a trance to comfort me. I sat completely still. I pictured the Simpson Lady's son on their own pot back in Pelahatchie. I pictured my legs around my father's neck. I pictured us drinking imaginary tea. I reached up under myself and gently touched my butthole with one of my fingers. I felt its outline and pretended it was Whatshername's pussy. I heard the audience scream inside the theater and wanted to get back to my seat. I pulled on my pants. I did not wash my face and hands. I did not look at myself in the mirror.

I walked out into the lobby and headed back inside for the end of the movie. "Where do you think you're going, young man?" Old Lady Jacobs asked from behind the snack bar. She had a greasy pageboy that never seemed shampooed, her blond hair having gone that dull gray that blondes go, a mottle of gunmetal strands always caught up in the black-framed reading glasses she mostly wore pushed up on top of her head. The only times she lowered the glasses were when ringing up ticket sales or when a customer wanted her attention there where she stood next to the popcorn machine and soda spigots. She also always had a flashlight holstered to her belt to pull out and shine in a moviegoer's eyes if we had our feet propped up on the seats in front of us. She was one tough little crone, but I had a soft place in my moviegoing heart for her. "You can't go back in there. No way," she said, leaning her elbows on the candy counter in front of her. She took her flashlight out of its holster and laid it on the counter next to her, like it was her pistol and she was going to try and negotiate with me first. "It's the last eight minutes. I've turned the lights all the way off, like the poster said," she told me. "No seating now. That's the rule. Who was that man that just ran out of here? By the looks of him he should be in that jail yonder and not in my theater."

I shrugged. I heard Audrey Whatshername shouting for help inside. She shouted it three times. I stared at Julie Andrews on the *Thoroughly Modern Millie* poster. I read Beatrice Lillie's name in big type toward the bottom of it. It said on the poster that Lillie played someone named Mrs. Meers in the movie. Julie Andrews had a black-and-white checked cap on. The audience inside loudly screamed. I jumped. Old Lady Jacobs laughed. "People are getting their money's worth, I guess," she said and re-holstered her flashlight. I turned my attention to the poster for *Hillbillys in a Haunted House*. An illustration of a King Kong–like gorilla was carrying a beautifully frightened blonde who wore a low-cut dress. She looked familiar. Someone in the audience screamed again. Others nervously giggled. Henry Mancini's score was building. Where had I seen the beautiful blonde before? That must be Joi Lansing, I reasoned as I reread the poster, but where had I seen her? The word *Hillbillys* in the title jogged my memory. Of course: She played Gladys, Lester Flatt's glamorous wife, on *The Beverly Hillbillies*. I thought of my aunt with the same first name and all those movie magazines she always made sure she had for me to read. I thought of Uncle Toy and his glass eye and how he liked to give me a nickel so I could punch in that Ferlin Husky song he liked so much, "Timber, I'm Falling," on his jukebox. I thought of Aunt Drucy telling her juke joint customers to put that dead soldier in a vat of cooking grease. I kept staring at Joi Lansing's big breasts and knew that my dead daddy wouldn't like them. I looked at the word *Hillbillys* once more. I wondered why it was spelled incorrectly. My mother would not approve. I wished I were back in that Lamar Theater lobby with her in Jackson looking at earlier images of Audrey Whatshername, who screamed again in the dark. I kept thinking about the Lamar and how I had tugged at my mother that day, begging her to bring me back to see Whatshername. I wanted, just one more time, just one more, to tug at my mother. Instead I sniffed the finger I had just used to touch my butthole. I thought of Audrey's outlined pussy. I thought of my eleven-year-old one. I kept my finger at my nose—was this how I smelled? this?—until the lobby doors swung open and the audience, laughing at how scared they had been, emerged.

6

Pee Wee Reese, Dizzy Dean, and Erik Estrada

When I first started to masturbate, I'd lie in my bath water and, before ejaculating, I'd put my face in the curve at the back of the tub so my voice would be acoustically enhanced by the porcelain, and I'd sing some of the songs I had sung at Trinity Methodist when I was younger and my soprano hadn't embarrassed me so. "The Church in the Wildwood" remained one of my favorites. I'd sing its lyric quietly to myself as I pulled on my penis:

> There's a church in the valley by the wildwood,
> no lovelier spot in the dale.
> No place is so dear to my childhood
> as the little brown church in the vale.

(Oh, come, come, come, come)
Come to the church in the wildwood.
Oh, come to the church in the dale.
No spot is so dear to my childhood
as the little brown church in the vale.

I was singing that verse and chorus over and over one night, after
my experience with Dr. Gallman at the Downtowner Hotel in Jackson, when I suddenly began to fantasize about him masturbating me
with his sickeningly smooth hand. The thought upset me, and I
quickly replaced it with Billy Graham's handsomer visage, his own
voice summoning me in his soothing North Carolinian accent when
he made his altar call, "Come, come, come, come," until that memory of my own voice, "Cum, cum, cum," teasing Bobby Thompson
back at our fourth-grade cafeteria table, overtook everything else and
I shot a hot stream of sperm into the bathwater. Gallman to Graham
to Thompson. It sounded like a double play my father would describe
when making me watch Roger Maris and the New York Yankees on
television on Saturday afternoons. Two men with the funny names of
Pee Wee and Dizzy were the commentators for the game. "Dizzy was
born up in Arkansas but we claim him here in Mississippi," my father
would brag. He would make me stop pretending I was vacuuming and
dusting the furniture when Maris, who, like my father, threw right-
handed but batted from the left, came to the plate. "Dizzy once broke
a toe, back when he played for the Cardinals—think it was during an
All-Star game—and had to come up with a whole new wind-up from
the pitcher's mound. Gave up his fastball for a change-up and a slow
curve. That's what you always got to do, Kevinator. When you break
a toe, come up with a new way to pitch. That pretty much sums up
everything in life. Baseball—can't beat it. People think I love basketball, but baseball's what broke my heart. That's the girl that got away.
Dizzy had 'im a brother that pitched in the majors, too, who went by

the name'a Daffy, like that goddamn duck you like so much. Dizzy and Daffy. Shit."

I lay in the tub that night and thought of my father and how he would feel if he knew that Dr. Gallman had put his hand down my gym shorts. Would he have beaten him up? Would he have beaten me? It had been a few months since I had seen Dr. Gallman, but his letters continued to come addressed to me at Route 3, Forest, Mississippi. I thought maybe he would feel as ashamed as I did about what had happened between us, but he soon issued an invitation to join him again for a sleepover when he was headed back our way in December for another son's wedding. Mom, of course, was excited by the news. In the intervening months I had almost told her about what Dr. Gallman had done to me but the accusation could never quite escape my lips. I was beginning to admit to myself, however tentatively, that I might as well take on the sexuality that being a sissy entailed. Why not just be what everybody expected I was, I concluded, which was resulting in a conundrum regarding Dr. Gallman each time I worked up the courage to let Mom know what he had done: If I told on him, would I, in effect, be telling on myself? What he had inflicted upon me conflated in my thirteen-year-old thoughts—wrongly so—with my own emerging sexual identity. Men like Dr. Gallman focus on boys like me just at that moment in our lives when we are beginning to question who exactly, in the deepest sense, we really are. They cut us out of the herd that they stalk wolflike at every turn. But they are not wolves. They are lost members of the same herd, having replaced the word itself in their religiously ordered lives with the more compliant *flock*, a connotative palliative more pleasing to all the targeted ears it falls upon. A perverting of language is a logical step for those who pervert their longings. Certain words—love, trust, understand—are utilized by men like Dr. Gallman once they've marked their prey (a perversion of a word itself) and are moving in for the kill. Kill is not a perversion of a word. Kill is exactly what I mean. Spiritual murders take place at the hands of such men. What must their most secret prayers be like, these men who pray and prey and pray and prey? Do they live in anguish? They cause it, but do they live in it? In my own most secret prayers I pray they do, even as I pray to be able to forgive them. To forgive him. Let me say it now: I forgive you, Dr. Gallman. But I will always hate you. Every time I get a hard-on, there is hatred for you in the blood that rushes there.

"How wonderful!" Mom said when I told her the news about his second invitation. I asked her if I had to go. "Of course, you do," she said. "Don't you want to?" I shrugged and let pass another opportunity to tell her what had happened. "You been slippin' a bit in your Bible readin'. Don't think I haven't noticed. You don't seem as interested in your Christianity. Christianity takes a heap'a upkeep—like me trying to mop this floor like the fool I am," she said. I watched her with her one good arm dip the mop into the bucket. Since her stroke, she couldn't wring the water from the mop's head so I'd kneel and do it for her. She insisted on being useful around the house, and trying to push a wet mop about the floor with that one good arm was one of the things she had come up with that she could still do, though I saw that it quickly tired her out. "Dr. Gallman will be good for you," she said. "You could use a visit with him. Get you back on track."

"I'll go if Kim goes," I told her, thinking I could use my little brother to run interference. If Kim were there, Dr. Gallman wouldn't try anything again.

"Well, we'll have to see if he wants to go and if it's all right with Dr. Gallman," Mom said, handing me the mop and asking me to finish up the job. "I'm sorry. I'm plumb pooped. I'm going out back to see what Pop wants for his supper. I can't eat no more of them stinky rutabagas we've had the last few nights. How does Sloppy Joes sound?"

I shrugged and finished up the mopping. Would I let that old man put his hand down my pants again? Would he give me another massage? Would we pray again on our knees? Would I take another of his sleeping pills so I wouldn't have to know what he was doing to me during the night? At dinner, I negotiated with Kim for his participation in my plan. After I let him have half of my second Sloppy Joe, he agreed to come along with me and we cleared it afterward with a phone call to Dr. Gallman, who, a few December days later, picked up my brother and me in his Mercedes.

This time we didn't spend the night in a hotel, but at his younger son's apartment in Raymond, the town in which Hinds Junior College was located. It was where my mother and Kim and Karole and I had lived in that old faculty house after my father's car accident, when she first read to me from Katherine Anne Porter inside her blue-green bedroom and pleaded with me to call for help on that night she could not take the pain inside her anymore. I had not been to Raymond since the night I had hidden behind the drapes when the gurney was wheeled from the ambulance into her room. When I realized that Raymond was where Dr. Gallman was taking us, I was even more upset at being back in that Mercedes. He had officiated at the wedding a few days earlier and had borrowed the place while his son was away on his honeymoon so that no one in his family could be aware of the furtiveness of his reasons for using the place as a kind of hideaway-in-plain-sight. There were two small bedrooms in the apartment, and when the time came to go to bed, I started to go into the room with Kim. A discussion ensued. Kim and I had seldom shared a bed before. The few times we had, when cousins were visiting for holidays, he complained that I kept him up because I kicked him in my sleep. Dr. Gallman told us to stop our fighting and that Kim could sleep by himself and I'd sleep with him. I wish I could say his suggestion met with more resistance from me, but I gave in much too readily, so readily, in fact, that it must have signaled to him that he didn't have to seduce me all over again once he got me behind the door that awaited us.

The minute we went into his son's bedroom Dr. Gallman stripped down to his boxer shorts. I stripped down to my white Hanes briefs. I did not put on the gym shorts I brought along. We climbed into his son's bed, our bodies brushing up against each other as we settled in under the covers. Dr. Gallman immediately turned toward me and pulled his penis from his boxer shorts and pressed himself closer. He began to hump me and put his hand down my briefs. I did not want to be erect, but I could not stop it from happening. This time my Pela-hatchie trance did not work. So I tried instead to think of images of my dying mother, of Mom when I caught a glimpse of her in the bathroom when she was hospitalized after her stroke and the nurse was cleaning her up, of what my father's head could have looked like when he flew from his Volkswagen and his skull was instantly crushed, the sound of his own blood—the last sound he must have heard—sizzling momentarily, it had to have sizzled, next to his ear embedded in the bubbles of tar pocking yet another Mississippi blacktop in the unrelenting August heat. All the images were of ill-ness. Of death. They were the images of my childhood. But none of them worked. They did not make me feel again like a child. I just got harder. Dr. Gallman began to masturbate me. He kissed me on my shoulder. I lay completely still on my back and stared at the ceiling. For the first time, *I felt nothing*. I let myself go blank. Dr. Gallman's cock grew larger. Bits of his pre-cum began to ooze from him onto my leg. His saliva thickened on my shoulder. He grabbed me tighter be-fore running his smooth old palm down my scrotum in an attempt to touch my sphincter, to open it, with his longest finger. I put my legs together as tightly as they would go. He gave up his search and put his hand again around my cock. He stroked me over and over. He humped me harder. He ejaculated on my leg. I ejaculated on my stomach. His mouth opened wider and it took as much of my shoul-der as it could inside itself, careful not to bite down on me though I felt his teeth shudder against my flesh. I never stopped staring at the ceiling. I waited for him to take his hand away, to remove his mouth where he now slobbered with relief. He lay against me. He would not move. I slipped from under his arm and went to the bathroom and washed my stomach. I washed my leg. This time I did look at my face in the mirror. I looked at my face in the mirror for a very long time. I decided not to go back into the bedroom. I went into the living room and lay shivering on the sofa. I heard Dr. Gallman open the door. I closed my eyes. He came and stood over me. I listened to his breathing. I pretended I was asleep. He let me pretend. He left and got a blanket. He put it over me, gently tucking it around my body. I listened to his breathing again as he stood staring down at me. I would not open my eyes. He sighed, a sound mixed with desire and exhaustion and disgust. He went back into the bedroom to his son's bed.

The next day, Dr. Gallman dropped Kim and me off at the first matinee of *The Cross and the Switchblade* at the Jackson Mall Cinema but did not come in himself. I sat watching Pat Boone play a street preacher named Wilkerson from Pennsylvania who puts the love of Jesus into the lives of two warring gangs in New York City. I kept staring at the red socks Pat Boone was wearing in the movie and wondered what Dr. Gallman was up to while Kim and I shared the bag of popcorn he gave us the money for. Were Dr. Gallman's feelings hurt because I slept on the sofa? Was he was now looking for another boy out in the mall as my replacement? Finding an unlocked church in the neighborhood so he could kneel alone at yet another altar? Was he shopping? Having his shoes shined? Hitting up some businessman for a contribution to that college he worked for up in Kentucky? Was he calling his wife from a pay phone? Or was he—this was what I decided he was doing—smirking at his good luck? Suddenly a scene in the movie gripped my attention. I looked up. Erik Estrada, who played Nicky, the meanest member of a Spanish gang called the Mau Maus, awoke from a nightmare in his apartment and was filmed wearing only a tight white pair of briefs. Why couldn't he be the one who stuck his hands down my pants and ejaculated on my leg and put his mouth so hungrily against my shoulder? Pat Boone, after banging on Erik Estrada's door that night, gave a sermon to the rival gangs. "I'm here to talk about love," he told them. "That's right: *love*. That word that bothers you. It's a *sissy* word to most of you. But love is the gutsiest word in the English language. You pretend you don't want anybody to touch you. But inside you are crying out for love." I laughed at Pat Boone. Kim punched me on my arm.

Dr. Gallman was waiting for my little brother and me in the mall after the movie. He took us to a bookstore and bought us each paperback copies of the *Good News for Modern Man* Bible, which all the cool church kids back in 1969 carried with them on Sundays. *Good News for Modern Man* was a translation of the New Testament written in language we could understand better than all those "thees" and "thous" in the King James Version. Dr. Gallman noticed me admiring his Montblanc pen when he signed the credit card bill for the Bibles. "You want this?" he asked. I hesitated accepting it. "Take it," he said, and put it in the front right pocket of my jeans, letting his hand linger there for a few extra seconds. He did not drive us back to Forest in his Mercedes but instead took us to the Greyhound bus station downtown, close to the Lamar Theater. I did not know it at the time but when he put us on that Greyhound to Forest I would not see him again until thirteen years later when I returned home from New York City to attend my grandmother's funeral. (I would never receive another postcard from him, another letter, or another phone call.) He attended the funeral and came to our house afterward. We sat across from each other in the living room yet did not exchange one word. He did not even look at me, though I made a point of staring right at him, the way he had sat up behind the pulpit in Harperville that night before his sermon when he couldn't take his eyes off me and I was convinced he was seeing directly into my twelve-year-old soul.

He finally got up from his chair in the living room and excused himself, I alone knowing it was because of my unflinching, accusatory stare. As he turned his back on me, he pointedly sighed in that way he had when he stood over me while I pretended to be asleep on his son's sofa in Raymond, the sound—an even richer mixture of exhaustion and disgust and desire—sending a long-ago shiver through me. Without saying a word, he had the final say. It was as if he had only just put me on that Greyhound bus, a premeditated gesture—all his gestures were premeditated—of rejection. I certainly had felt rejected as I tried to read my *Good News for Modern Man* paperback on the bus home to Forest that day after the matinee of *The Cross and the Switchblade* but was getting too nauseous with motion sickness as my eyes scanned the verses laid out like paragraphs. I took Dr. Gallman's Montblanc from my pocket and wrote "$70 \times 7 = 490$" in the margin of the eighteenth chapter of Matthew. I wondered if I would have to do as Jesus said, and forgive Dr. Gallman that many times. I skimmed the next chapter, my woozy eyes falling upon more of Jesus's words. "There are different reasons why men cannot marry," He said. "Some, because they were born that way; others because men made them that way; and others do not marry for the sake of the kingdom of heaven. Let him who can accept this teaching do so." I looked over at Kim in the seat next to me. He had fallen asleep. We were passing through Pelahatchie on Highway 80 and I caught a glimpse off that old two-lane of the green-shingled house we had lived in and the ersatz log cabin next door where I had looked into the Simpson Lady's bathroom window and become my father's teammate. I gripped Dr. Gallman's Montblanc tighter and wrote the same five letters in Matthew's margin that my mother had so indelibly instructed me to write across her stationery when we stayed up late together: SISSY, I wrote as I had written then. I took Dr. Gallman's Montblanc and traced over each letter, making them even more pronounced in the margin. I heard my mother's voice overriding Jesus's. "Look at the muscles those S's have. Look at the arms on that Y." I tried to recall what else she said that night, but all I could remember were the muscles and the arms.

7

Dusty Springfield, Cloris Leachman, and Miss Diana Ross

When I was fourteen, going on fifteen, I spent most of my time playing sports and trying not to get a hard-on in the locker room, where I often found myself pulling on or off a smelly jockstrap. It was my freshman year, my one year of truly trying to fit into small-town life, when I accepted fully my dead father's mantle. I doubled as tail-back and safety on the football team. I was point guard on the basketball team. And I won first place in all the Little Dixie conference track meets, where I still ran the 100-yard dash and 220-yard dash as well as anchoring the 440-yard and 880-yard relays. In fact, I had run those races at the conference finals all bruised up with a big black eye from a car wreck I had had close to home the Sunday before, when I skipped church and went to pick up Kim and Karole after the service at Trinity. I'd been trying to find any kind of rock on the AM radio in the old used Dodge that Pop had bought me when I got my license. I had taken my eyes off the road for just a moment to fiddle with the dial. When I looked up I had run off the road onto the shoulder of a steep ditch and been thrown to the other side of the car. I grabbed the steering wheel and pulled myself back over to the driver's side and sped across the road. The car then jumped the other ditch, crashing into one of the poles that held the barbed-wire fence around the Derricks' cow pasture. My face smashed against the wheel. Stunned, I jumped from the car and ran, bawling, all the way home. By the time of the track meet at the end of that week I really had a shiner but had shaken off the shock of the wreck—I kept thinking how close I had come to having my own skull smashed on a patch of country asphalt—and felt that my roughed-up appearance butched up the sissy residue I could never quite shake, no matter how many blue track ribbons I won, first downs I made on end-around runs, or assists I made on the hardwood to Bobby Thompson so he could take the shot.

But a year of playing all those sports was all that I could take. I quit every one of them when I was a sophomore and concentrated on graduating from high school early, especially after I consciously admitted to myself that I was a homosexual, saying the four words silently to myself: "I am a homosexual." Earlier in the year, I had started hanging out with an older guy—in his mid-thirties, maybe—who still lived with his mother in Forest. I had met him at a revival at the First Methodist church that summer after I spotted him in his white linen suit and was impressed at how he was keeping the choir ladies in stitches. His name was Joe Rex Dennis and he was no doubt a homosexual, the kind small towns tolerate as best they can. I'd never been happier to make anybody's acquaintance. He knew instantly, of course, I was what I was and helped me reach the same conclusion. He was in the process of getting his master's degree in English and writing his thesis on the works of Flannery O'Connor.

His first act of kindness—he never made one sexual pass at me—was to give me a collection of her stories. He also adored Leontyne Price and constantly played her albums, but never "Melancholy Baby," like Frank did. Joe Rex took Leontyne much too seriously for that. He played only selections of her arias (preferably recorded live so he could revel in the sound of the ovations as much as the voice that led to them) or, often, he would make me sit and listen to her in whole operas, mostly by Verdi, though he'd put the needle down on Gershwin's *Porgy and Bess* and Puccini's *Tosca* from time to time. But Verdi's *Aida* was his favorite. I liked three other of her Verdi operas just as well: *Un Ballo in Maschera*, *La Forza del Destino*, and, of course, *Il Trovatore*, in which she made her great Metropolitan debut. Joe Rex filled me with Leontyne lore and pointed out the metaphors in Flannery. One day in October, when I was looking at the *Jackson Daily News* sports pages while listening to *Aida*'s "O patria mia," I spotted a picture of football players from Jackson Prep who were going to dance in a production of *The Nutcracker* in December and were already rehearsing for their roles. I was amazed by the photo, and Joe Rex told me that one of the boys was like us and that he knew him personally. I still had never had sex with another guy—only with Dr. Gallman and the stranger at Audrey Whatshername's movie, and they did not count. Although I wasn't sure how to label those experiences, I nevertheless reasoned that I shouldn't call them sex. I begged Joe Rex to introduce me to the boy in the picture. He set up a phone call for us, and when I went with a group of friends to the Mississippi State Fair that weekend, I snuck off and met the hunky Jackson Prepper. During the halftime of a televised Ole Miss football game, I had my first freedom-of-choice sex with another guy. He was friends with a couple of male music professors at Millsaps—"old-lady lovers," he called them—and had arranged for me to rendezvous with him at their house. They gave us our privacy in their study, even furnishing us with clean sheets to put on the fold-out couch they sensed we would be folding out. It was that very next Monday at school when I admitted who I really was. I was in biology class dissecting a frog, the smell of formaldehyde wafting through the room, when the thought hit me, when I said those silent words: "I am a homosexual."

From that sweet-sixteen moment on, all I could think about was getting to college and away from Forest. By going to summer school twice, I was able to skip my senior year and head straight to Millsaps in Jackson to major in Theater. I had also applied to NYU and the University of Missouri, thinking I might want to study journalism, as I had had such a great time writing stories and conducting interviews for the high school newspaper I had helped found. I had successfully convinced the rest of the staff to christen the paper *After Eight*; it was my secret tribute to *After Dark*, the magazine I had begun to read around that same time at Frank Hains's urging, for it was also around this time I had been cast in the New Stage production of *The Medium* and Frank entered my life. Ivan Rider, New Stage's artistic director, had almost given up on finding a boy with the right exotic quality to play the role until I walked into that *A Midsummer Night's Dream* cast party to which Joe Rex had taken me at Bleak House. When I told Ivan and Frank I had just won the Best Actor award at the state's high school drama festival at the University of Southern Mississippi, the deal was cinched. It took a lot of coaxing by me and Joe Rex and Frank and Ivan to get my grandparents to agree to let me drive the family Plymouth (that old wrecked Dodge was, well, a little dodgy) the eighty-mile round trip every day for a whole month of rehearsals and performances at the highly regarded theater, which staged its productions in an old church, the audience sitting in pews newly utilized, churches and pews an inescapable aspect of my young life even as I was beginning to escape them. I'll always be grateful to Mom and Pop for letting me be a part of that production. They recognized how much I needed to take my first tentative steps away from them, from

Old Highway 35 where we lived, from a Mississippi country life that could not keep me captive much longer. "This is something good I can ponder on later in life," I told Mom, citing her "Alice Blue Gown" days as part of my argument. She convinced Pop that all the gas I would burn up that month would be money well spent. I adored the attention the production brought me. My picture as the mute gypsy boy was all over the Jackson papers. And young men—many more beautiful than I—waited around after the show each night to tell me how good I was in the part. But most of all I loved hanging out afterwards with the New Stage crowd, for whom Miss Welty gladly served as a kind of den mother.

Those were halcyon days of literate discussions and witty banter and sucking dick, sometimes all three at the same time, especially if I went to bed, as was my wont, with Carl Davis, that dashing bisexual advertising executive who looked like Robert Redford and acted in many of New Stage's productions. He was as debonair to me in his late-thirties demeanor as he was slightly tortured by how I was making him feel. "Rather foolish," he told me once, as we lay naked in each other's arms after one of my performances. "But rather grateful, too. I'm not sure which is more troubling. Are you trouble?" I shrugged. I turned toward him and, like Dr. Gallman had done to me, took as much of his shoulder as I could inside my mouth and felt my teeth shudder against him. "Make me cum," I whispered single-mindedly. "Make me cum again, Carl. Make me cum."

I also started to sneak into the gay bar in Jackson back when I was sixteen, going on seventeen, or going on whatever age you wanted me to be. One had to be eighteen to get into a club, but I got around that by slicing the raised numbers off my new driver's license and rearranging them so my rejiggered birth date would make me old enough. I glued the rearranged numbers back on and slipped the license back into its plastic sleeve in my wallet. It looked a little haphazard but did the trick. The old couple whose son owned the gay bar located up a flight of rickety stairs in a dilapidated building located on a deserted side street in downtown Jackson—Mae's Cabaret was its name—would look at me kind of funny but go ahead and let me in. They always worked the door for their son, and during my fourth or fifth visit there they asked me if I had ever lived in Pelahatchie. Shocked by the question, I just stood staring at them. "It's okay, honey," said the little round, big-haired woman. "I recognize your name on this driver's license. And who can forget that pretty face. We're Mr. and Mrs. Myers. 'Member us? Jack, that's my son who owns this place—he's Mae—used to be the manager when he was in high school for the basketball team for your daddy when we lived over yonder. Ever'body called him 'Tip' back then. Small world, ain't it? Lord, what would Coach Sessums say if he knew you was spendin' time at Mae's."

Her husband, wearing thick-lensed glasses and his usual pair of overalls, looked me up and down. "I knew you'd end up in a place like this when I saw you doin' them cheers with them Pelahatchie Chiefs cheerleaders when you wasn't but knee-high to a June bug," the man said. "Jack wanted to be a cheerleader hisself but we made him settle on bein' the manager for Coach Ses. Boy cheerleaders ain't looked at with much respect 'round these parts, I told him, if ya' catch my drift. I ain't got nothin' agin boys like y'all—shoot, I give him the money to open up this queer bar once we was out of Pelahatchie—but you got t'member where you livin'." He looked at me some more. "You can't be no eighteen neither by my figurin', but go on ahead inside. Once dick-suckin' gets a'holt'ya, ain't nothin' gonna keep you away from it. Safer in here than a truck stop out on I-20." His wife hit him on his shoulder but laughed at his irreverence. "Coach Ses'd never forgive me if I didn't keep a eye out fer'ya," he said. "You behave in here. We gotta a drag show tonight goin' on. Wait till you see that colored boy from Corinth we got doin' Gladys Knight's 'Midnight Train to Georgia.'"

"Carthage," his wife corrected him. "The Lady Naomi's from Carthage."

"Wherever," he said. "Naomi's my favorite. 'At boy'll knock your socks off when he throws that suitcase down from the stage and it opens up and all his extra-large lingerie comes a'fallin' out along with some of them rubber dicks. That's when he starts makin' his tips. Here," the man said, handing me back the dollar out of the cash box I had just given him. Mae's Cabaret didn't have a cash register at the door. "After he throws that suitcase down on the dance floor and falls on his knees right behind it—Jack give him some old kneepads to wear under his gown that he must've stole from Coach Ses and one of them Chiefs he coached, 'cause that colored boy, he ain't little neither, not by a long shot, falls right on his knees from way up on the stage down to the dance floor, that's a right fer piece, crowd goes wild, you'll see—you go on over and stuff this here dollar I'm givin' back to you into the Lady Naomi's fake tits. That's the way it's done. Go on now. Have fun. Line's formin' behind'ya."

I took the dollar. I sat in a corner and sipped at the Coke I got at the bar. The place didn't have a liquor license, but sold something called setups from the bar for the older people who brought their own liquor in brown paper bags. I was often offered liquor by old drunks trying to pick me up but I always had my eye out for boys closer to my age. There weren't that many to be found at Mae's. But every now and then one would wander in and we'd pair off in the parking lot. That night I looked for Jack, that pudgy, pimply-faced basketball team manager who'd been so mean to me back in my father's locker room. I'd been waiting my whole life to hit him back like he'd hit me, on the top of his head, almost ruining that first visit my father had allowed me down there underneath the gym. I saw a door open that led backstage and, though he was backlit by the narrow hallway's bare bulb, I could tell it was Jack. Even pudgier—he looked more like his mama now—he still had that same walk, a determined waddle that gave him, oddly, an air of authority, whether it was needed to run a high school basketball team or Jackson's only gay bar. He waddled right by me. I almost put a foot out to trip him. But as I drank Coke after Coke that night and watched him greet his regular customers and handle the varied egos of the drag queens about to perform and keep his eyes on the bartenders hovering at the cash register behind his bar, I gained a new respect for him, and even a newfound fondness. He was no longer pimply faced, but he still had those same doe eyes I remembered, that seemed so full of a contemptuous recognition whenever my father made him tend to me. Back in that Pelahatchie gym he often looked like a deer caught in headlights, but now, here at Mae's where he felt at home, he looked more relaxed, less wide-eyed, a heavy-lidded jadedness lending him a Bambi-after-a-few-beers leer. He kept checking on his mother and father at the door and making sure they were comfortable, steadily supplying them with soda and snacks, a bag of pork rinds for his daddy, his mama munching on any Lay's product he put in front of her. Sometimes he'd stand off by himself and contemplatively watch the disco ball turning in the light above the dance floor as it glittered and speckled the faces of Mae's denizens so thankful to have a place we could be ourselves for a few hours, an inner sanctum more precious to us than any locker room, cigarette smoke taking the place of steam as it rose around us in a haze-enhanced world, the only world back in the early 1970s that would have us. He said "darlin'" a lot, something he had not said when sitting on my daddy's bench with those basketball players, and wore a muumuu and purposefully bad makeup later when he lip-synched to Vestal Goodman singing "I've Found a Better Way" off a Happy Goodman Family gospel album. I tipped him the dollar his daddy had given me instead of tipping the Lady Naomi, that fat colored boy from Corinth or Carthage—it didn't really matter where he came from. We had all come from the same place, somewhere that didn't want us. When I stepped into the spotlight to stuff the dollar into Jack's pudgy palm he held my hand a long moment and stared into my eyes. A look of shock—a recognition no longer contemptuous—registered beneath his wig and badly applied eye shadow. The crowd whooped with delight, thinking he was flirting with a beautiful teenage boy who had happened into the place, but we both knew we were looking into the eyes of our earlier selves. He hesitated before hitting me on top of my head for old times' sake, this time both of us acknowledging the flirtatious sting the gesture was meant to leave behind. Later, in the corner of Mae's parking lot, I jerked off somebody in the backseat of his mama's old Studebaker, and as I stared at the discarded candy wrappers on the floor as he shot his load in my hand, I thought of that gallant ballplayer on my father's high school team who defended me against Jack Myers back when he had pimples and dared to perform in his mama's muumuu only in private.

Mae's Cabaret became my refuge throughout the two years I went to Millsaps—even though I had a girlfriend I met while in line at the registrar's office my first day on campus during freshman orientation. She was in front of me wearing a halter top and I couldn't take my eyes off of the lovely array of freckles across her shoulders and back. When she turned to say hello, I instantly fell for her. I don't know why. It still confuses me. But I can truthfully say she is one of the few people for whom I felt real love. The sex was good, too, and we weathered the requisite pregnancy scare. But my truer self was homosexual and I kept returning, behind her back, to Mae's and to men. I also joined a fraternity at college, Pi Kappa Alpha, and had sex with two of my fraternity brothers. The sex with a younger one was more of a lark after a drunken night of stealing plants from old ladies' porches around Miss Welty's house on Pinehurst. The sex with an older one, however, was more meaningful to me. It took my whole freshman year to seduce him but I would not give up. He reminded me of Bobby Thompson, who still filled my thoughts. Young gay boys fall first for boys we want to *be* more than boys we want to *fuck*. Both Bobby and my Pike brother fit the bill, not only with their smooth-bodied blond-haired beauty compared to my increasingly hairy-chested brunet looks, but with their lives of privilege compared to my hardscrabble one. They were both preppy, both effortlessly popular. The first time I slept with my older Pike brother was, I kid you not, after we went to see Woody Allen's adaptation of *Everything You Always Wanted to Know About Sex (But Were Afraid to Ask)* together at the Paramount Theatre when it finally came to Jackson. And we kept sleeping together sporadically for the rest of my time in college—whether it was in our respective dorm rooms or at Frank's when I'd stay at his house while he was away in New York seeing shows for his arts column in the *Daily News*. I even once showed him Frank's collection of pornography in that secret trunk, knowing it would make Frank crazy if he knew I was doing it, but also knowing—I had checked it out many times myself when Frank wasn't around—that there was enough pussy in there to get my Pike brother horny. He wasn't as queer as I was, just queer enough to make love to me, or, more precisely, to allow me to make love to him. For me, at that time in my life, it was enough.

Indeed, it was more than enough, for when it stopped I was devastated. Gossip had started to percolate around campus about the two of us. My girlfriend and I had broken up, and people were beginning to notice that my Pike brother and I were spending way too much time together. By that time, I had decided not to hide the fact I frequented Mae's Cabaret, which was, I guess, a rather brave stance for any eighteen-year-old to take back in the early seventies. The only regret I had about my openness was that it was putting so much distance now between my Pike brother and me. One night at Mae's, while Shirley & Co.'s "Shame Shame Shame" was blaring from the sound system, I was drowning my sorrow at losing both a girlfriend and what passed for a boyfriend in my life with a series of a liquored-up Cokes (Jack let me borrow one of his bottles of Bacardi) when I heard a voice ask, interrupting one of Shirley's shouted "shames," if the seat next to me was taken. I looked up. At first all I could see was a giant Afro encircling the guy's head in the light reflecting off the disco ball behind him, a massive halo of frizzy hair like that overly serious actor on *The Mod Squad* whose Afro was so big it was like a fourth lead character. The guy's voice, unlike so many surrounding me in Mae's, was not effeminate at all. His overabundance of cologne, however, was bordering on the feminine, such a perfumy presence at odds with the physique so obvious beneath his tight polyester shirt and even tighter low-slung jeans. "Do you mind?" he asked, pulling out the chair. "I've been watching you. You look so sad. It seems you could use some company. My name is Frank, by the way. Frank Dowsing."

He reached out to shake my hand and almost crushed it in his giant palm as I smiled at the pun I didn't say aloud but certainly thought as I stared at that "Dowsing rod" inside his jeans. "I know who you are," I said. Frank Dowsing was a star at Mae's. In fact, he was a star all over the state of Mississippi and a much braver soul than any sissy eighteen-year-old hiding out in a gay bar on yet another Saturday night. He was not only the first African American to play football at Mississippi State, but the first African American to be chosen Mr. Mississippi State by the student body. He was an all-SEC defensive back who was also an all-American. I was still interested in sports and had read everything there was to read about him in the pages of the *Clarion-Ledger* and *Jackson Daily News*. I knew he had been drafted by the Philadelphia Eagles the year before but had decided to go to med school instead—he was an academic all-American as well—because he was dissatisfied with the round the Eagles drafted him in. He also still held the SEC record for the 100-yard dash with a time of 9.5 seconds. His marriage to his childhood sweetheart in the campus chapel at Mississippi State up in Starkville had been written about in the papers. His recent divorce had not received as much coverage. And he was handsome, as handsome as anybody on *The Mod Squad.*

He sat down across from me. Gloria Gaynor began to sing "Never Can Say Goodbye." I smiled at him. "That's better," he said. You're even sexier when you smile. You should smile more often."

I offered him what was left of Jack's Bacardi. He declined the offer. "You sit down next to me more often, I'll smile more often," I told him, putting the last bit of rum in my plastic cup. "My name is Kevin, by the way," I kept flirting, kiddingly echoing his own introduction. "Kevin Sessums."

"I know who you are, too," he told me. "I've been watching you for a while. Not just this evening. But I was afraid to approach you. I just couldn't take you looking so sad tonight, though." He slipped his huge black hand beneath the table—Gaynor still wasn't saying good-bye—and touched my leg, gently, briefly, before running a finger across my instantly hard cock. I wanted him to keep his hand there, but he just as quickly removed it. He was too much of a gentleman to feel me up in public. I looked over to where he had been sitting and noticed stares as well as whispers sweeping through that section of the place. Although up those rickety stairs Mae's was for all the gays and lesbians who wanted to congregate in Jackson, once inside we all self-segregated. The blacks had their tables on one side of the bar. The whites had ours on the other. Seldom did we mingle. But every-body, white and black alike, watched Frank when he came into the bar. There was no hotter gossip that year than his being a homosex-ual and so open about it. He was the kind of person one had to look at when he entered a room, not only because he was a sports celebrity but because he had that charismatic swagger with which sports celebrities are born. It's part of their DNA. Before they ever run back a touchdown or hit a home run or win a basketball game at the buzzer, they charismatically swagger those first few steps they ever take toward their mother's outstretched hands, hoping their fathers are watching, their athletic prowess built on such physical trust, such hope for their father's eyes. Because Frank was already an object of rapt attention at Mae's, the Saturday-night regulars were extra vigilant not to miss what was going to happen between him and that aloof white boy who always sat alone over in the corner while downing Jack's rum and ruminating on his own loveliness. When the Hues Corporation began to sing "Rock the Boat," Frank asked me to dance. A loud whoop, derisive and appreciative at the same time, went up from a table of over-the-top black queens who had been fawning over him earlier. From the white section: silent frowns. My response? *Fuck 'em all.* I forgot all about Pike brothers and my confusing heartbreak at not having a girlfriend as Frank and I began to dance and continued dancing right through Barry White's "Can't Get Enough of Your Love, Babe." We both hated ABBA so when "Waterloo" came on we sat back down and talked till the bar closed.

Frank told me he had come out of the closet on his way to the Hula Bowl, a game played by a roster of collegiate all-stars, the year before, when he had a stopover in San Francisco where he had his first homosexual experience. At the Hula Bowl he discovered that four of his teammates were gay and were quite open about it. He decided during the second half of the game that he would come home and get a divorce and be exactly who he was. He also decided not to sign with the Eagles. "It really wasn't because of the draft round, that's just something I told the press," he said. "I concluded it would be tougher being an out homosexual in the NFL than being an out homosexual in Jackson, Mississippi, and that's saying something." For the first time that night, he too looked sad. It was my turn to reach under the table and touch his leg. We held hands. I thought we were going to have sex later but he told me he wanted to have a proper date. He asked me to go out for dinner the next Saturday night. I gladly accepted.

I could barely think of anything else throughout the following week. I had never slept with either a sports celebrity or a black man, and I'm not sure which excited me more. I told the other Frank in my life all about it when we had dinner at Bleak House that week, and he was beside himself with excitement for me. Frank Hains was exclusively into black guys, but his interest tended mostly toward younger, lither, more ladylike boys. I'd met several of them and, though they were always quite sweet, they were just a little too sweet for my taste. At dinner that night, it was the first time I ever heard the expression, "Once you go black, you never go back," when Frank Hains began to regale me with how such men tasted in an epidermal sense. "Maybe it's the chocolate connotation, but they are quite literally more delicious. I can't explain it," he said. "Perhaps it's the musk in their melanin. Whatever it is, trust me, it's marvelous. *Marvelous.* You won't be disappointed. Your diet is about to change, dear boy. Thank God such lusciousness is not fattening or I'd be as big as Montserrat Caballé."

But Frank Dowsing's allure for me was bigger than just his beauty. I had to admit to myself that sleeping with Frank Dowsing would be a way of doing penance for insulting Matty May so deeply with my use of the N-word that she left my grandparents' employ and, in turn, my life. If I truly were not bigoted—my whole life, since Matty walked away from me in Uncle Benny's cotton field, had been spent proving that point to myself—then I would suck Frank Dowsing's dick and anything else he wanted me to do. It would be more than a sexual act on my part; it would be a political one.

Saturday arrived. He picked me up in his Ford Torino, which I took as a good omen, as it was the same kind of car that Bobby Thompson drove in high school. We went to the T.G.I. Friday's that had just opened in Jackson. We had a hard time eating our meal because people kept recognizing him and asking for his autograph, especially football-loving fathers who were there with their sons. After dinner we went back to Frank's apartment in the black section of town around Jackson State. I was expecting a butch place full of wooden furniture and trophy cases. Instead, there were overstuffed pillows and peacock feathers in vases and a poster of Diana Ross. He made me a Bacardi and Coke without asking what I wanted to drink, and put an album of duets between Ross and Marvin Gaye on his turntable. We slow-danced until we fell into bed together. His chiseled body broke my fall. We stripped each other's clothes off down to our white underwear. I went to slip his pair of underwear down his massive thighs but he stopped me and pulled me toward him. The first time his full lips found mine—we still had not kissed—I felt devoured. I've never wanted anyone as much as I wanted him in those first few moments of our making love. Frank Hains was right. He did taste slightly different than the white boys I had had sex with. More luscious. Yes, muskier. Then, suddenly, he wanted to fuck me. I had never been fucked before. I told him so, and that I didn't think I was ready for it, especially from a cock the size of his. He put a finger to my lips to quiet me then stuck it inside my mouth so I could suck on it. He took the wet finger from my mouth and ran it along my sphincter before sliding it inside me as far as I could take it. "Please," I whispered. "No. I can't. I can't." He pulled his finger free and licked it now himself. "That's okay," he said. "Reach down under the bed." I did as I was told and retrieved a bottle of Vaseline Intensive Care lotion and a perfectly folded white terry cloth hand towel. "Beat me off with that lotion," he said. I poured the Vaseline Intensive Care into my palm and started masturbating him. He shot all over his stomach. "Want to lick it up?" he asked. I had never done that either. "Try it," he said, pressing my head down toward his row of abdominal muscles. I tried licking it, but wiped most of it up with the towel. "You're sweet," he said.

"You, too," I told him. "Literally."

We laughed and I lay next to him. We listened to Miss Ross, as he kept calling her, and Marvin Gaye sing a couple of more songs. He got out of bed to clean up in the bathroom, then went to change the music on the turntable. "Who's that?" I asked when he climbed back into bed. "Dusty Springfield. This is her new album called *Cameo*. I love this song. I went to high school in Tupelo, you know," he said as Dusty did her version of Van Morrison's "Tupelo Honey." We lay in silence and listened to her sing. I kept touching his Afro.

"Do you like going to the movies?" he asked me when Dusty was finished singing about his hometown. "We should go to one next Saturday. How about *Uptown Saturday Night?* I've been looking forward to that one. Or the picture that was filmed here last year by Robert Altman. I've been reading about it a lot."

"*Thieves Like Us,*" I told him, keeping it to myself that I had been picked up by a man working with Altman at Poet's, a restaurant where local hipsters hung out. I had had a brief affair with the man, even going to watch the dailies with him a few times and listening to Altman hold court, once viewing a scene not used in the movie of a naked Keith Carradine and Shelley Duvall jumping up and down on a bed, wanting Carradine's bouncing cock a lot more than I wanted the crew member's. "*Uptown Saturday Night'*s fine," I said.

"What's your favorite movie you've ever seen?" Frank asked me as he kept gently touching my sphincter, my legs slowly parting for him as he continued to massage me there, the same way I had begun to massage myself back in that bathroom stall at the Town Theater during the last unseen part of *Wait Until Dark*.

Although anything Audrey Whatshername starred in was in the running, and I had gone back to see *Cabaret* three times at the Capri Theatre close to Millsaps the year before, I came up with another answer. "*The Last Picture Show,*" I said.

"But that's in black-and-white," he said, sounding like Mrs. Fikes complaining about *Who's Afraid of Virginia Woolf?*

"So? Look at us," I told him.

"You've always got a funny answer for everything, don't you," he said, laughing before pulling me to him so we could kiss some more. "No. Really now. Why did you choose that movie?" he asked when he took his tongue back from where I tried to keep it inside my mouth.

When I was fifteen I had convinced Mom and Pop to let me take our Plymouth to Jackson to see *The Last Picture Show* with Bobby Thompson. When he said he could go, I had been as excited about the approaching day as I had been about having dinner with Frank Dowsing. I pretended I was having a real date with Bobby. When we got to the Paramount Theatre and the movie started, our elbows touched on the shared armrest between us as Cloris Leachman's face grew sadder and sadder in close-up and Timothy Bottoms cried at the death of a street urchin and Cybill Shepherd, like Bobby, allowed her beauty to be admired. Afterward, I often dreamt of seeing *The Last Picture Show*, but in my dream the street urchin lived and Cloris Leachman laughed and I held Bobby's hand. "It reminds me of Forest like that Dusty Springfield song reminds you of Tupelo," I told Frank. "What's your favorite movie?" I asked.

" 'They call me *Mister* Tibbs!' " he robustly exclaimed, using a totally different yet familiar voice. "Do you know what that's from? That's from my all-time favorite movie." He said it again: " 'They call me *Mister* Tibbs!' "

"*In the Heat of the Night*," I said. "That's Sidney Poitier. You sound almost just like him. Do you like Sidney Poitier?"

"I worship Sidney Poitier even more than I worship Miss Ross," he said. "If Sidney Poitier made albums, I'd be playing them right now. The same year I saw *In the Heat of the Night*, I saw *Guess Who's Coming to Dinner* and *To Sir, With Love*. I was sixteen and had just enrolled at Tupelo's white high school under the freedom-of-choice program. I was in that first small group of Negro kids who integrated the place and was one of only three Negro players in all the white public school system to be playing football in the whole fucking state. I was scared shitless, man, but every time I saw Sidney Poitier on screen I was less scared. He's got more dignity in his little finger than most white folks—no offense—have in their whole bodies. Someday I hope to be half the man that Sidney Poitier is. He got me through some pretty dark times. He still does. That's why I want to see *Uptown Saturday Night* next weekend. He directed it. Sidney Poitier is *the man*. He's my inspiration."

I sat up and straddled him. I put his hard dick along the crack of my ass and told him all about Matty May and how much she loved Sidney Poitier, too. I told him how I had offended her on the morning after the Academy Awards, when I was in second grade, by calling him a nigger. I told him how I had slipped up and used the word again in her presence. I told him about the day picking cotton at Uncle Benny's farm. I told him, in a way, that being in bed with him was a way of making up to her. Frank Dowsing said nothing as he lay beneath me and I told him all of that. He then pushed me off his crotch where his cock, becoming softer and softer, still lay inside my crack. He sat on the edge of the bed. I massaged his massive shoulders. I kissed his neck. "Don't," he said. "Don't."

"I'm sorry. I didn't m-mean to . . . ," I started to apologize, my stutter still surfacing whenever I became unsure of myself.

"Don't say you're sorry. That just makes it worse," he said.

"M-makes what worse?" I asked.

Frank Dowsing stood before me now in all his naked glory. Dusty Springfield was singing the last song on her new album. "That's all I am to you?" he asked. "I'm the buck who makes you feel better about yourself?" His flared nostrils flared even more. "Fuck you, man. Fuck you."

"Okay," I quietly said, not taking my eyes from his. "Okay. Fuck me. Do it. Try."

Neither of us said anything for a few long moments as we attempted to decipher what had happened suddenly between us. He couldn't help it—he finally had to smile at me, if only slightly. I smiled back. He then reached out and touched my face. I turned his hand over and kissed his palm, as different a palm as humanly possible from the palm that Dr. Gallman had used against me. I lay on my stomach and spread my legs. He poured the Vaseline Intensive Care into that palm and worked it into me. I arched my back toward his finger opening me up. He mounted me. I tried not to cry out at the pain he was causing me, the pain I accepted as the penance I had come seeking. With each of his thrusts into me, I kept repeating silently to myself, "Poi-ti-er Poi-ti-er Poi-ti-er," trying to approximate the dignity, threadbare, though still not thwarted, with which Matty May had ended up grunting out the name when she was picking that cotton for Uncle Benny. Poi-ti-er. Poi-ti-er. Poi-ti-er. I repeated the name with her same determined rhythm, her same grim obedience, trying to turn all that pain behind me into something sublime. It had just begun to work—was this pleasure I was feeling? was this trust?—when Frank Dowsing shot his second load of the night, this time deep into my receptive body. "Stay inside me," I heard myself say. "*Stay,*" I said aloud. "*Stay. Stay.*"

8

Lewis Carroll, William F. Buckley, and Yvonne De Carlo

The following day, I called Frank Hains from the pay phone in my dorm floor's hallway. I had promised to call him the minute I got back to my dorm so I could give him, like Pee Wee or Dizzy, the play-by-play of my date. I made sure to whisper into the receiver whenever a door opened on the hall but was so giddy with my accomplishments that I even blurted out that I had been fucked for the first time. "Dear boy, this calls for a celebration," came Frank's voice through the telephone. "I am simply dying to meet the young man. I've heard his name spoken from time to time by the guys on the sports desk at the *Daily News*. Frank Dowling."

"Dowsing," I corrected him.

"Oh dear. Mustn't make that mistake when I meet him. I tell you what, why don't the two of you drop by tonight?" he asked. "I'm having some of the girls over for dinner, but you and Mr. *Dowsing* could come for dessert or a drink or two. Say around nine thirty or ten?"

"Which girls?" I asked, knowing he meant some of the New Stage gang.

"Oh, it's just Eudora and Charlotte and Jane and Karen," Frank said. "It'll be a hoot. They'll get a kick out of meeting him. It'll liven up the evening. I'll tell them to be on their best behavior. Or would you prefer they be on their worst?"

I thought about the invitation for a moment. I already knew how sensitive Frank Dowsing was. Would he feel as if he were being put on display? Hell, he had played football in the SEC. He was on display every Saturday, in front of thousands of appreciative white people. Five more wouldn't hurt him. "I'll have to call him," I told Frank. "He already asked me to go to a movie next week. Do you think I'll scare him off if I call him so soon?" Frank Hains always liked for me to ask him questions of that nature. "Aaah, appealing to my sagacity," he said once. I hadn't known what the word meant and he handed me a dictionary from his kitchen's glass-covered bookshelves and told me to look it up. He worked on his column "On Stage" there at the big round kitchen table under the lamp that hung over it, so the kitchen bookshelves were stuffed with reference books as well as cookbooks. An S-word, I remember thinking, when he handed me that dictionary and, in that moment, I missed my mother terribly. I wish I could say that Frank Hains was a father figure to me, but it was my mother's absence I was aware of when I was in his presence. There was a steely diffidence to him that reminded me of her, although he was much more cultivated than she. She aspired to be cultivated, but was always just that: an aspirant. He was also, I dare say, a tad more maternal. But more than anything else, it was the way he made me feel when I was with him, which, up until that point, I had felt only when I was with her. *Seen*, is the first word that comes to mind. Gently guided. Unjudged. Joe Rex had been more like a buddy to me. But Frank—who, like Joe Rex, never made a pass at me—was the older man who helped me begin to heal from the experience of Dr. Gallman, who had *seen* me, of course, but for his own nefarious purposes. Frank Hains was my first true mentor for he did not have any ulterior motive except, maybe, in nurturing me, to expand his already generous spirit. We simply loved being in each other's company. When we were up late one night, telling each other the secrets of our lives—him curled up in the kimono-like robe he loved to wear in his reading chair, me lying on the low-slung sofa as if I were at a therapist session, an Erik Satie album turned down so faintly on the stereo one could barely tell that a piano was being played—I told him about Dr. Gallman's molestation of me and Frank flushed red with indignation. I'd never seen him so angry before. Frank didn't get angry, not like that. Well, when Nixon's face came on the television he could get pretty worked up (this at the height of the Watergate scandals) but that anger—Frank was devoutly liberal—was cultural in its animosity. Hearing my Dr. Gallman story, he could barely contain his contempt for the man. Frank himself had always had an appreciation for young boys, but, according to him, he had never crossed the line into pedophiliac scandal. He had even received a National Pop Warner Award for his work with youth back in the late fifties. "Why is it that the ungodly always reach for the God mask?" he asked, tightening the sash around his kimono. "When will the world stop being fooled by such men?" Standing in the hallway of my dorm, I waited on the other end of the phone for his advice about the skittish football player I was bringing into our midst, "our sphere," as he called it. There was certainly no anger in his voice when his reply came over the line. He sounded as excited as I was feeling at this new prospect in my life, and, by extension, in his. "Call him," he said. "Call him the minute you hang up with me. He should know you're interested. You've been reading *Cosmo* too much. I'll tell the girls you're coming. See you later. Signing off."

Frank Dowsing agreed to meet me in my dorm room that night and walk down the hill from Millsaps to Frank Hains's house across from the Jewish cemetery. "Bleak House?" he asked when I described the place to him over the phone and told him what we all called it because of its outward appearance. "The Dickens, you say." We laughed at his joke before hanging up and I spent the rest of the day unable to study, thinking about seeing him again. I closed my English Lit anthology and instead played Jackson Browne and Dan Fogelberg albums—I didn't have any Diana Ross or Dusty Springfield in my collection—while I fantasized about the night I had spent with him. When he arrived, he told me he had to "give an account for his behavior the night before." I was a little confused but told him to proceed. He prided himself on his manners, he informed me in a stilted, rather comical way, and I was beginning to think I was in an adaptation of Jane Austen over at Jackson State's theater department, since pride mixed with my stumbling attempt at alleviating any vestiges of my own prejudice the night before had resulted in an attraction that neither of us could deny. "Please accept my heartfelt apologies for my rudeness last evening," he said, and slightly bowed before me. I looked puzzled. I started to say something but he put his finger to my lips. He continued in his overly solicitous manner. "I ejaculated twice last night," he said. "You did not ejaculate once. That was not very gentlemanly of me." His Darcy-like demeanor cracked; a raffish grin appeared on his face. He cleared his throat, carefully, and regained his composure. "Rather selfish of me, in fact," he said, the rest of his roguish seriousness settling once more upon his brow. "Quite self-centered on my part. Uncharitable. I think we should rectify the situation before we head down to Bleak House." I started getting hard thinking he was going to fuck me again. Instead—with the flourish of an early nineteenth-century Englishman pulling a silk handkerchief from the brocaded pocket of his breeches—he pulled my penis from my jeans. He knelt in front of me. He placed my penis inside his

mouth until the situation of which he spoke was rectified. He swallowed every bit of the result of such a rectification. He stood and put
my penis back inside my pants for me and took out a pack of Juicy
Fruit gum. Ever the gentleman, he offered me a piece first before un-
wrapping one for himself. "Ready?" he asked, next offering me his
arm. "Now, who are these bitches I'm about to meet?"

"Well, there's Frank Hains." I said, still a bit dizzy from what had
just happened yet having the presence of mind to let go of his arm
when we walked into the hallway and made our way out onto the
campus.

"No. I know about him. Every Negro homosexual in Jackson
knows who he is. His taste is legendary, especially down around Far-
ish," he said, naming a downtown street where Jackson's blacks lived
and owned businesses. "And, of course, I know Eudora Welty. I'm a
little nervous about meeting her," he said, as Miss Welty was at the
height of her renown back then, having just won the Pulitzer Prize
for *The Optimist's Daughter* and the National Book Award a couple of
years earlier for *Losing Battles*. "I met Margaret Walker Alexander at a
dinner party recently," he said, mentioning the Jackson State professor who wrote *Jubilee*, the African-American answer to *Gone with the
Wind*. "She was formidable. Probably more formidable than Eudora
Welty *in her person*. But I'm still quite nervous. Thanks for inviting
me, though."

"You're welcome. Jane Petty'll be there. She's a rich divorcee. An
amazing actress. She played Edna Earle in *The Ponder Heart* at New
Stage and she and Frank were supposed to have been a great George
and Martha in the very first production New Stage ever did, *Who's
Afraid of Virginia Woolf?* She's really pretty. Kinda like Hope Lange."

"Who?"

"Did you ever watch *The Ghost and Mrs. Muir*?" I asked him, hating the question the minute it came out of my mouth. It didn't sound
like something you asked an all-American football player.

"No. I missed that one," he said, chuckling. He stopped to open the passenger side of his Torino and reached into the glove compartment to get his Afro pick so that he could even out his hair where my hands had pressed it to his head after he decided his Mr. Darcy imitation had done its work and he went for my dick.

"She's a blonde, Jane," I said, watching him primp in his car's side mirror. "Then there's Karen Gilfoy. She's not a blonde. She's tall and lanky and a lawyer. Got a great voice. She performs at New Stage when there's a musical or a Gershwin or Cole Porter revue or something. She looks like she'd have a good hook shot," I said, trying to make up for the Hope Lange remark. "Who else? Oh, yeah. Charlotte Capers. She's kinda the ring leader. She runs the archives at the Old Capitol or something like that. She's the big dog. Not Miss Welty. She's had an 'Episcopal pageboy,' as Frank calls it, ever since her father was the rector at St. Andrew's back in the nineteen-twenties. He also told me once she's like Eve Arden as Prince Valiant, whatever that means. You missed a spot right there," I said, thankful for an excuse to stop my babbling. I took the pick from him and gently touched his Afro with it just above his left ear.

When we arrived at Bleak House the door, as usual, was unlocked and gales of women's laughter were wafting through the entrance hall. The soundtrack to Lerner and Loewe's *Gigi* was playing on the turntable. I took Frank's hand and led him into the kitchen where all the merriment was taking place. "You've arrived!" Frank Hains said when he saw us coming toward them. "Ladies! Ladies!" he said, clapping his hands for attention. "Best behavior!" he instructed them. They continued to giggle. There was an empty bucket of Kentucky Fried Chicken sitting in the middle of the table. Frank had made a big dish of his special macaroni and four cheeses. The remains of the salad they had eaten lay limp at the bottom of a big wooden bowl. A bottle of Dennery's salad dressing—Dennery's was the name of a favored restaurant in town—was next to the two bottles of bourbon they'd obviously been enjoying. Maurice Chevalier and Hermione Gingold were singing, "Yes, I Remember It Well," from the stereo's speakers. "Let me turn this down," said Frank Hains. "We were just making up names for each other based on the stars in *Gigi*. Ladies, you all know Kevin. This is a new friend of his, Frank *Dowsing*."

"Go, Bulldogs!" shouted Karen Gilfoy, evoking the mascot name for the Mississippi State football team. "I'm 'Leslie She-Does-Carry-On,'" she said, slightly slurring the name they had come up with for her based on Leslie Caron, *Gigi*'s star.

"I'm 'He-Manly Gingold,'" said Miss Capers. "And that's 'Maurice She-Valley,'" she said, pointing to Miss Welty, who grimaced at the name.

"That wasn't my idea," Miss Welty apologized. "I liked 'Lerner and Loewe Though I Walk through the Maurice Chevalier of Death.'"

"Is that because you fear no evil?" Frank Dowsing asked her.

"I'm sitting at this table, aren't I?" she said.

Miss Capers laughed louder and again piped up. "Oh, come on, Eudora. I think 'Maurice She-Valley' would be a good *nom de plume* for all that porno Henry Miller wanted you to write on the side."

"Good God," said Miss Welty, who had once welcomed Miller to Jackson when he was passing through but did not allow him in her home at her mother's insistence. "Let's not bring that man into the conversation. We're having fun."

"And who are you?" I asked Jane Petty.

"We're having a hard time coming up with a pun for Eva Gabor," she said. "And Louis Jourdan has us completely stumped."

"I've got it!" exclaimed Miss Capers, and to the tune of "Shortnin' Bread" sang, "Mama's little baby loves Louis Jour Louis Jour, Mama's little baby loves Louis Jourdan."

All the other women joined in: "Three little children layin' in the bed, two were sick and the other 'most dead. Sent for the doctor, the doctor said, feed dem children some Louis Jourdan. Put on the skillet. Put on the lid. Mama's little baby loves Louis Jourdan!" They raised their glasses and clinked them beneath the kitchen table's hanging lamp.

Frank reentered the room. "And what are they calling you?" I asked him.

"Well, since I'm the host, we thought I should have the director's name. So Charlotte suggested 'Vincente *Femmelli*' instead of Vincente Minnelli. But I think it's simpler just to change the first name."

"To what?" asked the other Frank.

"Liza!" he said and slightly struck a Fosse pose. Again glasses clinked.

On the table was a piece of paper with a long list of paired letters on it. "What's that?" I asked as soon as things had calmed down and more proper introductions had been rendered. Frank Hains found two extra chairs for Frank Dowsing and me and, attempting to be two of the girls, we pulled them up to the table.

"We were coming up with all the writers we could think of who went by their initials, then each of us was going to name our favorite," said Liza, née Frank. "Can you think of anymore?"

I looked at the list:

E. B

T. E.

P. D.

T. S.

A. E.

W. H.

H. G.

C. S.

e. e.

D. H.

V. S.

V. S.

E. M.
A. L.
A. A.
J. B.
G. K.
C. P.
J. D.
E. L.
P. G.
J. G.

"I can," said Frank Dowsing. "Does Y. A. count?"

"Who?" asked Miss Welty.

"Y. A. Tittle?" asked Miss Capers.

"Yes, ma'am," said Frank Dowsing. "I read a book of his once about being a quarterback I checked out of the Tupelo library."

"Put him down," said Karen.

Jane Petty picked up her pen:

Y. A.

"Are you from Tupelo?" asked Frank Hains.

"I'm really from a little town outside Tupelo," said Frank Dowsing. "Palmetto. I'm sure you've never heard of it."

"I have. I went to Palmetto once when I was working for the W.P.A.," said Miss Welty. "Churchgoers."

"Eudora's the only saint you'll ever meet that doesn't go to church," Miss Capers told my friend.

"Hush, hush, sweet Charlotte," said Miss Welty, tapping her finger on the rim of her glass as a signal for Miss Capers to top her off with a little more bourbon. "Hush up."

Frank Hains said it was time to pick our favorite writer from the list. I studied it and have to admit I could only figure out who five or six of them were supposed to be. "Who's C. P.?" I asked.

"Cavafy. That's one I came up with," said Frank Hains.

"Of course you did," said Miss Capers.

"I have to go with T. S. Eliot as my favorite on here," said Jane. "He at least wrote a play."

Karen said, "I'm tempted to go with Y. A. But I think I'll pick J. D. Salinger. Not because of Holden, but because of Franny and because of Zooey."

"I'm for D. H. Lawrence," said Frank Hains. "For the censorship issues alone. Kevin?"

"A. E. Housman," I said.

"That's an odd pick, son," said Miss Capers. "I was thinking maybe you were more an e. e. kind of boy. Why'd you pick him?"

"The preacher read a poem of his at my daddy's funeral when I was about six or seven years old," I told them all. "My aunt Vena Mae made a fuss about how beautiful it was afterwards and insisted the family all get copies of it. The preacher obliged and my grandmother kept her copy in a drawer all these years. She gave it to me when I moved here to go to Millsaps. 'To an Athlete Dying Young.'"

"I know that poem," said Miss Welty. "There's a beautiful, simple line in it, if I'm recalling it correctly, describing the pallbearers at the young athlete's funeral: 'townsmen of a stiller town.'"

"Yes, ma'am," I said. "That's it."

"You know Housman doesn't have an *e* in it," she told me. "People are always making that mistake when they spell his name."

"Jean Harlow once met Noël Coward," said Frank Hains, getting out a carton of Seal-Lilly vanilla from the refrigerator's freezer compartment. "'Oh, *Noël! Noël!*' she exclaimed," he continued, pronouncing the name as if it were the French term for Christmas. "'It's such an honor to meet you, *Noël!*' Noël Coward looked at her with not a little disdain and said, 'Dear girl, the *e* is silent like the *t* in Harlow.'" We laughed and all raised our hands when Frank asked who wanted ice cream.

"I saw your daddy play basketball once or twice, Kevin," said Karen. "Have I ever told you that? I was at Millsaps at the same time he was at Mississippi College. Has he informed you that his father was also a sports star, Frank?" she asked my guest. Frank Dowsing shook his head and looked at me with a cocked eyebrow. He touched my leg beneath the table. "I came to see you, too, in a play at the Christian Center," she told me, using the name for the auditorium at Millsaps that the students there preferred to shorten to the CC. "It was that infernal *Infernal Machine* by Cocteau that Lance Goss loves so much," she said, naming the head of the theater department at Millsaps. "You were great, though." She turned again to Frank Dowsing. "He played Anubis, the Jackal, the Egyptian God of Death, and wore this skimpy little costume that showed off his body. But I'm sure you've seen even more of the little jackal by now. I was in that damn play back when I went to school up the hill there. Back in 'fifty-three or 'fifty-four. I played Queen Jocasta."

"Honey, you're still playin' her," said Miss Capers. "Let's get back to this list. I was about to choose E. B. White because y'all all know how ol' Char can weave a web. But I think I have to go with P. D. James. Somebody's got to stick up for us women. She's the only dame on the list, as far as I can tell. Now *that's* a mystery. Mr. Dowsing?"

"May I choose someone not listed?" he asked, studying the page of initials.

"Sure," said Miss Capers. "You've come up with yet another one we've missed?"

"W. E. B. DuBois," he said.

"Well, if we're going to allow three initials then I'm going to have to go with that S.O.B. Henry Miller," said Miss Welty. She and Miss Capers clinked their glasses. Miss Welty then turned the page of initials her way. She slumped deeper in her seat. "This is much too difficult. It really depends on what night I'm looking at such a list for me to come up with an answer for my favorite."

"Try Sunday," said Miss Capers. "It's Sunday."

"Hush up," said Miss Welty, still studying the list. "V. S. would kill me if he knew I were about to make this choice," she said.

"Pritchett, not Naipaul," Jane whispered to me, though I had no idea who either was at that point in my life.

"Sorry, Victor," Miss Welty continued. "I have to go with E. M. Forster. *A Passage to India* tips the balance on Sundays. Have you started reading that, like I asked you to, Kevin?" she asked. "*Maurice* is not first-rate Forster, even though I understand the reasons why it would be the only work of his you've read," she said, finally eyeing Frank Dowsing with the interest that the rest of her friends had been eyeing him all night. "Promise me—*A Passage to India*."

"Yes, ma'am. I'm writing a paper right now on *The Red Badge of Courage*," I said.

Miss Capers moaned, "Ugggh, *college* . . ."

Frank Hains served us all our bowls of Seal-Lilly ice cream. Karen Gilfoy poured the remaining bourbon in her glass over her two scoops of vanilla. The discussion turned to politics and the state's old war-horse senators up in Washington, John Stennis and James Eastland, and whether they were about to retire. Governor William Waller was roundly hailed for having the courage to honor slain civil rights activist Medgar Evers by proclaiming a Medgar Evers Day. Miss Welty, an early integrationist, was especially moved by Waller's actions since she had stayed up late the night of Evers's assassination in 1963 to write one of her most talked-about short stories for *The New Yorker*, "Where Is the Voice Coming From?," a harrowing account of that assassination from the point of view of the killer. It meant a lot to her, that proclamation. The ladies also went on and on about how lovely Waller's wife was and what a great job she was doing restoring the governor's mansion. The list of initials on the table led to a discussion of writers who went by three names, and I told everyone that my mother used to read to me from *Pale Horse, Pale Rider* and *Sex and the Single Girl* as bedtime stories. "Katherine Anne Porter and Helen

Gurley Brown—well, that explains a lot," said Miss Capers. Porter was one of Miss Welty's first champions and the two of them had a complicated friendship. I tried to get her to tell me some stories about Porter but she turned the conversation to Robert Penn Warren and the night she and Miss Capers had gotten blind drunk with him when he looked them up in Jackson.

Frank then put one of Ethel Waters's early 78-rpm recordings on the stereo, and again insisted she was one of the great geniuses of the twentieth century, though he hated that she had ended up appearing on Billy Graham crusades and "singing about that goddamn sparrow every chance she got." In fact, the one time that Frank's publisher at the *Daily News* made him retract a column was when he ranted in print about Billy Graham preempting a broadcast from the Metropolitan Opera on a local television station. He had pictures of Ethel Waters framed in the house and had collected every one of her records he was able to find, storing them in their alphabetized place in the room that housed his extensive record library. "Waters is the Welty of my collection," he said one night when he was showing me some of her prized LPs down in the "W" section. He always called her the Black Swan because that was the name of her first record label. "They all stole from the Black Swan," he said that night when we were gathered around his kitchen table. "Mildred Bailey. Ivie Anderson. Connie Boswell. Even Ella. Did any of you ever see her on that episode of *Route 66* she did? One of her great performances. Better than *The Member of the Wedding*. Maybe even better than *Pinky*." The Black Swan began to sing "Suppertime," from the 1933 Irving Berlin and Moss Hart revue *As Thousands Cheer*. It's a song, Frank Hains pointed out when he first played it for me, about how a woman is going to tell her children that their father has been lynched. We all sat in silence and listened to her sing it.

"How've y'all been able to stand livin' in Miss'sippi all these years?" I asked when none of the raconteurs around the table seemed to know exactly what to say at the end of the song, especially in the presence of the new person I had brought into their sphere.

Frank Hains got up to put a more upbeat Ethel Waters song on the stereo. "How about some 'Heat Wave'?" he asked. "Eudora!" he shouted as he headed for his record library. "Didn't William F. Buckley ask you something like our resident little smart-ass there just had the audacity to ask us all, back when you were on *Firing Line?*"

"Heavens to Betsy! Must we invoke that man's name tonight?" huffed Miss Capers, pushing her chair back and grabbing the empty bucket of Kentucky Fried Chicken to throw in the trash. "I warned Eudora about going on that show," she said, alluding to the *Firing Line* episode filmed at Mississippi's ETV studios that Miss Welty had agreed to appear on with Walker Percy because it was being filmed at ETV. Frank had directed for the station his own highly praised adaptation of several of her short stories, *A Season of Dreams*, and hosted a program there called *In Conversation with.* . . . Buckley, moreover, had himself agreed beforehand that politics would not be discussed, only literature. "Heavens to Betsy!" said Miss Capers again when she plopped back down.

"Betsy—that's a good name for him," said Frank, reentering the kitchen as Ethel Waters began singing in calypso-like rhythms. "Henceforth at Bleak House he will forever be spoken of as Betsy Buckley. So . . . ," he said, putting a hand on one of Frank Dowsing's shoulders and leaning against him, "when Eudora got on the set with Betsy he sandbagged her with a series of political questions. One of which, if I'm recalling this correctly, was something like, How can you as a person of *sensitivity* have lived in Mississippi during the time you've lived here? To which Eudora replied, in essence, 'How could one not have?'"

Everybody looked at Frank Dowsing for his reaction to Frank Hains's story. Everybody but Miss Welty. She sat staring at her vanilla ice cream. She ate a spoonful. "I think," Frank Dowsing said, "you have to be a privileged white person to have the luxury of a reply such as that."

"Well, Frank is not quoting me exactly—my thoughts on the subject lost some of their complexity in his journalistic penchant for succinctness—but your point is well taken," Miss Welty stated before a discussion could ensue or an uneasy silence settle in around the table once more. "Good for you, Mr. Dowsing," she said, then looked up from her ice cream and right at him. "I knew I liked you the minute you said I feared no evil."

"Touché," said Frank Dowsing.

"Honey, nobody's fencin' here," said Miss Capers.

"How about some Sondheim?" asked Frank Hains. "I think it's time for the Frank Hains *Follies*." One of his fondest memories was escorting Miss Welty to see *Follies* when they happened to be in New York during the same week. He found the album in his library in "record time," as he liked to describe the alacrity with which he could locate a choice among the thousands arranged in their room. The first song, "Beautiful Girls," began to fill the house after the orchestra played its prologue to the show.

"Except for seeing Jane there as Edna Earle in Frank's version of *The Ponder Heart* at New Stage," Miss Welty said, "attending *Follies* on Broadway with him was one of my best nights in the theater—though the production, finally, was neither this nor that. But perhaps that was its underlying allure for me."

Throughout the subsequent numbers, the ladies around the table discussed other favorite theater experiences of theirs, and the latest bits of New Stage gossip. "I'm gonna skip over these next few songs to get to that Yvonne De Carlo one," Karen said, and got up to do just that. As she came back into the kitchen she was singing along with the truncated version of "I'm Still Here" that was recorded for the Broadway album. "Good times and bum times, I've seen 'em all and, my dear, I'm still here," she sang.

Yvonne De Carlo took over for a few lyrics, then Jane prompted Miss Welty, "This is your part coming up, Eudora. Go!"

"I've slept in shanties, Guest of the W.P.A.," Miss Welty sang. "But I'm here! Danced in my scanties, Three bucks a night was the pay, But I'm here . . ."

The rest of us applauded her and, as the song continued, the women, the two Franks, and I sang along when we thought we knew enough of the words. Karen really belted out the names, "Herbert and J. Edgar Hoover" at one point, then turned her attention to Miss Capers. "Charlotte, you've got to sing," said Karen when she noticed her buddy was biding her time to join in. "Come on. Sing!"

Miss Capers downed the rest of what was in her glass and, squaring her shoulders, croaked out her own lyrics over De Carlo, giving Sondheim a run for his money. "Singing's not something I've ever dared, 'cause—*merde!*—I sound like Melvin Laird. But friends never gave a damn nor cared, so I'm here!"

I thought Miss Welty was going to fall off her chair with laughter. We all were laughing and trying to see who could now sing the loudest, after Frank scampered into the next room to retrieve the lyric sheet inside the album sleeve. I began to clear the table of the empty glasses and ice cream bowls. I turned from where I was standing at the kitchen sink and saw them all now with their arms around each other—Frank Dowsing especially included—as they headed toward the end of the number. The lamp hanging above the table bathed their faces in a glow of sheer happiness. "Lord knows at least I was there, and I'm *here*!" their voices rang out. "Look who's *here*! I'm still *heeeeeeeeeeere!*"

That night, that song, those lyrics, those women, those dear two Franks, that moment I turned from the sink and glimpsed pure joy for a second or so has echoed throughout my life. I wondered what they all would look like in bedsheet togas singing another Sondheim number. The last time I had been privy to such joy was watching my mother rehearse her secret performance just for me, all those years before. Who would be the last person standing from this group, I also wondered, for I had been already conditioned to consider when everybody, including myself, would die. Who among us would still be here? The first to go was Karen Gilfoy who, after a career as a judge, died a recluse and alcoholic. Miss Capers, by then residing in a nursing home, was the next to pass away, dying suddenly of a heart attack right before a Christmas Day she had hoped to spend with Miss Welty. Jane Petty, living life to the very end on her own terms, succumbed to cancer after stopping treatment and refusing sustenance for the final two weeks of her existence. Miss Welty, outlasting them all, died in 2001 of complications from pneumonia at the age of ninety-two. She even outlasted the two Franks.

Mr. Dowsing never graduated from medical school. After a few more dates, he and I became bar buddies. He liked his young white boys too much and I couldn't stop him from cutting a sexual swath through Jackson's small gay community before he moved on to New Orleans and Atlanta, where he became—I heard through the grapevine when I'd come home for visits from New York—a pharmaceutical salesman. We finally lost track of each other and I was heartbroken to hear from Joe Rex, who himself ultimately died of a suspected drug overdose alone in a hotel room, that there were rumors around Jackson that Frank Dowsing had contracted HIV and, suffering from AIDS, had moved back home to Tupelo. This is what his obituary said in the fall 1994 issue of the Mississippi State University alumni newsletter:

Frank Dowsing Jr., of Palmetto, the first African-American football player at Mississippi State and the only African-American Mr. Mississippi State University, died July 11, 1994. He was 43. . . . Dowsing enrolled at Mississippi State in 1969 and played defensive back under Coach Charlie Shira, subsequently being selected all-SEC and all-American. He graduated with honors in 1973. Before illness forced him to retire, he was district manager with AT&T in California. On his return to the Tupelo area, he became very active in Palmetto CME Church and had enrolled at Memphis Theological Seminary. He was instrumental in starting a scholarship program, which the Tupelo-Aberdeen CME District named after him prior to his death. Dowsing was a steward of Palmetto CME Church, a Sunday-school teacher, founding president of the church's Mass Choir, and a lay leader for Palmetto's Lay Council and the Aberdeen-Tupelo Lay Council. Acquaintances, former teammates, and coaches have described Dowsing as a pioneer whose quiet determination earned him universal respect as a positive influence on race relations in the state.

Those last words could have been written also about Frank Hains. He marshaled his arts and entertainment pages to advance inclusion. He abhorred violence. When President Kennedy was assassinated he used his column to cry out at its senselessness:

The assassination of President Kennedy was one of those unbelievable acts of mindless malice which shocks not only by its viciousness and by its tragic waste but also by a frightening realization which it brings. It is the realization that there can exist within one human animal—within one who is one of us—such disposition to violence and hatred. Indeed, no man is an island. Every man shares in the responsibility for that which is in every other man. When any man hates other men, all of us are befouled by his hatred. When any man carries his hatred to the extent which allows him to kill, any one of us who actively pours out hatred for any man adds the pressure of his own finger to that which pulls the trigger: any one of us who is passively indifferent to those outpourings of hate is guilty of failing to stay that pressure."

Rereading those words now makes it even more difficult for me to write about Frank's death. How do I start? How do I explain it? Though I had suffered through the deaths of both my parents and at the undenied hands of Dr. Gallman, nothing in my short life could have prepared me for what still awaited me. I wish now, as I write this, I could summon some of Yvonne De Carlo's boastful, infectious pride at having stuck around long enough to bear witness. But I feel more like Frank's beloved Black Swan singing about what she's going to tell her children when they get home for supper.

On the Sunday morning of July 13, 1975, I awoke to the smell of bacon frying and the sound of Julian Bream, the classical guitarist, playing Bach. How could I not feel at home in a house filled with such a smell, such a sound, or in the presence of a man who chose to fill his home simultaneously with each? I felt, yes, *at home* with Frank Hains. I guess that's the best, most basic way to put it. I was comforted by his taste, his take on life, the grace with which he honed his vast curiosity. He had offered me the front bedroom of Bleak House to live in that summer while I worked as a salesman at the Jeans West store at the Jackson Mall in order to earn some extra money for my move to New York City in August. Frank had been instrumental in convincing me to audition for the Juilliard School of Drama as well as the drama school at Circle in the Square. He knew that Millsaps was turning into a frustrating experience for me. "You're much too much a free spirit to spend four years at that Methodist prison up the hill," he joked one time, while we sat up late having one of our heart-to-heart talks. "Lance Goss doesn't understand someone like you. He much prefers Tab Hunters to James Deans in his department. You're talented enough to get into a school in New York." The discussion that night veered into finances, as all my discussions back then tended to, and I told him I didn't have enough money in the bank to buy a round trip ticket to New York if I got accepted for one or both of the auditions. He got up from his reading chair, tying his sash about his kimono so it wouldn't flap open to reveal his naked body beneath it, and found his checkbook. He pushed his reading glasses down on his nose from where they so often rode on top of his balding head. He wrote my name on the check and signed it. He left the amount blank. "Once you get the auditions and find out how much the plane ticket on Delta will cost, you fill in the blank with the right amount," he said, handing me the check. "I trust you. Now let's come up with what you should audition with. They'll probably want something classical and something modern." We decided I'd do the "Now I am alone. O, what a rogue and peasant slave am I" soliloquy from *Hamlet* (he lent me a recording of Richard Chamberlain's television version to listen to) and speeches from Leonard Melfi's one-act *Birdbath* and Israel Horowitz's *The Indian Wants the Bronx*. I got an audition for both schools and called Mom and Pop from New York and told them what I was doing once I was up there, afraid to let them know beforehand. They had gotten accustomed to my surprising them with my headstrong ambition and after I received a scholarship to Juilliard they accepted the fact that I was going. I never asked for their permission. I simply let them know that it was the latest phase in my life. The amount of love and trust it took for them to let me go to college at seventeen was nothing compared to the amount it took for them to let me move to New York City only two years later. Frank, of course, was ecstatic for me, though saddened that I would not be around much longer for our heart-to-hearts. He wouldn't hear of my paying him back the money for the ticket.

"Is that bacon?" I asked as I entered the kitchen that morning bare chested in my gym shorts, knowing he usually ate only a bowl of corn flakes before dashing out the door to the office or tending to whatever was on his ongoing to-do list. "What's the occasion?" I asked.

"Oh, I just felt a little like Berenice Brown when I got up. All I could think about was *pork*. You just know Berenice liked her bacon," he said, referring to Ethel Waters's character in *The Member of the Wedding*. "Want some coffee?" he asked and poured me a cup, having taught me to like it "strong and black," he said once, "like that dashing Mr. Dowsing. I wish you two had worked out."

I told him that Sunday morning Frank Dowsing and I had, in fact, been hanging out together the night before at Mae's Cabaret and that we talked about the night I had brought him to dinner at that very table. "He's still upset that he might have insulted Miss Welty," I said.

"Dear boy, Eudora's a tough old bird. She can take care of herself," said Frank, draining the bacon strips on the sports pages of the combined *Clarion-Ledger/Jackson Daily News* that the two papers' one publisher put out on Sundays. "You want an egg or two?" he asked, having also taught me to love how eggs could be poached, not just scrambled or fried.

"How 'bout I make us some pancakes," I said. "I saw some Aunt Jemima in a cabinet, I think."

"I'm not sure that's still good. It's been in there for a while. Can pancake mix go bad?" he asked.

"I don't think so," I told him and proceeded to make a batch. We sat down to our bacon and pancakes. I had failed to check to see if we had any syrup but Frank solved the problem by sprinkling sugar on the pancakes and cutting up some strawberries he had left over in the refrigerator from the daiquiris he had made us on Friday night. We were just beginning to relax again in each other's company since we had had a falling-out at the beginning of the summer. He had asked me whether, if he directed a production of *Butterflies Are Free* at the Vicksburg Little Theatre, I would star in it as the blind boy, Don Baker. I said sure but then backed out when I realized I had to earn some money that summer and would have to work most nights at the mall. He accused me of waiting too late to tell him—which I did, a

few days before rehearsals were supposed to start—but ended up forgiving me, as I knew he would, when he found another boy for the
part just in time.

"How's Carl?" he asked, mentioning the bisexual advertising executive who was my one sexual constant in all my time in Jackson. Carl
never went to the gay bar. The only time he really did anything gay
was when he went to bed with me. He had even had affairs with many
of his leading ladies at New Stage. In addition, he was carrying on a
sporadic romance with my best friend at Millsaps, Lynn from House of
the Rising Son. She had gone up to New York to study at the American Musical and Dramatic Academy but was back to get her college
degree at Millsaps and had been Lance's latest version of Jean
Cocteau's Jocasta. "I think Carl is really in love with you," Frank said.

I shrugged and ate some strawberries off his plate. "He gave me a
key to his apartment this summer," I told him.

Frank smacked me on the arm with a quickly rolled-up arts section
of the Sunday paper. "You scamp. Don't you hurt him. I think he must
be Presbyterian. That's my theory, at least. He seems predisposed—
predestined, whatever—to be a little tormented by his status as Jackson's resident sex symbol. I saw some of the photos he's taken of you.
I'm telling you, the man holding that camera is in love."

"He's really special," I said.

"Uh-oh," said Frank. "That means you're *not* in love."

"I'm moving to New York in four weeks," I said. "He's moving to
Houston to join the Alley Theatre."

"Non sequiturs," said Frank.

"No, I'm not in love with him. But I think Lynn is."

"Well, that's complicated," said Frank. "Didn't you say she was going home with you to Forest today? What is that I see up your sleeve,
dear boy, on that shirt you're not wearing? I think I've told you to
wear a shirt when eating at my table, have I not? Though I really
shouldn't be complaining about the view."

"There's this guy in Forest. His name is Bobby Thompson," I said, mentioning the person I was really in love with, who would always remain the unrequited object of all my fantasies. He had become friendly with Kim and Joe Rex while I was away at college, and through them I had reignited my friendship with him. I explained all that to Frank. "I introduced B-b-bobby to Lynn the other night when he was in town," I said, my reemergent stutter signaling my unease at the subject. "There was a spark between them. She admits it. I figure it would even out the score. If I'm sleeping with the m-man she loves, then she should get a shot at sleeping with the one I do since he's sure not a homo. He's playing d-d-doubles with my little b-brother in a tennis tournament later today. My little sister is in the tournament, too. I think she might be a lesbian. I hope so. Then we're all going to church tonight. Joe Rex is in one of his religious phases," I said, Frank having known Joe Rex slightly through another mutual friend. "There's a revival goin' on with some preacher he's high on at the First M-methodist church. It'll be like old times."

"Doubles with your brother? Church? Jesus!" Frank said, shaking his head. "There's too much transference *goin' on* in that story for me to take it all in at this hour," he continued, mocking my country accent, which also had a tendency to resurface along with my stutter.

"Huh? Transference?"

"Never mind. When are you leaving?" he asked.

"I thought I'd maybe catch an early movie first—I like going to the movies by myself—and then pick Lynn up and head on over there. Maybe I'll see *Jaws* again," I said.

"I could sit through *Nashville* for a second time," Frank said. "That's the only recent movie I could sit through more than once. Still deciding whether that's the masterpiece I think it might be. And I'm looking forward to Pacino in *Dog Day Afternoon* next month and Woody Allen's *Love and Death*, if it ever makes it to Jackson. I read a great line from it the other day. Woody says to Diane Keaton, 'I was made in God's image? Take a look at me. You think He wears glasses?' She goes, 'Not with those frames.' Made me think maybe I should get some new glasses myself. These make me look like Gloria Steinem's ugly sister," he said, pulling his big black-framed ones from a pocket in his kimono. "If *Love and Death* were playing here I'd insist you see that. But, alas . . ."

"Don't you think I've had enough of those fucking two things by now?" I asked.

"Oh, woe is me—the awful strain of being a nineteen-year-old," he teased me, then cupped my face in his hand. "I'm sorry. You have had enough of the the latter in your life, dear boy, yes, you have," he said. "More than I even. But one can never have too much of the former. Someone told me about a one-act comedy Woody Allen wrote recently, titled *Death*. Maybe he should write a one-act tragedy called *Love*. Who was it who told me that? Jane, maybe. I should make a note to try and order it from Samuel French," he said and, putting on his glasses, he added it to his to-do list. "You really should start seeing Woody Allen movies, though, Kevin—especially if you're going to be a New Yorker," he said, pushing the glasses up to where they rested atop his head. "A friend of mine in New York told me he did get a little bored at this one but he just closed his eyes and listened to the Prokofiev on the soundtrack."

"Didn't you say it was like Woody Allen's version of Leo Tolstoy when you and Miss Welty were talking about it the other night?" I asked, sounding as wary of the description as I possibly could. "She's the one who told you about the one-act."

"That's right. I remember now. She insisted it was probably more like his version of Bob Hope."

"Worse," I groaned. I cleared the table to wash the dishes.

"Let's see what's playing in town," said Frank, unrolling the arts section.

"What's your column about today?" I asked him.

"Oh, it's a rather dry one, but important. It's about the live Russian launch of the joint Apollo-Soyuz space mission next week. NBC is broadcasting it live, as well as the Soviet Union. It's the first time Russia has allowed a live broadcast of a space launch, la la la la, on and on and on. I interviewed this John Dancy chap who's covering it for NBC. Let's see. That Paul Newman movie *The Drowning Pool* is playing. *Return of the Pink Panther. Walking Tall: Part Deux.* God! *Gone with the Wind* is at the Lamar, can you believe it? I always like to see what's playing at the Showtown East drive-in. Perfect. It's a double feature of *The Longest Yard* and *The Klansman.* Guess they won't be playing the new Woody Allen there anytime soon. *Cabaret's* back— but you've seen that too many times. I think you should see *Day of the Locust.* They're running quotes in the ad from Judith Crist and Rex Reed and Vincent Canby. Can you imagine them as a threesome?"

"Maybe I'll just skip the movie and head over to Forest and watch more of the tennis match," I said, imagining what Bobby Thompson's butt was going to look like in his white shorts. Julian Bream and Bach had fallen silent. I began to hum "Alice Blue Gown" as I scrubbed the skillet in which I had made the pancakes.

"I know that tune," said Frank. "It's from *Irene.* I've never been a big fan of Debbie Reynolds, but I have to admit she pulled that performance out of her ass. Have you ever heard the rumors about Agnes Moorehead and her?"

"Samantha's mother on *Bewitched?*"

"Well, I wouldn't put it that way, but yes. Wait. I think I have some versions of 'Alice Blue Gown' other than that tiresome cast album of *Irene.* I'm pretty sure I do. I think there's a Teddy Wilson back there. A Chet Atkins version, maybe. Oh. Wait wait wait. I know—there's an amazing Irving Fazola."

"Who the fuck is that? Fa-whata?"

"*Fazola.* He was a big fat jazz clarinetist back in the thirties. I think he's better than Goodman or Pete Fountain or certainly Artie Shaw.

People called him 'Faz.' His real name was Irving Prestopnik but he got his stage name, get this, from the solfeggio. You know—do re mi fa sol la ti do. Get it? Fa. Sol. La. It became Fazola because of that damn accent those *Yats* down in New Orleans won't give up. He's marvelous. *Marvelous!* Wait. You'll see."

I chuckled at Frank's ability to get so excited about imparting his musical knowledge. Suddenly the house was filled with the strains of a version of "Alice Blue Gown" I never thought possible. I couldn't help myself. My hips and feet started moving with the music as Faz's fingers raced up and down his clarinet on the scratchy old album. Frank came swanning into the room, his kimono gathered in his right hand. "Come, come, come," he said. "Dance with me, dear boy! Dance with me!" I dried my hands on my gym shorts and we half-waltzed, half-jitterbugged around the kitchen, laughing and twirling in each other's arms to Irving Fazola's toe-tapping rendition of my grandmother's favorite song. "Who's leading whom here?" Frank asked as his glasses went flying off the top of his head as I swept him around the kitchen.

"Does it matter?" I asked right back. I let go of him after one final spin. When he bent down to get his glasses I playfully kicked him in his kimono as I started to Charleston. "I never could quite get the hang of this," I complained, trying to get my knees to bend inward as I kicked my legs out to the rhythm of the music.

"You'd still make a better Daisy Buchanan than that Mia Farrow," he said. "But I'm not sure you'd be as good as Betty Field."

"Who?"

Frank dramatically sighed and rolled his eyes at yet another thing he was going to have to explain to me. "She played Daisy in the nineteen-forties version of *The Great Gatsby*, opposite Alan Ladd," he said. "She's one of my favorite actresses. A George Abbott discovery. Married for a while to Elmer Rice. A hard-bitten kind of gal. You have a Betty Field quality yourself, dear boy, even in those gym shorts. Yes, you'd make a pretty good Daisy Buchanan, come to think of it."

"Fuck you. Just for that, I'm going to go see *Jaws*," I told him, and boogied back toward my bedroom.

"Any cute boys at Mae's last night?" he shouted after me.

"Just me," I said. "And the dashing Mr. Dowsing."

Frank and I remained in our respective ends of the house for the next hour or so. That was one of the secrets of our getting along so well. We knew when to steer clear of the other. He hated that I was so messy—my room looked like a tornado had hit it—but he said that as long as I kept my door shut he didn't have to look at it. After I got dressed I found him in his reading chair. This was his favorite spot in the house, where he read the books he was going to review for his own column or for the Sunday book supplement of *The New York Times*. (Nash Burger, an old friend of his and "the girls," was an editor there.) He and Miss Capers were in a bit of a competition to see who could write more reviews for the Sunday *Times*. Frank thought it somewhat distasteful to keep track of how many he had written, but always made sure that it was less than her tally since he knew it meant so much to her. Miss Capers wanted to get to 100, but at the time of her death she was, heartbreakingly, at 99. "Are you doing anything today?" I asked him.

"I might go into the office, but I'm more in the mood to have a lazy afternoon and catch up on these last two *Esquires*. There's that new Capote short story everybody's got their knickers in a twist about. And an Ann Miller thingamajig in one of them. Love Ann Miller. More Woody—can't get away from him. And let's see," he said, thumbing through one of the *Esquires* after pushing his reading glasses down on his nose. "Oh, yes. This interview with Nabokov here. I'll see if I can wade through that. And I want to listen to that Margaret Walker Alexander album again," he said, mentioning the author's spoken-word record he had written so effusively about a few days before in his column. On it, Professor Alexander read many of her poems, Frank's favorite being the title work from *For My People*, her first published volume, for which she won the 1942 Yale Award for Younger Poets. "You do know her husband, Mr. Alexander—Firnist, to his friends—is an interior decorator," said Frank, rolling his eyes a bit behind his glasses. He then attempted to take on the exaggeratedly dignified cadence and timbre of Margaret Walker Alexander herself but instead ended up sounding like his astonishingly good Malvolio did in New Stage's production of *Twelfth Night* back in February. "'Let a new world rise,'" he intoned, reciting a line from *For My People*. "'Let another world be born. Let a bloody peace be written in the sky.' La la la la. On and on and on . . .'"

I kissed him on the top of his head and started for the front door. "Drive safely," he called over his shoulder. "See you later. Love you!"

"Love you, too," I said. He was humming something when I left. It sounded a lot like "Alice Blue Gown."

I couldn't shake the thought of Bobby Thompson's butt, so on the way to see *Day of the Locust* I turned around to go pick up Lynn and head to Forest in my little white Mercury Comet, having traded in my old Dodge Dart. The year or two she had spent in New York had given Lynn more of a sophisticated edge than the rest of us in the Millsaps theater department, but she was not so sophisticated as to put up with Carl's bisexuality much longer. It speaks volumes about her that she valued our friendship enough to let it weather whatever obstacles were put in its way because of my continuing inability not to sleep with him, though I knew it was hurting her feelings. "Look, I understand—he's pretty irresistible," she said on the drive over to Forest when we discussed our sharing of him. "But it's time I moved on. Time we both did. Geography finally is going to force us to anyway. Though I'm not sure going to a revival at the Methodist church in Forest with yet another blond heartthrob is a step in the right direction for me. I've never found prayers and hymns and an altar call the best preliminaries for sex," she said.

"I don't know. They've always worked pretty well in my own life," I said, able to joke now, however privately, however bitterly, about Dr. Gallman.

"Don't tell me you're another one of these gay guys who've had sex with youth directors at their churches," she said. "Youth directors are the choreographers of Mississippi." We laughed and began to gossip about our classmates at Millsaps and in which part of New York City I should try to find an apartment, as she was an old hand at city living compared to me. Carl subscribed to *The Village Voice*, and I had been scouring the real estate ads for places to live while I was naked and sitting cross-legged in the middle of his bed.

"It's so expensive up there," I told her. "I've been living for free at Frank's. Carl pointed out an ad for a one-bedroom on Bleecker Street—that's in the Village, right?—that was $400! Can you believe it? Shit. I was hoping for something more in the 100-to-150 range. Carl only pays $150 for that great place he lives in in north Jackson."

Lynn looked out the window, her little upturned nose turned up a bit more at the mention of Carl's name yet again. "Let's shut off the air conditioner and roll down these windows," she said. "I want to feel my hair in the breeze." She was pretty irresistible herself so we did just that, and with her dark shag (shorter than my own shoulder-length hair) blowing about her face she was even more beautiful, her perfection sexier when she allowed herself to be mussed up a bit.

Bobby Thompson's butt was all that I had hoped for in the tennis match, but Lynn was right about the church service. It wasn't conducive to dating—though Bobby was certainly as beautiful as ever, sitting between us on the pew, a bit of the light coming through the stained glass adding a hue or two to his blondness. I began to get the giggles at one point, remembering another line from *Love and Death* that Miss Welty had mentioned to Frank when they were talking about the movie. ("If Christ was a carpenter, I wonder what he charged for bookcases?") I could tell that Lynn and Bobby bonded a bit in reaction to having been left out of whatever had amused me. After stopping to say our good-byes to Mom and Pop, whom we'd seen at the tennis match, we visited at the Thompsons' house for a while before heading home. We both regretted on the drive back to Jackson that we had tried to combine religion with sexual longing. Who the hell did we think we were, we concluded, after I told Lynn some more of the lines Frank had been spouting for the last few days from *Love and Death*, Woody Allen?

Still hungry and not out of conversation, we decided to head downtown when we got to Jackson and get something to eat at the Mayflower, a restaurant where a lot of the Millsaps students hung out, not only because it was one of the few places in town that stayed open late at night but also because of its funky charm. We finally got to Lynn's apartment on one side of an old shotgun house sometime after midnight. I walked her to her door and sat on the house's porch swing where we came to our whispered final truce about Carl: Carnality would be the only reason either of us slept with him during the weeks the three of us had left in Jackson. It was a pact that was easy for me to make, for it was basically the only reason I slept with him anyway. It was because her feelings for him were stronger than mine that I was dealing from a position of strength. Irony. The complexity of human emotions. Something Frank had earlier called "transference." All of that had replaced hymns and prayers and altar calls in both our lives, Lynn's and mine, since we had first met at the House of the Rising Son, barely teens, and dared to confide in each other without laughing, dead serious, our most theatrical of dreams. I kissed her good night on her cheek and headed back to Bleak House.

I parked next to the Jewish cemetery and bounded up the steps to Frank's vast old front porch satisfied by the events of the day. I'd been able to be in Bobby Thompson's presence and not completely ache for him, as I was beginning to realize the limits to his blond charms. He wasn't bland exactly, but after my time away from Forest, fucking, it seemed, everything that moved, I realized that Bobby Thompson was sort of a tabula rasa presence in my life, someone on whom I could project the purer longings of my past. I also felt better about being a big brother to Kim and Karole (whom I had mostly ignored in the solitary sorrow I lived in after our parents' death), since I had made the effort that day to see them in their tennis tournament. They had been basketball stars—they must have gotten Daddy's gene—during high school, and selfishly I had missed most of their games. I had not let political arguments ensue, either, during my time with Mom and Pop that afternoon. And I had sat inside a church without getting angry at Dr. Gallman. All of that, plus Lynn and I had de-Carled ourselves and Frank and I were back to our old routines, having truly forgotten about our *Butterflies Are Free* falling-out. But most of all, and on top of everything else, I was moving to New York City in a little over a month. Juilliard, by accepting me, had made me feel finally just that: accepted. I had certainly never really felt that way in Mississippi, though I had felt as close to it as I had ever come when Frank befriended me and included me in his dandy little sphere of like-minded Mississippians, all scaldingly smart, irrefutably liberal, capable of the kind of laughter that still lingers inside me long after the sound of it has subsided. I dared to feel happy as I bounded up the front steps of Bleak House that night. Even hope was making itself known.

Frank's screen door was slightly ajar and between it and the front door Carl Davis had left a paper sack full of fresh tomatoes for him with a note saying they were from his mother's own garden. The front door was unlocked, as I expected it to be. The house was also ablaze with light, which I was not expecting. I checked my watch. It was close to one A.M. I called out Frank's name, as I always did, to make sure he wasn't reading in the nude. That was a habit of his I was trying to break him of. No one answered. I heard an odd *tut tut tut tut tut* and realized it was the sound of the needle on his turntable at the end of one of his albums. One could only play a single album at a time and then had to pick the turntable's arm up at the end. I once asked him why he didn't get the "reject" fixed on it and he said, "Rejection, dear boy, has no place in this house." I went to pick up the arm, first putting the sack of tomatoes next to the Margaret Walker Alexander album resting on the top of the built-in cabinet on which Frank's turntable sat, the cabinet seeming to float in space and serving as a kind of divider for the house's dogtrot hallway and the living room. Professor Alexander's smiling face was on the cover but her last name was not. Only MARGARET WALKER all in capital letters was printed across it, the M and W and R with extra curlicues on them. The record on the turntable was a Mabel Mercer one she recorded with Bobby Short, called *Midnight at Mabel Mercer's*. I read a song title, "Wouldn't It Be Loverly?" as the record continued to spin and spin and spin. I thought of Audrey Whatshername in *My Fair Lady*, and hummed a snippet of the song. I turned off the stereo.

"Frank!" I called again. There was still no answer. Next, I noticed something odd: There were two comic books on the coffee table. Frank was not a comic-book reader. I picked up the sack of tomatoes and walked around the turntable cabinet into the living room and looked down at the comic books. One was something called *Doomsday +1*. In a balloon over the head of a female space warrior, her breasts quite pronounced, were these words: "The death-machine has broken through." One of Frank's impressionable young African-American friends, I assumed, must have paid him a visit and left his reading matter behind.

"Frank!" I called again, and walked into the kitchen. When I put the sack of tomatoes on the big round table I could see a blurry image of him lying on his bed through the back of the glass bookshelves. He appeared to be nude. Perhaps he had fallen asleep after he'd had the date he'd kept secret from me. I stepped into the hallway to call his name again and to tell him to put on some clothes. That is when I saw what I will see for the rest of my life. Frank Hains was lying face-down on his king-size bed. The whole mattress was soaked with blood, a giant congealing pool of it. His hands and feet were tightly bound with several of his silk neckties. His mouth was gagged with a handkerchief and another necktie held it in place, pulling his head backward where it was knotted down below with the ties that bound his wrists behind his back. The crown of his head was completely gone, red masses of brain matter spilling from it and running down his neck, splattering the sheet with even more blood. A crowbar lay on the bed next to him. He made no sound. There was no movement. I started toward him and heard a loud creak, the way Bleak House could creak when one stepped on one of its old floor boards too heavily. The sound seemed to issue from Frank's room, as if someone were hiding beyond the open door and was now coming for me. I panicked. I ran from the house. I jumped in my car. I sped instinctively toward Carl.

The thing I remember about that night as much as I remember Frank Hains's blood-soaked bed, as much as I remember what was left of his gelatinous head after that crowbar had done its work, as much as I remember how his body had been bound and gagged with his own silk neckties, as much I remember the instant nausea that those sights can induce in a teenage boy who discovers them, was the way my foot shook on the gas pedal after I cranked up my old Comet and headed straight to Carl's. It was like my grandmother's foot, palsied with incomprehension and anger and yet more imminent sorrow, bearing down on her sewing machine's pedal all those years before, when she didn't think she could take one more sissy demand from me but went along with Matty May's and my Halloween costume idea just to shut us up, so tired was she from taking care of my dying mother in the goddamn hospital. Unable to utter "goddamn," she had instead kicked my hand away that day for the very first time when I tried as usual to help her foot press the pedal, our favored ritual forever altered. I wished I could kick myself away that night as I continued to speed toward Carl's. I wished I could put that witch's costume back on, and be that age again, and head to the carnival still unaware of how it would all turn out. It was as if the shock and fright of finding Frank had puddled in a frenzy down around my right ankle. And yet the car—red leather interior, no power steering, a radio that longed for FM—did not jerk and sputter as I turned onto the Interstate. It seemed instead to head more smoothly onward with each spastic brush of my scuffed Bass Weejun against the gas pedal. That's the core of the memory that night, of all my memories really: the eery smoothness of the ride.

I could not get the image of Frank's bludgeoned head out of my mind. It looked so much like the image I had come up with when Dr. Gallman had begun to molest me that second time and I, trying not to get hard, had attempted to imagine how my father's bashed-in head must have looked when it hit the pavement after he flew from his Volkswagen. Trying not to think of Frank, I thought of that day my father had had his wreck while I tried to keep my own little car on the road as I increased my speed, the Comet's steering wheel always vibrating in my hands whenever the speedometer approached seventy, on its way to eighty. We had been visiting with Mom and Pop the day of my father's accident. My mother was squinting at her McCall's magazine, sunning herself in a lawn chair in the front yard. She was letting me wear her sunglasses while I perused a Better Homes and Gardens. My father told us he was going to look at some Black Angus cattle he was thinking about buying with Charlie "Chunkin'" Ward, a cattle farm their latest get-rich-quick scheme. My mother did not like the idea but knew not to argue. I wanted to go with him and hopped up from my own lawn chair and headed for his Volkswagen Beetle. I climbed into the passenger side as he was trying to get the

thing to crank. "You're not going with me," he flatly stated. I repositioned my mother's sunglasses in a more fashionable angle on my
nose. "Oh, yes, I am," I said, feigning that flirtatiously obstinate tone
that my mother so often took with him. "No, Kevinator. No, you're
not," he warned me. I punched on the radio when the car suddenly
started up. Ferrante and Teicher were banging out the theme to *Exo-
dus* on their pianos. I grabbed the seat, determined not to let go. My
father, getting out, slammed his door shut and fiercely strode over to
my side of the car. My mother looked up from her *McCall's*. "Out!
Now!" he ordered me. "No," I said. "Goddamn you," he groused, his
voice tinged with the anger that so often overtook it when he had to
deal with me, a son whose effeminacy had become downright willful.
He swung my door open. "Goddamn you," he said again. "Goddamn
you, Kevin." It was the last thing he ever said to me. He pulled me
from the car and slammed me onto the ground. He climbed back into
the Volkswagen and sped off down the road, his tires screeching as he
shifted gears and floored the tiny car as fast as he could make it go.
My mother picked me up and brushed me off. She grabbed her sunglasses where they had fallen off my face and put them back on me.
"You don't want to go see any nasty old cows," she said. I was determined not to cry. *I wish you were dead*, I remembered thinking about
my father as I continued to speed toward Carl's. *I wish you were dead.
I wish you were dead. I wish it. I wish it. I wish it*. Less than twenty minutes later, he was. Frank's head kept morphing into my father's that
night—back and forth, back and forth, back and forth. Had my father's distaste for my sissy presence saved my life back then? If I had
not gone to Forest, could I have saved Frank from his similar fate?
Was God loudly speaking to me in the silenced lives of such disparate
men? Was there a voice of God to hear? I sped faster. "There is no
goddamn fucking God," I spat out the words as I approached the exit
I'd been waiting for. "G-god-d-damn you, Fr-frank," I began violently
to stutter. "God-d-damn you," I kept on stuttering, hearing for the

first time not only the angry tone my father's voice could so often take suddenly surfacing there in my own, but how troubled that anger sounded. "G-g-god-d-damn you, g-god-d-damn you! God! God! God! God! God!" I began to repeat over and over, banging the steering wheel with each "God!" that came out of me.

When I got to Carl's, I tried to insert the key he had given me into the lock on his front door but my hands were shaking so badly I was having a difficult time getting the lock to work. The tremor from my ankle seemed to have risen now through my whole body. It had taken all my powers of concentration to get to his apartment, and now that I was there I had begun to hyperventilate to such an extent that I felt as if I were about to faint. The doorknob turned in my hand. I flipped on a light. I ran to Carl's bedroom where he was already asleep. "Ca-ca-ca-ca-ca . . . ," I tried to get his name out but sounded instead like those flummoxed crows that flew toward Mom and Pop and me, the whole complaining flock of them, on that awful November afternoon of my childhood. Carl awoke at the sound of my stuttering attempt to say his name. He sat straight up in bed. When it dawned on him I really was there in his bedroom and was in distress, he jumped to his feet. He was well over six feet tall. His hair was so blond and his skin so fair he almost glowed before me the dark. His uncircumcised penis was half erect from the dream I had awakened him from. There was a lupine sharpness to his features, even when bleary like this from sleep. His eyes were icy blue. He put his hands on my shoulders and tried to calm my trembling. "It's Fr-frank," I was able to say. "Something has happened to Fr-frank. He's d-d-dead, I think. I'm n-not sure. Awful. It's awful."

Carl dressed quickly and got enough information out of me to know that there was blood involved and that what I had witnessed sounded sadomasochistic, certainly traumatic, most likely tragic. He told me to follow him in his car over to Bleak House in my Comet. When we got there, he next told me to wait in the hallway while he checked the bedroom. He came right back out and seemed, even paler, about to be sick. We stared into each other's eyes for several long seconds and knew that no one else would ever know what we were feeling right then, right there. We did not have to speak. He took deep breaths, as if he were about to dive under water, and went back into the bedroom. He came back out and put his arms around me. "I think we're too late, buddy," he whispered in my ear. "I think we're too late. I'm going to call the police."

I stared at Margaret Alexander's smiling face and listened to Carl tell the dispatcher the address of Bleak House. Within a few minutes we heard two police cars arrive. Carl went running outside and hurried the policemen, a Sergeant Bartlett and an Officer Russell, into the house. Sergeant Bartlett, after checking on Frank, then told Officer Russell to get back on his car radio and tell the ambulance it wasn't needed. He next telephoned for someone from the coroner's office to be sent over, as well as investigators from the Jackson Police Department's Crimes Against Persons unit and the Mobile Crime Lab. Soon the house was teeming with people. Frank's body was wheeled out on a gurney. He was still lying facedown, still bound, but a sheet had been thrown haphazardly over him. I was sitting on the living room's low-slung sofa and the last I saw of him was his elbow, bent back behind him where his hands were bound, sticking out from under the sheet. Carl was by my side with his arm around me. An investigator named Fondren arrived on the scene and introduced himself to us. He wanted to ask me some questions. He started to sit in Frank's reading chair. "Don't!" I suddenly blurted at him. "No. Don't sit there. Just don't. Don't."

"It's okay, son," he said. "It's okay. I don't have to sit," he softly said, and came and stood in front of the coffee table. "You're the one who found the body?"

"Yes, he is," said Carl.

"And who are you?" Fondren asked him.

"I'm a good friend of Kevin's," Carl said. "His name is Kevin Sessums. I'm Carl Davis. We are both friends of Frank's. Kevin is living here."

"Oh, you are," said Fondren, interested enough in that detail to make a note on a pad he pulled from his hip pocket. "And where were you all day, Kevin?"

"Forest. I was in Forest with some friends. We went to church," I said.

"Good for you, son. That's where you should be on Sunday," Fondren said.

"Sir, this front bedroom looks ransacked," a young policeman told him.

"No, that's my room," I said. "I'm a pig."

Fondren smiled and made another note. "Do you see anything out of the ordinary in the house, Kevin?" he asked. "Anything at all."

"These," I said, pointing at the comic books on the coffee table between us. "Frank doesn't read comic books and these weren't here when I left today." I started to hand him the top one, *Doomsday +1*.

"Don't touch that," Investigator Fondren said. He said it again: "Don't touch that."

"Excuse me," I said. I went into the bathroom. I locked the door.

"Don't flush!" he called after me. "There might be a salvageable fingerprint on the handle. Don't touch that, either. Don't touch it."

I lay on the floor, fetal-like, and cooled my face against the tile. "Don't touch that," I had heard that *Wait Until Dark* man say to me as the actors who only pretended to be police were scaring Audrey Whatshername up on the screen inside the Town Theatre when I was eleven. "Oh wouldn't it be lo-ver-ly . . . ," I quietly sang to myself. "Lo-ver-ly. Lo-ver-ly. Lo-ver-ly. Wouldn't it be lov-er-ly . . ." Unlike that day at *Wait Until Dark*, I did not have to pee. I did not have to cry. I did not have to vomit or shit. I just wanted to be alone, to do something secret like lying in the fetal position with my face on Frank's bathroom floor. I needed a secret to calm me down. Secrecy was how I coped. I turned over and put the other side of my face on the cool tiles.

Carl knocked on the door. "Are you all right in there?" he asked. "You want me to come in?"

"No, I'll be out in a minute," I told him, my voice echoing slightly against the tiles and mixing with the static from the walkie-talkies on the cops' belts that crackled out there around Carl. I stood and washed my face with cold water. When I opened the bathroom door, I saw the young policeman who had been in my room now sitting in Frank's reading chair. I grabbed him by his shoulders and pulled him up. "Get the fuck off," I said. "Don't sit there."

The rookie looked over at Fondren. "Maybe you should take the boy to your place for the night," Fondren told Carl. "Does he have anywhere else to go?" Carl nodded no. I hated being talked about as if I were not there. "I have all your information here," Fondren said. "I'll contact you tomorrow, Mr. Davis. I'm sorry about your friend."

When Carl and I got back to his apartment we climbed into bed nude, as we always did when we slept together, and, still in shock, I fell fast asleep in his arms. The next morning, Carl, having been awake all night watching me sleep, told me I should telephone my grandparents and let them know about Frank before they read it in the newspaper or heard about it on the television. I didn't bother to get dressed. I walked into his kitchen where the phone was and called home. Mom picked up. "Hello, it's Kevin," I told her. I did not try to make small talk. "Mom, I have something I have to tell you. Frank has been m-m-m-m. . . ." I tried to say "murdered" but could not get the word out of my mouth. Finally I began to cry, then sob, then fall to my knees, my naked body sliding down the wall till I sat crumpled on the floor. I handed Carl the receiver I held over my head. Still naked himself, he took it from me and explained to my grandmother what had happened and that he was taking care of me, for her not to worry, that I was going to be okay. I could not stop crying. Carl picked me up and carried me back to his bed. We began to make love and for a few blissful moments my tears subsided, but then I started crying again and could not stop. After a half an hour or so of my increasingly convulsive sobs, Carl called his doctor who agreed to come over and give me a shot to help me sleep.

My eyes flew open several hours later. I had one thought only: Frank's trunk of pornography. I had promised him I would get rid of it if anything ever happened to him. *I had promised him.* I sprang from Carl's bed and walked into the living room. He was napping on his sofa. The afternoon's edition of the *Jackson Daily News* was on his coffee table. A banner headline was above the name of the paper across the very top of the front page: DR. JONES, 'LITTLE PROFESSOR OF PINEY WOODS,' DIES AT 92. Jones was an African-American educator who had started Piney Woods Country Life School as an open-air classroom with fallen trees and logs as classroom benches and built it into an exemplary institution of learning for his people during the darkest days of segregation. Right below Dr. Jones's headlined obituary was a huge picture of Frank in a black turtleneck and herringbone sports jacket. Underneath the picture was his name and under that: SLAIN AT HIS HOME. The headline next to it read, NEWS ARTS EDITOR FOUND MURDERED. The story took up most of the front page. I picked up the paper and read the first few paragraphs:

Frank Hains, 49, *Jackson Daily News* arts editor and a well-known figure in Mississippi drama circles, was found murdered early today in his 616 Webster St. home.

A police spokesman said death apparently resulted from a blow with a blunt instrument on the back of his head.

Police information officer Sgt. Johnny Dickson said at noon there were no suspects and no leads in the case.

Dickson said the body was discovered about 1:12 A.M. by

Kevin Sessums, 19, a theater associate who was residing tem-
porarily with Hains.

I stopped reading the story when I saw my name and dropped the
paper onto the coffee table. Carl woke. I explained to him that I had
made Frank a promise about the trunk of pornography and I had to
go to Bleak House right then, that minute, before the police found it.
Carl tried to talk me out of it—he didn't think I was quite myself
yet—but he was so exhausted by then that he let me go. He also
knew me well enough to realize there was no stopping me. It would
have taken another call to his doctor and another shot to keep me
from walking out his door and getting in my Comet.

When I got to Bleak House it was still overrun with police. Yellow
crime-scene tape was up around the front steps. A photographer
started following me and snapping my picture. "Are you the house-
boy?" he started shouting. "Did you do it? Did you kill him? Are you
the murderer? You queer, too?" I pushed him out of the way. "Faggot!"
he muttered under his breath as I stepped over the tape. I walked up
onto the porch. A policeman tried to stop me but I pushed past him,
also. He chased me inside but Fondren was there with a colleague
named Covington. They were coming out of the record library and
Fondren told the policeman it was okay of me to be there. Every
room in Bleak House was covered in white fingerprinting dust as the
police continued to try to find any clues to the murder. I took Fondren aside and explained to him about the trunk. He said that they
had already found it.

"I promised Frank I'd get that out of here if anything ever happened to him," I begged. "It was really important to him that his family not find that. Please. Let me take it with me."

"Son, you can't remove anything from a crime scene," Fondren explained to me. Then he wanted me to tell his partner Covington
what I'd told him about the comic books still there on the coffee

table. I did as I was told, then begged again for them to give me the trunk of pornography. "Don't worry," said Fondren. "I'll make sure his family won't find it or see anything that's in there. I promise. Let me walk you out to your car. There's something I want to talk to you about. Is that a Comet you're driving?"

He and I climbed into the front seat of my car. Neither of us spoke at first, but sat silently and watched all the activity at Bleak House. He then turned and looked out his window on the passenger side at all the gravestones. "That's a Jewish cemetery," I told him. "Frank loved living across from that. He thought it was beautiful."

"I'm beginning to see Mr. Hains was one of a kind," he said. "I want to ask a favor of you, son. We've ruled you out for the murder. Your alibi's airtight. But when I start getting questions about you from the press—especially the TV guys, they're already curious about you—I want to say we've ruled nobody out. I won't say you're a suspect but I won't say you're not one, either. We've got an APB out on someone we're interested in. A real piece'a work. We want him to think we're not onto him so he'll slip up and we can throw the net over him. We think he might have gone down toward New Orleans. He was spotted around McComb. Is that okay with you? It might get a little nasty. Mr. Davis tells me you're about to move to New York City anyway. Can you handle it? Would you do that for us so we can catch your friend's murderer?"

I didn't even think about it. "Sure," I said, and shrugged. He was right. I was moving to New York in a matter of weeks. What did I care what a bunch of Mississippians thought of me?

"Thank you, son," said Fondren. "I guarantee you we're gonna get some justice here. You take care of yourself." I had a hard time doing that, for my next few days in Jackson were a blur of scandal and grief and fear. Fondren was right: The TV guys kept calling me the "house-boy," a moniker that had seemed to stick, and would not stop asking questions about me as they fanned the sadomasochistic and homosexual aspects of the case. If one only watched television, one would think I was the murderer.

———————

A week after my conversation with Fondren, an African-American acquaintance of Frank's named Larry Bullock was arrested in New Orleans, where he had fled, while sitting in the shade of a statue of Robert E. Lee. Bullock was a drifter who had ended up in Mississippi working at the blood bank located next door to the offices of the *Jackson Daily News* and *Clarion-Ledger*. He was from Indiana, where he had already been arrested for rape and sodomy, as well as two murders for which he was found not guilty by reason of insanity. I had to return to Jackson in February to testify at the trial, taking a break from rehearsals at Juilliard, where I had been cast as Edmund in *King Lear*. Bullock's defense was to put Frank on trial and prove that Frank was a promiscuous homosexual and that anybody could have killed him because he had so many sexual partners. The judge even allowed the trunk of pornography to be admitted as evidence. With my grandfather sitting in the courtroom, I had to go through the trunk and identify each piece of pornography I myself had looked at before; a sampling was then passed among the jury, most of whom averted their eyes in disgust when the magazines were placed in their hands. The comic books were also admitted as evidence—they bore Bullock's fingerprints—as was his admission of guilt to his half-blind cellmate, George "Tangle-Eye" Lamb, another acquaintance of Frank's, a character that Miss Welty could not have imagined but whom Flannery O'Connor most likely could have. Bullock had warned Tangle-Eye that he would kill him and his family, "even, he say, if he had to go to Timbuktu to find somebody to do it," if "Tangle-Eye" testified against him. But Tangle-Eye took the stand anyway, because "Larry threaten my mama and nobody threaten my mama, that ain't right. Naw, sir. Larry kilt Mr. Frank. He tolt me so. Mr.

Frank be a right-nice man. *A right-nice man.*" Jane Petty and Miss Capers and Karen Gilfoy and Miss Welty, in their capacity as Jackson's
reigning doyennes, had skirted the rules and pooled their resources to
hire a lawyer friend of theirs to aid in the prosecution of Bullock, not
trusting the elected district attorney to fully press the case because of
its homosexual aspects. Their lawyer friend—a man whose last name,
appropriately, was Royals—told the jury during his summation that he
understood their unease at the subject of Frank Hains's homosexuality.
"But try the correct issue. Don't try Frank Hains. He's already been ex-
ecuted," he said, as if maybe that were a good idea if the jurors themselves were thinking such a thought. Bullock was found guilty and
sentenced to life in prison. After the trial Royals told me not to worry
about the sentence. "He's such a crazy mean son of a bitch, Bullock'll
be dead soon," he said with a cold certainty. "Somebody in the state
pen at Parchman'll kill 'im." Royals proved clairvoyant. A few months
later, while exercising in the prison yard, Bullock was surrounded by a
circle of inmates while the one he had singled out to be his "bitch," the
tiniest but toughest one in lockup, stuck a shiv deep into his gut and
walked it around the circumference of his waist until he was disem-
boweled. Mom mailed me a clipping from the *Clarion-Ledger* that told
me of Bullock's murder. "Remember Galatians, Chapter 6, Verse 7,"
she wrote on the note she attached to the clipping. A message to Bullock? To Frank? To me? "'Be not deceived,'" she wrote. "'God is not
mocked: for whatever a man soweth that shall he also reap.' Have you
found a church to go to yet in New York City? You are in my prayers
several times a day. Find a church. It would put my mind at ease. Find a
church, and go."

For many years, however, the last church I ever set foot in was the
one at which Frank's memorial service was held back in that July of

1975. The service had been quickly organized for the Tuesday afternoon after his death at Northminster Baptist Church, where Karen Gilfoy was the choir director. Carl and Jane Petty and Miss Welty and Miss Capers and I all had to be escorted into a side entrance of the church, away from the press, who were lying in wait to snap our pictures. We were seated behind the baptismal font in a single-file row of folding chairs. Northminster's preacher did not know Frank and the service was quite brief. I sat there on my folding chair, staring at Miss Welty's stooped shoulders, and, as I had when staring at the ceiling while Dr. Gallman masturbated me and ejaculated on my leg, completely let my mind go blank. There were no tears. There would be no tears for years. I was all cried out.

Frank's family arrived and took his body back to Parkersburg, West Virginia, where he was buried in a place called Big Tygart Cemetery. I still wanted to stay in Jackson for a week or two more to finish my job at Jeans West, but was getting scared—Bullock had yet to be caught—that whoever killed Frank was coming after me next. Local writer and publisher, Patti Carr Black, the junior member of Frank's cultural claque of "girls," graciously offered me her house, around the corner from Miss Welty's, to live in for a few days while she and her twelve-year-old daughter moved in with Jane Petty. I accepted her kind offer, but each night I thought I heard noises outside the bedroom window and called my older Pike brother to come over to sleep in the house with me. Our sexual relationship was over but we were able to keep our friendship intact. For a night or two, Lynn came by and kept me company. Carl made sure to visit every day and offered to let me stay at his place so Patti and her child could have their house back. I decided instead to quit my job and head home to Forest, to spend my three remaining weeks with Mom and Pop and Kim and Karole before loading up a yellow rented Ryder truck and driving north to my new life in Manhattan.

On a Sunday afternoon, two weeks after Frank's murder, I told

Mom that I was going to drive over to Harperville to my parents' graves. We were washing dishes after we'd eaten our after-church lunch of roast beef and baked potatoes and fatbacked green beans and yeasty homemade buttered rolls. When Mom asked, "Want me to go with you, honey?" I told her that, no, I wanted to be alone with my parents, that it would be the last time I'd be seeing their graves for a while, once I'd moved to New York City. I cranked up my old Comet and pulled out of the drive. Instead of heading to Harperville, I found myself driving to Jackson. The emotional *nothingness* that had resurfaced at Frank's memorial service had settled inside me during the past few days in Forest. The feeling—the *lack* of feeling, really—would not budge. I couldn't even focus on packing for New York. I felt no excitement, none at all, at the prospect of my life completely changing in a matter of days. An hour later, I was parked not at my parents' cemetery but at that Jewish one across from Bleak House. I sat staring at the front porch and those old steep steps up which I had so often bounded before calling out "Frank!" to let him know I was home. I sat there for a long time. I kept looking from the Jewish headstones on one side of my Comet, back to Bleak House on the other. The Sunday *Clarion-Ledger/Jackson Daily News* was on the seat next to me. I had stopped to buy a copy to check the movie ads in case I wanted to see a film later in the day. I opened up the arts section and spotted the very last "On Stage" column that would ever run. Frank Hains's byline was still beneath its heading. His carefully drawn likeness that ran above each of his columns was still there, too. But the title of that last column was "In Memoriam" and it was written by Eudora Welty. I knew that she and her friends had become angered by the press coverage of Frank's death before I left town, especially another "In Memoriam" column by a colleague of his at the *Daily News*, Charles B. Gordon, who had written about "the poor fellow who stood charged with Hains's slaying." Gordon had also written that although Frank had lived a life of "books, art, music, and literature," it was also a life "slightly constricted and devoted to such a life's ramifications." This is what Miss Welty, a few days later, wrote for everyone in Mississippi to read. I sat in my Comet, a Mississippian, and read it.

For all his years with us, Frank Hains wrote on the arts with perception and clarity, with wit and force of mind. And that mind was first-rate—informed, uncommonly quick and sensitive, keenly responsive. But Frank did more than write well on the arts. He cared. And he worked, worked, worked for their furtherance in this city and state. He was a doer and a maker and a giver. Talented and versatile to a rare degree, he lived with the arts, in their thick.

So it was by his own nature as a man as well as in the whole intent of his work that he was a positive critic, and never a defeating one. The professional standards he set for art, and kept, himself, as a critic, were impeccable and even austere. At the same time he was the kindest, most chivalrous defender of the amateur. And it was not only the amateurs—it was not artists at all—who knew this well: his busy life, as he went about his work and its throng of attendant interests, was made up of thousands of unrecorded kindnesses.

I speak as one working in the arts—and only one, of a very great number indeed—who came to know at first hand, and well, what ever-present perception and insight, warmth of sympathy, and care for the true meaning, Frank in his own work brought to a work of theirs. The many things he has done in behalf of my own books I wouldn't be able to even count; his dramatic productions of my stories are among the proudest and happiest events of my working life. He was a dear and admired friend for twenty years.

Frank gave many young talents their first hope, sometimes their first chance, and I am sure he never could have let any talent down. He didn't let any of us down, but was our constant and benevolent and thoroughgoing supporter, a refresher of our spirits, a celebrator along with us of what we all alike, in the best ways we were able, were devoting our lives to.

What his work contributed—the great sum—had an authority of a kind all its own. I wonder if it might not have had a double source: his lifelong enchantment with the world of art, and an unusual gift for communicating his pleasure in it to the rest of us. Plus the blessed wish to do it.

We are grateful.

I read that line one more time: We are grateful. I turned the page. I looked at the movie ads. Suddenly, vividly, a memory surfaced. I looked up at Bleak House. In that closet where Frank had hidden his locked trunk of pornography, he had also kept a framed copy of his very first "On Stage" column. "I had it hanging in the house for a while," he told me when he showed it to me once, when he was digging around in that closet trying to find something else. "But I finally thought it a bit tacky and self-aggrandizing," he said. He handed it to me to read. For the very first paragraph of that very first column, he had chosen to quote from *Alice's Adventures in Wonderland*: " 'Where shall I begin, please your majesty?' he asked. 'Begin at the beginning,' the king said gravely, 'and go on until you come to the end: then stop.' "

Parked in that Comet that day, I shook my head bemusedly, just as Frank would so often shake his head at me. The *nothingness* was lifting. I did not go to a movie that afternoon. I waited until I arrived in New York City two weeks later and on my first day there bought a ticket to a matinee. Sitting alone, beginning at the beginning, I watched *Love and Death*.